# BEADWORK

# BEADWORK

## A WORLD GUIDE

CAROLINE CRABTREE AND
PAM STALLEBRASS

**RIZZOLI**
NEW YORK

ONE

TWO

THREE

FOUR

FIVE

PAGE 1: Heavily beaded item of religious apparel made by the Yoruba of western Africa.

PAGE 2: Small panel of mirrored embroidery, from Afghanistan, incorporating *gul-i-peron* and a twisted thread and bead fringe.

PAGE 3: French mourning wreath of beads on wire, early 20th century.

PAGE 5: Beads from Norman Hartnell's workrooms in their original small cloth bags; one bead would be stitched to the outside of the bag to identify the contents.

PAGE 6, ABOVE, RIGHT: Athabaskan gauntlets trimmed with coyote fur, North America.

PAGE 6, LEFT: Kirdi apron, Cameroon.

PAGE 6, BELOW, RIGHT: Lakota Sioux moccasins, North America.

PAGE 7, ABOVE, LEFT: Necklaces with human figures, Sabah, Borneo.

PAGE 7, ABOVE, RIGHT: Transylvanian man's hat with band of loomed beadwork and bead cockade.

PAGE 7, BELOW, LEFT: Hair tassels of beads and sequins from North-West Province, Pakistan.

PAGE 7, BELOW, RIGHT: Small pouch, Micmac, Woodlands region, North America.

Designed by David Fordham

First published in the United States of America in 2002 by
RIZZOLI INTERNATIONAL PUBLICATIONS, INC.
300 Park Avenue South, New York, New York 10010

ISBN 0-8478-2513-2

Printed in Singapore

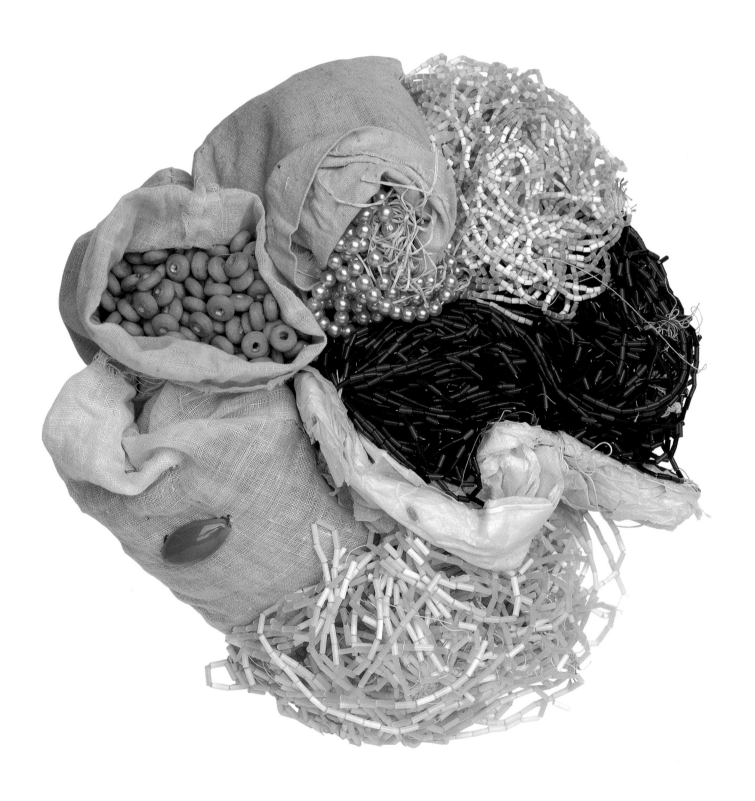

# CONTENTS

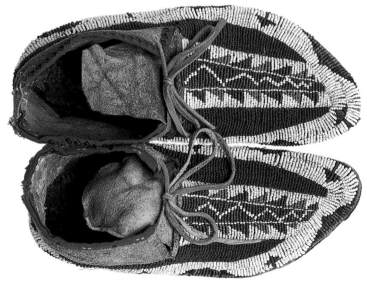

# INTRODUCTION

I N BEADWORK, very small, usually uniformly coloured, beads are transformed into intricate articles or embellishments. Each bead is just an element in the larger pattern and the overall design creates the impact, rather than the individual bead. The artistry and skill lies in the design, construction and execution of the article. Beadwork from different areas is usually readily identifiable by the design, colour and size of the beads, the use to which they have been put, and also the methods of construction. For centuries, people all over the world have created complex patterns using only beads and thread. The beadwork discussed and illustrated in this book has been categorized according to the geographical region in which it was made. In the last section descriptions and examples of various methods of construction are given as an aid to identification.

ABOVE: *Wallet of one-bead netting, from Afghanistan, lined with silk and metallic braid.*

RIGHT: *Small hard seeds have been cut and threaded by the Azande people from the Democratic Republic of Congo, so that they knock together and make a rippling sound when worn for dancing.*

## FROM BEADS TO BEADWORK

T HERE ARE many books that focus on individual beads, their manufacture, history and cultural significance. Others concentrate on regional and historical jewelry, but here our aim is to draw attention to objects decorated with, and constructed from, the tiny glass 'seed' beads that are so often overlooked. We have attempted to give a brief overview of the history and manufacture of these beads. Making small beads, whether from precious stones or glass, is a highly technical skill, so they have only ever been manufactured in a few centres. Beads became highly desirable trade items and could be found all over the world – the trade routes they travelled are outlined at the beginning of the sections – as part of existing forms of textile creation and decoration.

The beadwork illustrated here shows the great diversity of its uses, and of the designs and techniques employed. The wealth and diversity of traditional beadwork from around the world still in use or in private and public collections is revealed. This book is by no means an exhaustive survey, but a starting-point to inspire the beadworker, collector and designer to delight in creations made using the humble seed bead.

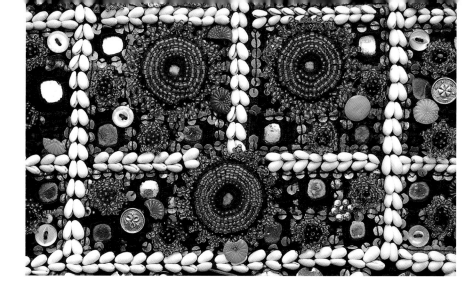

RIGHT: *Red-on-green beads – some of the first drawn-glass beads made in Venice to imitate and replace the Indian beads sold to the East African market. These beads were found on the Scilly Isles, England, and are from a late 16th-century wreck of a Dutch East India Company ship.*

ABOVE: *Detail of a woman's blouse (choli) from the Chauhan caste, Sind, Pakistan. The blouse is heavily decorated with rosettes of small glass beads, white shells and mirrors.*

BELOW: *Necklaces of Job's tears seeds made by the Akha tribe, northern Thailand. The Akha use the seeds both in their natural colours and also whiten them by leaving them in the embers of a fire.*

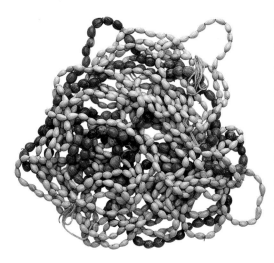

## THE HISTORY OF BEADWORK

THE HISTORY of beadwork is older than the history of glass 'seed' beads. Though the English name would suggest that some of the earliest beads were made from seeds, and this is indeed so, the tiny drawn-glass beads were named 'seed' beads because of their size; as small as seeds, or even grains of sand. In most European languages, the word for bead has its origins in the word for 'pearl' – perle, perla, perola, pareltje, parlstav – a further indication of the origin of pre-glass beads. Before the widespread manufacture and trade in small glass beads, minute beads of stone, shell, small hard seeds, clay, faience, tiny ('seed') pearls and precious stones were highly desirable trade items, traded throughout the ancient world. They were used not just as a decorative element in themselves, but threaded into larger constructions, or stitched onto textiles and incorporated into already existing forms of textile decoration – the very beginnings of beadwork. Stitched beadwork of this type, using shells and seeds, has been found in Stone Age sites in Israel; and a complex structure of finely worked beads of shell and malachite is part of the Chimu culture of Peru (AD 1000–1470). In Africa, particularly, beads have been made from organic materials (shells, seeds, bone) for centuries – some of the earliest known beads were made from ostrich eggshells and date from 10,000 BC; in India, ostrich-eggshell beads have been found which date back to 2,300 BC.

RIGHT: *Akha woman's jacket (detail), from Thailand, decorated with appliqué, embroidery, buttons, coins and Job's tears seeds stitched to the fabric like beads. Both mature and elongated immature seeds have been used on this garment.*

OPPOSITE, BELOW, RIGHT: *This is a contemporary photograph of a Maasai woman in Tanzania. The beads on her neck ornament are threaded onto thin wire, with leather spacers to keep the rings in place. The women and girls often wear large numbers of these neck ornaments and many strings of beads, which flip up and down when they dance.*

## CONSTRUCTING BEADS

SMALL BEADS, of any material, whether easily available shell or more valuable pearl or semi-precious stone, have to be drilled to make a bead; the smaller the bead, the more exacting the task. By the early Neolithic period (7000–5500 BC) bow drills were used to perforate stone beads in the Indus Valley. In the South Pacific and the Philippines beads of coloured corals and shells were employed from 1000 BC onwards – possibly earlier – and worked into complex netted structures for belts, armbands and other regalia. Clay beads were made on the islands, and some of the earliest glass seed beads found their way to this region from southern India and were combined with the beads of other materials into the beadwork structures used for ceremonial gift exchanges. Clay and faience represent another stage in the development of beadwork, as these materials are shaped into beads rather than cut and drilled. In particular, faience, a ceramic of quartz

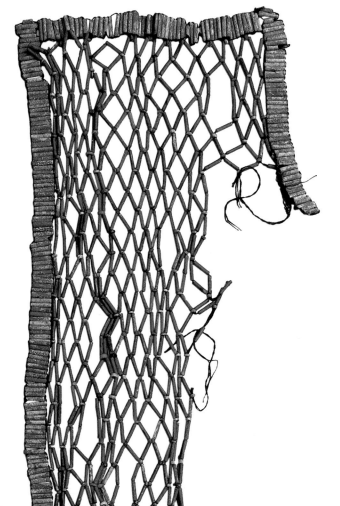

ABOVE: *Mask of faience beads, from Egypt, used to cover the face of a mummified body.*

LEFT: *Mummy net of faience beads for covering a mummified body, New Kingdom, 1500–1000 BC.*

RIGHT: *Franzina Ndimande has travelled extensively, giving lectures on Ndebele customs and traditions. (Photograph by Peter Rich)*

sand with a coloured glaze – considered to be the forerunner of true glass – represents the first mass production of relatively inexpensive beads. Invented in Egypt or Mesopotamia in around 4000 BC, faience beads were produced in large quantities for an expanding market, allowing ordinary people to own adornments constructed from many small components – beadwork, if not for the masses, then certainly for a larger section of the population who could not afford the more costly precious stones. Multi-coloured collars of faience beads can be seen in Ancient Egyptian wall paintings.

## CONSTRUCTING GLASS SEED BEADS

TRUE GLASS seed beads are produced by making a long, fine, hollow 'cane' of glass, which is cut into short sections and the cut edges smoothed to produce the familiar rounded bead. The earliest true glass seed beads, small beads made by drawing canes of hollow glass, were produced from around 200 BC in various locations in India and exported along the major trade routes to Zanzibar, Kilwa in Tanzania, Kisiwana, Malindi in Kenya and the island of Lamu in East Africa between AD 200 and 1600. The beads reached Sumatra in around AD 100, and Malaysia and Vietnam in about AD 1000, and became one of the most important trade items in this region, traded by Arabs, and later by the Portuguese,

ABOVE, LEFT: *Man from Mangareva, the largest islet of the Gambier group in the South Pacific, with beaded ornaments.*

BELOW, LEFT: *Beads, shells and buttons stitched onto discs of thick cloth make up these gul-i-peron, or dress flowers, used to decorate bodices of the loose, smock-like Afghan women's traditional dress.*

BELOW, RIGHT: *A large, circular netted cover, possibly for a low table, from Pakistan. The beads are almost certainly Bohemian.*

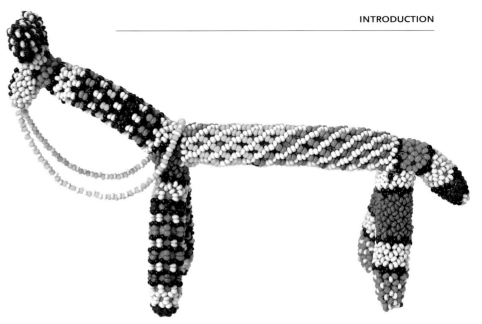

for over 1,500 years. The beads were always scarce and highly prized; some have been found in royal tombs in China and Korea. Skilled artisans left southern India in the first century AD, settling in Sri Lanka, Thailand, Vietnam and Malaysia, taking with them the knowledge of beadmaking. Large quantities of glass beads were made in Arikamedu in southern India – drawn-glass beads continued to be made until the 12th century AD – and in other areas of the sub-continent until the 16th century, by which time Venetian craftsmen and European traders were dominating the manufacture and distribution of drawn-glass seed beads.

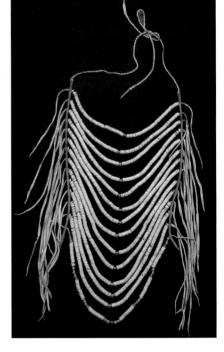

ABOVE, LEFT: *Utimuni, nephew of King Shaka, painted by G. F. Angus in 1849.*

LEFT: *Selection of beads used by the Xhosa, Zulu and Sotho women before and after the arrival of glass beads in South Africa. They are, from top to bottom, Job's tears, hand-rolled clay beads, and different types of seeds.*

TOP: *Horse with bridle constructed of netted beads over a framework of tightly bound grass, southern Africa.*

ABOVE: *'Loop' necklace of shell beads, worn by men as a breast ornament, Crow tribe, North America.*

LEFT: *Well-dressed Xhosa man in the middle of the 20th century.*

LEFT: *Girl, from a Panamanian folklore show, wearing a beaded headdress.*

RIGHT: *Pair of child's moccasins of Iroquois work, North America.*

BELOW, LEFT: *Shona fertility figure from Zimbabwe. She was covered in a variety of objects all adding to her significance.*

BELOW, MIDDLE: *Central Asian, probably Afghan, camel decoration.*

BELOW, RIGHT: *Girl in dancing costume at a Nazareth Baptist Church gathering near Durban, KwaZulu Natal.*

BOTTOM: *Section of tambour beadwork used on a Western European garment, early 20th century.*

## CONCLUSION

IN MANY societies beadwork was, and still is, an indication of shamanistic power, status, wealth or religious belief. Beadwork can indicate age, marital status or regional origin. Though the history of bead trade was often the history of colonization, the development of beadwork is a vivid testament to the triumph of skill and artistry used to produce articles of adornment with distinctive and cultural significance. We owe a debt of gratitude to the often anonymous artists who created these wonderful artefacts, and to the collectors and museums who let us photograph their collections. We hope that this book will inspire further study and appreciation of the wealth of beadwork from around the world.

# BEAD MANUFACTURING CENTRES

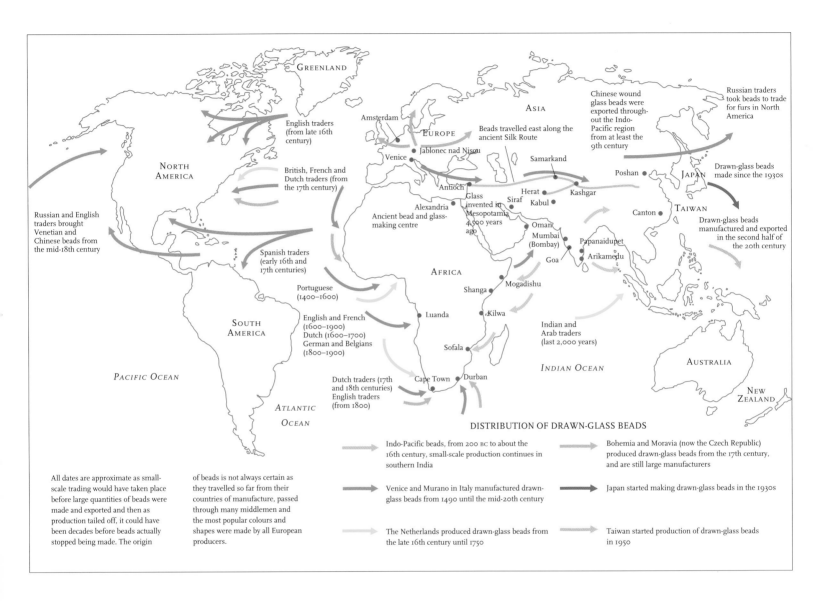

GREENLAND

ASIA

EUROPE

Amsterdam

Venice

Jablonec nad Nisou

Chinese wound glass beads were exported throughout the Indo-Pacific region from at least the 9th century

Russian traders took beads to trade for furs in North America

English traders (from late 16th century)

NORTH AMERICA

British, French and Dutch traders (from the 17th century)

Beads travelled east along the ancient Silk Route

Samarkand

Poshan

JAPAN

Drawn-glass beads made since the 1930s

Antioch

Alexandria

Ancient bead and glass-making centre

Glass invented in Mesopotamia 4,500 years ago

Herat

Siraf

Kabul

Kashgar

Canton

TAIWAN

Drawn-glass beads manufactured and exported in the second half of the 20th century

Russian and English traders brought Venetian and Chinese beads from the mid-18th century

Oman

Mumbai (Bombay)

Goa

Papanaidupet

Arikamedu

AFRICA

Spanish traders (early 16th and 17th centuries)

Portuguese (1400–1600)

Shanga

Mogadishu

English and French (1600–1900) Dutch (1600–1700) German and Belgians (1800–1900)

Luanda

Kilwa

Sofala

Indian and Arab traders (last 2,000 years)

SOUTH AMERICA

INDIAN OCEAN

AUSTRALIA

PACIFIC OCEAN

Dutch traders (17th and 18th centuries) English traders (from 1800)

Cape Town

Durban

NEW ZEALAND

ATLANTIC OCEAN

DISTRIBUTION OF DRAWN-GLASS BEADS

All dates are approximate as small-scale trading would have taken place before large quantities of beads were made and exported and then as production tailed off, it could have been decades before beads actually stopped being made. The origin

of beads is not always certain as they travelled so far from their countries of manufacture, passed through many middlemen and the most popular colours and shapes were made by all European producers.

→ Indo-Pacific beads, from 200 BC to about the 16th century, small-scale production continues in southern India

→ Venice and Murano in Italy manufactured drawn-glass beads from 1490 until the mid-20th century

→ The Netherlands produced drawn-glass beads from the late 16th century until 1750

→ Bohemia and Moravia (now the Czech Republic) produced drawn-glass beads from the 17th century, and are still large manufacturers

→ Japan started making drawn-glass beads in the 1930s

→ Taiwan started production of drawn-glass beads in 1950

## GLASSWORKS AND TRADE ROUTES

THERE IS evidence of glass production in Mesopotamia dating back at least 4,500 years. The glass was composed of one part sand and three parts ash of the Chenopodium plant, a salt-loving plant that grows in the desert. Extremely high temperatures, reached by using forced draught kilns, are needed to melt the raw ingredients, and, probably for this reason, the ancient glassmaking sites such as those listed below are often found near metalworking sites. Glassworks have been found in Egypt at Tell el-Amarna, capital of Akhenaten, dating back to 1365 BC. In 1200 BC the Phoenicians settled on the north-western coast of Syria and northern Palestine. They were perfectly positioned

ABOVE: *Sandal of faience beads, Egypt, probably dating from the New Kingdom, 1500–1000 BC.*

BELOW (FROM LEFT TO RIGHT): *Lapiz from Afghanistan; garnets from India; terracotta from Mauritania; turquoise from Afghanistan (though probably Chinese); Iranian carnelian (over 1,000 years old); brass from Africa; old bedouin coral.*

OPPOSITE: *Handmade beads, Papanaidupet, India.*

to trade goods from the east with European countries, and factories were built to make glass beads for trade. During the Hellenistic period Alexander the Great (356–323 BC) founded Alexandria, in Egypt, which became famous for the quality of its glassmaking. Later when it was conquered by Julius Caesar skilled artisans were sent all over the Roman Empire, thus spreading the secrets of glassmaking. It is not known whether glassmaking technology spread to China, or whether it was independently invented there, but the Chinese were producing glass by 1000 BC.

Beads were one of the first articles to be made by glassmakers, and glass beads became an early trade item. By 200 BC Indian glassmakers had invented an ingenious method of mass producing small beads. Knowledge of this technique spread to Sri Lanka and various sites in South-East Asia such as Oc-eo in Vietnam, Vijaya in Sumatra and other sites in present-day Thailand and Malaysia. These beads, now known as Indo-Pacific beads, are one of the most successful trade items of all times, and were traded from China in the east to Africa in the west by Muslim traders from the Persian Gulf ports of Oman and Siraf. Massive quantities of glass beads were made at these sites, and they must have been prestige items as they were found in royal tombs in China and Korea. There is a special type of glass bead that is still used in Indonesia as a wedding gift from a groom to his bride – they are orange-red in colour, and are known as 'mutisalah' or false pearls in Timor, and as India reds in Africa. The red colour in the beads is made by adding copper (cuprous) oxide to the glass ingredients. This colour was greatly desired in both Africa and Indonesia. When the Portuguese started trading along the east coast of Africa the natives were not interested in anything they had brought to barter, so 'barros miudas', literally earthenware beads because they were the colour of red clay, had to be bought from India until copies had been made in Europe.

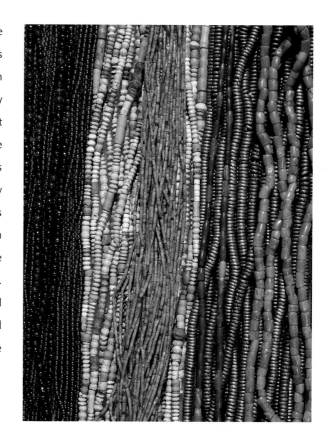

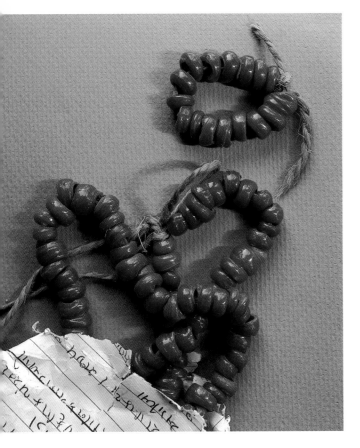

Until the end of the 15th century the Islamic world, India and China were the wealthy trading nations. Henry the Navigator of Portugal, spurred on by dreams of wealth from the lucrative spice trade, encouraged Bartholomew Diaz and Vasco da Gama, among others, to discover a sea route to India. Up until then the spices had come overland by camel caravans, Arab middlemen added to the cost and valuable cargoes were lost and delayed by wars. By the end of the 15th century Columbus had already reached America, and Da Gama had rounded the Cape of Storms, later renamed the Cape of Good Hope, and landed in India. The Portuguese were closely followed to the East by the Spanish, French, British and Dutch. By 1850 Europe dominated world trade and had established colonies in Africa, America and Asia. Glass beads were a universal trade item, and many different styles were made by the bead factories in Europe to suit local preferences. A large number of the styles were copied by the various factories, so it is not always easy to tell the origin of the beads, but in some cases old trade routes can be traced through the history of beads.

## THE MANUFACTURE OF SMALL GLASS BEADS

THERE ARE hundreds of different designs of beads made all over the world, but essentially four methods are used to make small glass beads suitable for beadwork. They can be wound, drawn, moulded or blown.

ABOVE: *Furnace-wound beads from Gujarat, India. They are sold by weight – the little ring on the right was to make up for a shortfall.*

BELOW: *Lamp-wound beads made by outworkers in Zelezný Brod, the Czech Republic. Tiny little roses of thin glass canes and sheets of silver foil covered with clear glass decorate the beads.*

## WOUND BEADS

WOUND BEADS are made individually by winding molten glass around a rotating copper wire or metal mandrel. The spike is coated in clay or dipped in salt so the glass bead does not stick to it, and the completed bead can be removed when cool. The beads can be furnace wound, where a small amount of molten glass is picked up on a rod and wound onto the mandrel right in the heat of the furnace, or pre-formed rods of coloured glass can be melted with a small burner while they are wound onto the mandrel. The latter are called lamp-wound beads, and the greater degree of control that can be exercised while making these beads means that thousands of different designs can be created, depending on the skill of the maker. The final shape can be perfected by turning the molten bead in a half-mould. It is not always easy to tell if a bead has been wound, but any bubbles or discrepancies in colour running at right angles to the hole are a good indication. Wound beads have been made for thousands of years, and in many parts of the world. The fact that they are made one at a time increases their cost, and it is difficult to make them as small and even as drawn-glass beads.

## DRAWN-GLASS BEADS

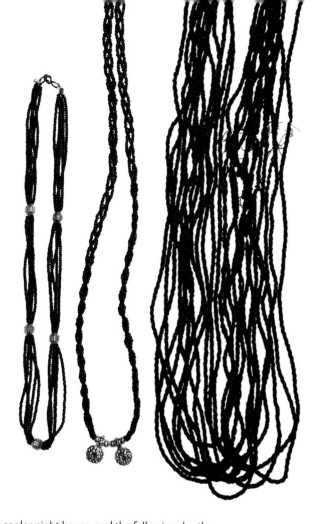

**D**RAWN-GLASS BEADS, where dozens of beads can be produced at the same time, were first made over 2,000 years ago in the coastal town of Arikamedu, in the south of India. In the village of Papanaidupet, 130 km (80 miles) north-west of Madras, beads are still made in the same way (see p. 26). Torben Sode, from Denmark, visited the village and his description of the process gives us a fascinating glimpse into the past: 'Forty to fifty kilos of glass ingredients are melted in a furnace. The molten glass is gathered onto the end of a two-metre [6¹⁄₂ ft] long, hollow metal rod, or lada, and then reheated in the furnace. When the correct cone shape has been formed by rolling the glass on a low wall, an iron rod is pushed through the hollow lada and hammered right through the molten glass, which is then placed in the furnace again, and drawn out the opposite side by the puller. He draws out the continuous hollow cane, breaking it off in one-metre [3 ft] long pieces.'

ABOVE: *Short lengths of striped hollow glass canes from the Jablonex factory in the Czech Republic.*

ABOVE, RIGHT: *The smallest beads in the world are handmade in Papanaidupet, southern India, to be threaded into the* mangal sutra *(see the two different types on the left), the wedding necklace of central and southern India.*

BELOW, RIGHT: *Large, roughly drawn and cut beads that have not been heated to round off the edges.*

The drawing of the glass is done during the cooler night hours, and the following day the hollow canes are cut into small, bead-sized lengths and mixed with cow-dung ash, and then heated in a large clay pot to round off the edges. The ash prevents the beads from sticking together, and stops the holes from closing up. The beads are pounded in a wooden mortar to clean off the ash, and then washed, sorted and strung. The art of hand drawing glass beads has survived in Papanaidupet because the mechanized factories in the north of India cannot make the very tiny beads for the *mangal sutra* necklace traditionally worn by the Tamil farmers' wives.

Some drawn-glass beads are cut, and not rounded off by heat or abrasion. They are known as snapped canes.

Nearly all the beads used for beadwork are made using variations of this process. They are often known as 'rocailles', which is French for little rocks, or seed beads. In West Africa they were known as pound beads because they were weighed out when sold. Each bead is usually a single colour, but it is possible to make a drawn-glass bead with two or more layers. Drawn-glass beads with red glass over a white core were popular in North America, where they were called 'red-under-white', and in southern Africa where they were known as 'white hearts'. It is also possible to draw out canes with stripes of a different colour, the white beads with blue stripes are favoured by the *sangomas*, or traditional healers, in South Africa. The stripe and any impurity or bubble in drawn-glass beads is always parallel to the hole.

BELOW, LEFT; AND BOTTOM (DETAIL): *Blown-glass beads used in a bridegroom's wedding veil, Gujarat, India.*

BELOW, RIGHT: *These press-moulded 'sweetie' beads were made in the Czech Republic for the West African trade. Molten glass, decorated with strips of coloured glass rods which form stripes, is pressed into a pear-shaped mould to make these beads.*

## PRESS-MOULDED BEADS

THE THIRD method of manufacturing beads for beadwork is moulding. A rod of glass is heated to melting point and placed in the lower piece of a mould. As the handle is lowered by hand or mechanically, the upper half of the mould clamps the glass, squeezing the molten glass into the metal or wooden former. Beads made in this way are very regular in shape. In cheaper moulded beads a line is sometimes visible where the two halves of the mould came together. If they are carefully finished off this is not visible.

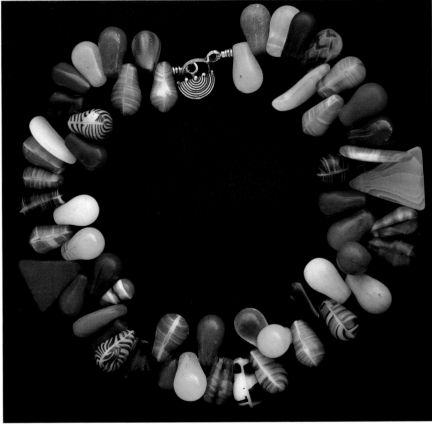

## BLOWN-GLASS BEADS

BLOWN-GLASS BEADS are normally too big and fragile for beadwork, but in India, small, regular blown-glass beads can be made using a special mould. The molten glass is drawn out to form a tube, and this is placed in the mould. Air is blown into the tube, forcing the glass into the mould which makes a row of beads. These used to be silvered on the inside with fish scales, and filled with wax to strengthen them. Now silver nitrate is sucked up the pipe before the beads are broken off. These little beads are mostly used for embroidery.

RIGHT: *Section of beadwork of faience disc beads, Egypt, from the New Kingdom, 1500–1000 BC.*

BELOW, RIGHT: *Faience beadmakers sifting the beads from the ash after firing, Egypt.*

BOTTOM: *Contemporary Japanese bag entirely made of delica beads.*

## FAIENCE BEADS

FAIENCE BEADS are still made by hand in Egypt, using a process that has hardly changed for over 5,000 years. To make the beads, a mixture of quartz, steatite, kaolin, feldspar and salt is ground to a very fine powder, which is sifted, then mixed with water to make a fine paste. Larger beads can be shaped individually out of this paste, but for small beads the paste is pressed into a thin cylinder around a length of rice straw. The beads are made by cutting through the paste, at intervals. The straw is not cut. For very small disc beads this is done by rolling the cylinder of paste over the edges of blades set into a stone, a bead width apart. The paste is rolled in talcum powder to give a smooth surface, and placed in the sun to dry. The beads are then left in fires of animal dung for several hours, which burns away the straw, leaving the fired beads.

## DELICAS

DELICAS ARE small, very evenly sized drawn-glass beads developed by the Miyuki factory in Japan in 1982, in imitation of the metal beads widely used in Europe during the 19th century. Delicas have two distinguishing features – they are not the 'doughnut' shape of traditional seed beads, but are cylindrical in shape, as tall as they are wide, and have, in comparison to their size, a larger hole than standard seed beads. This allows several threads to pass through the bead, an advantage when working a complex piece. The delicas are exceptionally even in size, not varying between one batch and another, or one colour and another, as seed beads frequently do. The factory has developed their own method of cutting the beads to ensure this evenness of size. Delicas are increasingly popular, despite their greater cost, and could be said to represent a real innovation in the art of beadmaking.

# European Manufacturing Centres

In 1291 the glass workshops were moved to the nearby island of Murano because of the constant danger of fire from the furnaces in Venice itself, which was built almost entirely of wood. The seclusion also helped keep the secrets of glassmaking safe. The artisans were confined to the island, but were given privileges usually only accorded to noblemen.

It is thought that beadmaking began at the beginning of the 14th century in Murano, but it was only in 1490 that drawn-glass beads, *margarite*, were produced. These beads did not have to be made individually like wound-glass beads, but could be mass produced. Molten glass, made up of local sand, crushed river pebbles and plant ash, was pulled out into long, hollow canes, and then cut into short little tubes. After being mixed with sand, lime and coal they

## Venice

The Venetians were the leading European glassmaker until the 20th century. Their tradition of glassworking dates back to Roman times. The industry re-emerged during the 9th century when specialist craftsmen, many from the Benedictine order, were working on the mosaics in the Basilica di San Marco and other churches and palaces, and quantities of glass tiles were needed. By the 13th century Venice was the most important centre for glassmaking in the Western world. Additional glassmaking skills may have come from refugees from Syria after Tamerlane (1336–1405) moved artisans out of Syria to Samarkand in Uzbekistan. All beadmakers belonged to a guild that preserved the knowledge of the skills needed to produce *conterie*, glass beads. It also maintained the quality of its products and looked after its members. No one could set up a beadmaking *bottega* (shop) without being a full member, and the tools of the trade could not be removed from the Venice lagoon area. If a glass worker moved out of the area he could be considered a traitor with a possible death sentence.

were heated to round off the sharp edges. Some of the holes close up in this process, and these beads were taken out to be used in decorative pictures and on furnishings. The good ones were polished with oiled bran and then threaded to be sold. It was these small beads that became a major trade item that was so eagerly sought after in Asia, America and Africa. Explorers, traders and missionaries took them on expeditions to exchange for food, labour, ivory, gold and furs, and as enticements to attend church.

The tiny beads also found a ready market in Italy. During the 16th and 17th centuries women in Naples and Milan decorated clothes with *margarite* to such an extent that it was banned by the Senate, restricting their use to hair ornaments. Printed patterns became available at this time and cushions, frames and altar covers were covered with beadwork.

The Venetians did not sell their own beads – they were sent by sea to agents in ports on the Black Sea, in the Mediterranean and north-western Europe where they were bought for redistribution. This makes identifying the origin of beads in old pieces of beadwork very difficult.

By the 16th century bead production in Italy was becoming a serious threat to the industry in India. Exact copies of

OPPOSITE, ABOVE, RIGHT: *Detail of a basket of Venetian beads threaded on wire, c. 1675.*

OPPOSITE, LEFT: *Detail of English beaded box, c. 1660, with Venetian beads embroidered onto satin.*

OPPOSITE, BELOW, RIGHT: *The beads in the window of this Venetian shop in Campo San Maurizio chart the history of beadmaking in Venice, from the glowing new 'perle Veneziane' to old drawn-glass fringe samples hanging up on the left, and three-dimensional flowers made from small beads threaded onto wire.*

Indian bead sizes, colours and shapes were made to be sold in the Indo-Pacific area. During the next 300 years Venetian beadmaking and export peaked, but by the end of the 19th century they were feeling the competition from other European centres. In 1898 many of the factories amalgamated to form the Societa Veneziana Conterie in order to survive, and they continued very successfully until the middle of the 20th century. Between 1932 and 1955 nearly four million kilograms of glass beads and rods were exported to Africa alone. Soon after this they became unable to compete with Bohemia in the mass production of beads.

Many beautiful wound-glass beads, 'perle Veneziane', are still being made in Venice, but the drawn-glass seed beads are no longer produced there. The history of glassmaking can be seen at the museum on the island of Murano, a short vaporetta ride from Venice.

Glassmaking in all its forms is very much a part of Venice. Beads, old and new – some seed beads, or the larger fancy beads that were traded in West Africa and new 'perle Veneziane' – are on display in the shops that can be found in tiny winding alleyways, over the canals or in magnificent piazzas.

ABOVE: *Girdle, inkciyo, worn by Xhosa women in South Africa. Old Venetian beads are more porous than Czech beads and absorbed the colour of the ochre rubbed onto their bodies, becoming a soft off-white colour.*

BELOW: *Multi-layered drawn-glass beads known as chevrons. These are Venetian chevrons which were traded into the Democratic Republic of the Congo at least 300 years ago.*

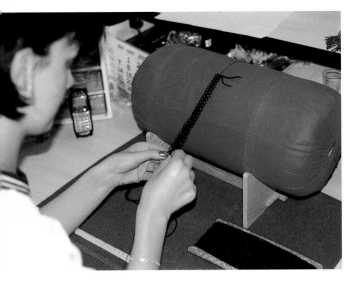

## BOHEMIA

**B**OHEMIA lies in the northern part of the Czech Republic, with Germany to the north and west and Moravia to the east. Glass beadmaking is a skill that has been practised there since the 9th century and probably even earlier. The beautiful rolling hills of this region are still covered in forests of beech and oak, which fed the furnaces melting the glass ingredients; and the ash from the furnaces provided the alkali for the glass. There are large and small glassmaking workshops throughout this region and their products, from tableware and chandeliers to works of art, can be found in shops throughout the country.

Despite the Venetians' secrecy, their beadmaking skills had spread to France, Germany and Bohemia by the 17th century. In the middle of the 20th century Bohemia eventually became the leader in the field. To begin with, the making of drawn-glass beads, or 'seed' beads, was a family business, with different families specializing in the various stages of production – the drawing of the canes, the cutting and the finishing, but in 1945 the Communist government consolidated these small businesses to create one large factory, equipping it with modern machinery. All the seed beads are now made at the Ornela factory in the village of Zasada. The marketing is managed by Jablonex in the town of Jablonec nad Nisou.

The raw materials used for making glass – quartz sand, soda, potash and the chemical colourants – are melted together. Originally, a glob of molten glass, called a gather, was picked up on the end of a hollow metal rod. The glass was pierced with a metal rod through the hollow rod to create the hole, then quickly pulled out into a hollow cane about thirty metres (100 ft) in length while heat was directed at the point where the glass was stretching. The faster the cane was stretched, the smaller the diameter of the cane. Nowadays, the molten glass is extruded mechanically, making it easier to control the size of the canes, but the striped and multi-layered beads are still hand drawn, a process requiring great skill and experience.

The long canes are broken into pieces one metre (3 ft) in length and cut in a guillotine into small sections that will, after finishing, form the beads. The sharp 'shoulders' have to be rounded off to make

ABOVE, LEFT; AND ABOVE, RIGHT: *Small design studio Yani, Zasada, the Czech Republic, which creates new beaded braid designs; women in Železný Brod making lamp-wound beads (shown above, right) in a home studio for Jablonex, Jablonec nad Nisou, the Czech Republic.*

LEFT AND RIGHT: *Manufacturing processes at the Ornela factory, Zasada, the Czech Republic – double-layered drawn-glass 'white heart' beads (left) and rocailles (right) coming out of heat tumblers.*

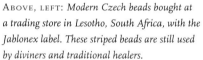

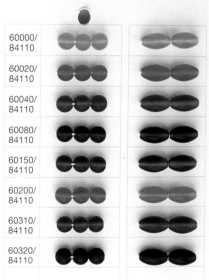

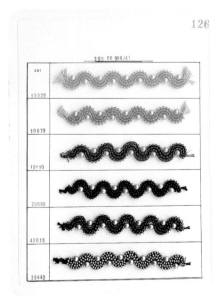

ABOVE, LEFT: *Modern Czech beads bought at a trading store in Lesotho, South Africa, with the Jablonex label. These striped beads are still used by diviners and traditional healers.*

ABOVE, CENTRE: *A spider made with bead-covered wire from the Yani studio, Zasada, the Czech Republic.*

FAR RIGHT: *Contemporary netted bag, from Egypt, using imported Czech beads.*

BELOW, LEFT; AND BELOW, RIGHT: *Sample card of moulded glass beads; sample card of glass-bead braids; both from Jablonex, the Czech Republic.*

the familiar doughnut shape of Czech beads. They are mixed with limestone which coats the beads and fills up the holes, and then heated to melting point while being rotated in a drum, slowly cooled, washed in acid and polished. The limestone stops the molten beads from sticking to each other, and prevents the holes from closing up. Some beads have different pearl or iridescent finishes applied to their surface. The silver-lined beads are soaked in a solution containing silver and after drying they are tumbled so that the only silver left is in the hole. The beads are then graded into sizes and packaged.

Moulded glass beads are also made at Ornela in the Czech Republic. The round 'princess' beads were marketed in South Africa, and larger, pear-shaped beads in West Africa. The Czechs researched their target markets and replaced shell, teeth

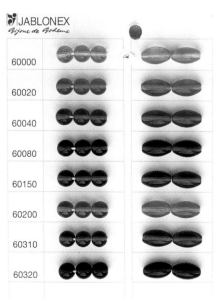

and other natural materials with glass beads imitating their shape. Some glass beads were made to look like stone beads to compete with turquoise sales in the North American market, and with their glass-cutting skills they reproduced faceted stones like garnets.

After the collapse of communism in 1989, small businesses were developed by many of the people who had been employed by Ornela and had a knowledge of the beadmaking industry. One designer set up a studio with her daughter to design and manufacture jewelry and Christmas decorations. Outworkers are employed to fulfil the orders. It seems that every other house in the area is involved in some way with beads and beadmaking. Other home businesses produce intricate lamp-wound beads that are exported all over the world. There is such a demand for these beads that local home textile production has mostly been replaced by beadmaking.

Unlike Venice, there is not much evidence of beads in the surrounding area, but there are shops at the Jablonex headquarters in Jablonec nad Nisou and at the Ornela factory in Zasada. A display of glass and costume jewelry can be seen in the museum in Jablonec nad Nisou.

TOP LEFT: *Large beads covered with seed beads; made at the Yani studio, Zasada, the Czech Republic.*

LEFT: *Pair of gauntlets from the Plateau region, North America, decorated with cut-glass beads from Bohemia.*

TOP RIGHT: *Modern bead-covered Christmas decorations made for export at the Yani studio, Zasada, the Czech Republic.*

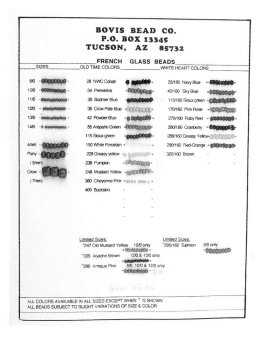

## GERMANY, FRANCE AND AUSTRIA

Many skilled German beadmakers left the Czech Republic after the Second World War and settled in Germany and Austria, where they set up factories. There is a Glass and Jewelry Technical School in Kaufbeuren, Germany, to serve the large beadmaking community. Many lamp-wound beads are produced, but it is the moulded beads that are of special interest to beadworkers. Manual machines are used in small businesses to press-mould beads.

As long ago as the 17th century Louis XIV's minister, Colbert, was luring Venetian artisans to France to make luxurious items for the French court. Glassmakers were among them, mainly to make the newly invented ornate glass mirrors. Today, there are two factories in Lyons making drawn-glass beads – one, Chaudemanche, specializes in unusual colours.

## THE NETHERLANDS

During the 17th century a Dutchman, Jan Heinrixszn Soop, applied to the government for permission to make glass beads. He had managed to smuggle some master glassmakers with their tools out of Venice, and set up a factory in Amsterdam. The first beads were very rough, but soon the quality rivalled that of Venice.

ABOVE, LEFT: *French glass bead charts from Tucson, Arizona, North America.*

ABOVE, RIGHT: *Punti woman's headband, from Hong Kong, using French beads.*

RIGHT: *The unusual colours of these beads from the Chaudemanche factory in Lyons, France, make them highly desirable to beadworkers all over the world.*

# ASIAN MANUFACTURING CENTRES

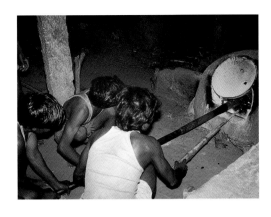

Some of the oldest bead manufacturing centres can be found in Asia, and beads are still made there using age-old methods in many sites, but today small drawn seed beads are only produced in India, Taiwan and Japan.

## INDIA

Small beads are made in two regions in India – in Papanaidupet, Andhra Pradesh, in the south, and Varanasi, Firozabad and Purdalpur in Uttar Pradesh, in the north.

It is thought that beadmakers from Arikamedu, the historical site of beadmaking in the ancient world, migrated to Papanaidupet some time during the 16th century as the old sites at Arikamedu were abandoned. Here, drawn-cane glass beads are still made by a process that has remained the same for 2,000 years. Though the industry is in decline, due to competition from the industrial production of beads in northern India, a few furnaces survive, making what are perhaps the smallest seed beads in the world. These exceptionally tiny beads, which cannot be manufactured by machine, are strung into the *mangal sutra* (see p. 17), the wedding necklace found in central and southern India.

In Firozabad, hollow, blown-glass beads have been made since 1960 – prior to this they were imported from Bohemia. These light, fragile beads are mainly used for the decoration of garments. Furnace-wound glass beads and lamp-wound beads are made in Purdalpur. The technique for making these was introduced in Varanasi in 1938, by a Czech couple. For twenty-five years there was a training programme at Benares Hindu University in Varanasi, but eventually the training programme was superseded as new beadmakers learned their skills from established workers. The lamp-working technique spread to Purdalpur, where lamp-worked beads are gradually replacing furnace-wound beads.

In Varanasi, as well as lamp-worked beads, the production of seed beads began in 1981 using machinery imported from Japan, to meet the ever-increasing demand for beads in the sub-continent. These had previously been imported from the Czech Republic and

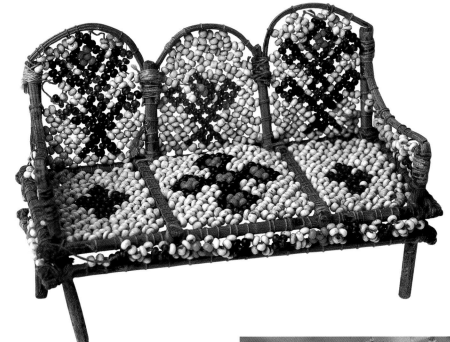

OPPOSITE, BELOW, LEFT: *Hollow blown-glass beads, from Firozabad, north India, metalized with silver nitrate.*

OPPOSITE, RIGHT (FROM TOP TO BOTTOM): *Beadmaking by hand, Papanaidupet, southern India. Melting the glass in the furnace and preparing the 'gather' (top); making the hole through the conical 'gather' of glass (second from top); drawing the thin glass tubes (third from top); cutting the glass tubes into short cylindrical pieces (bottom).*

ABOVE, RIGHT: *Settee for a doll's house made of cane and Indian beads.*

RIGHT: *Pisar potyda (money bag) made and worn by Banjara women in central India – each woman's bag is beaded to her own design.*

BELOW, LEFT: *The owner of the bag (see, right), wearing traditional Banjara dress, Mhetre Nagar Tanda, near Sholapur, India.*

BELOW, RIGHT: *Contemporary bag of Japanese delica beads; made by a Japanese beadwork designer.*

Japan. The production of beads around Varanasi provides employment not only for those who work in the factories or small workshops, but also for thousands of women employed as outworkers who string the beads ready to be sold. Seed beads produced there are sold throughout India, and also exported to Europe, though India still imports beads both from the Czech Republic and Japan.

## TAIWAN

BEAD manufacture began in Taiwan in the second half of the 20th century, using machinery purchased from Japan. Taiwanese beads are sold at very competitive prices, and very widely in Africa.

## JAPAN

SEED bead manufacture began in Japan in the 1930s, though mass production did not begin until after the Second World War. The oldest manufacturer of glass beads in Japan is the Miyuki factory, who re-started production of seed beads in 1949. Seed beads have been exported from Japan since 1955. In 1982, the technicians of the Miyuki factory developed the 'delica' bead, which represents a major innovation in beadmaking. Both delicas and high-quality seed beads are manufactured in large quantities and exported throughout the world.

# AFRICA

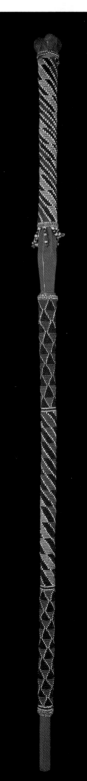

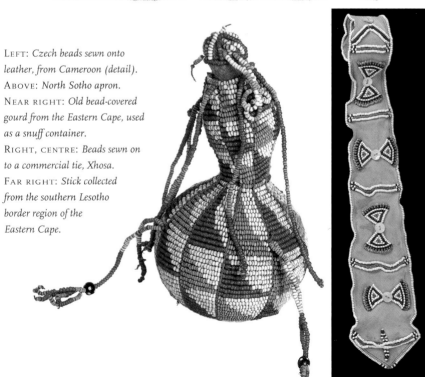

LEFT: *Czech beads sewn onto leather, from Cameroon (detail).*
ABOVE: *North Sotho apron.*
NEAR RIGHT: *Old bead-covered gourd from the Eastern Cape, used as a snuff container.*
RIGHT, CENTRE: *Beads sewn on to a commercial tie, Xhosa.*
FAR RIGHT: *Stick collected from the southern Lesotho border region of the Eastern Cape.*

# THE HISTORY OF BEADWORK IN AFRICA

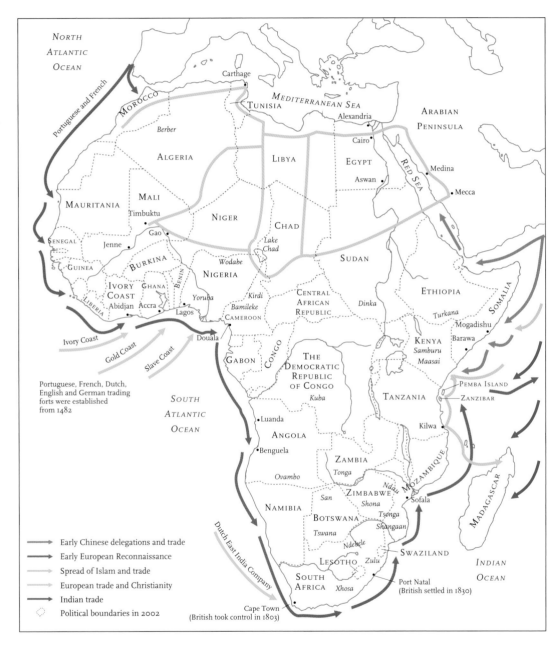

ABOVE: *A newly married Mfengu woman, from the Peddie district in the Eastern Cape, wearing a triangular scarf,* iqhiya, *decorated with mother-of-pearl buttons.*

BELOW: *Made of ostrich eggshell and marine shells, this is a reconstruction of a necklace found at a Late Stone Age archaeological site on the South Cape coast and is estimated to be 20,000 years old. The conus shells have had a hole cut with a straight tool, but the small beads have been bored with a stone or metal awl, threaded onto sinew, and then ground into a round shape on a grooved stone.*

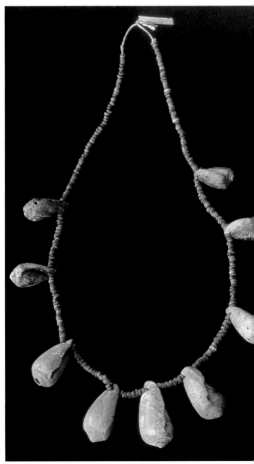

A FRICA IS A land of stark contrasts. Her vegetation ranges from equatorial forests to dry deserts, from high alpine regions to wide open grasslands. The people who live there are as divergent as the terrain, ranging from hunter-gatherers to members of sophisticated computer-driven societies.

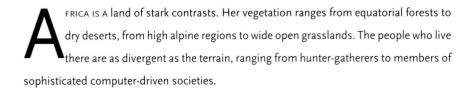

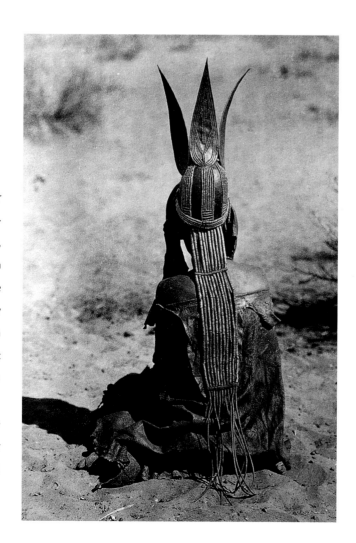

## TRADE ROUTES

**N**ATURAL BARRIERS of deserts, the Sahara and Namib, and Central African jungles could have separated the north from the south and the east from the west, but for thousands of years internal and coastal trade routes have linked these areas. It is recorded that in 2300 BC Harkuf, an Egyptian governor of the Old Kingdom, went on an expedition to the Congo Basin. At the time the Egyptians were already trading from Red Sea ports and overland across the Sahara to the west and south to Nubia and the Sudan, where gold was mined.

TOP: *Bridal headdress from Sale, Morocco. Tiny seed pearls decorate the headdress, and strings of pearls would have been hung from the bride's temples to her chest, and her face would have been painted with designs echoing the pearl beadwork.*

ABOVE: *Here, beads cover a natural-fibre vessel made by the Tutsi of Rwanda.*

RIGHT: *This photograph was taken by Alfred Duggan Cronin in 1936 and shows the incredible headdress, ekori, of a married Herero woman in Namibia. Small hand-beaten metal beads are sewn in rows onto the cap and 'petals' of shaped leather are sewn onto the top. Bands of slightly bigger beads are worked together to hang down the back.*

The Phoenicians established trading centres in the Mediterranean where, among other goods, glass beads were made and traded. The Berbers, the original inhabitants of north-west Africa, opened up trade routes south across the Sahara and to Sudan, Morocco, Tunisia and Libya, using horse-drawn chariots. The city of Carthage in Tunisia grew rich trading gold from sub-Saharan Africa, and agricultural produce from Egypt. When the Romans conquered the north of Africa and took control of the trading routes they introduced the camel to the Berbers, helping them to expand their trading network. With the conquest of Maghrib in north-west Africa by the Arabs in AD 705 Islam spread throughout the area. Through military skill and jihads the Almoravid Empire was created, spreading from Spain, through the Sahara as far south as Timbuktu in Mali.

In the mid-16th century the Songay Empire, now Mali, was extending its power base in the savannah region at the southern end of the Trans-Saharan trade routes. The Niger river provided transport for trade goods. Indian cowries and beads crossed the Sahara from

RIGHT: *Large Tsonga calabash (gourd).*
FAR RIGHT: Millefiori *trade beads from Venice.*
BELOW, LEFT: *Modern Zulu bangles for sale.*
BELOW, RIGHT: *Zulu beadwork, late 19th century.*

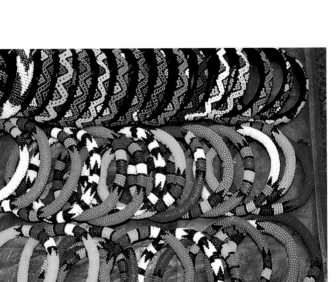

the east coast of Africa. About this time Europeans started trading around the West African coast and their arrival moved the centre of trade from inland to the coast, leading to a decline in the sub-Saharan empires.

The Portuguese were the first European power to start trading in West Africa. They wished to take the gold trade from the Arabs to avenge the invasion of their country by the Moors, and to find a sea route to India. Soon they were joined by the French, Dutch, English and Germans who established trading forts along the coast, all vying with each other for the lucrative African trade. They brought manufactured goods, including textiles and beads.

For almost 2,000 years Indian and Arab traders have been bartering up and down the eastern coast of Africa. Drawn-glass beads made in Arikamedu in the south of India from 200 BC onwards were becoming the largest trade item in the Indo-Pacific area, including the east coast of Africa. During the Dark Ages in Europe, Islam was extending its teachings and trade from Spain in the west to Pakistan in the east and Mozambique to the south. Beads from the Middle East, India, South-East Asia and China were traded throughout this area and beyond. Glass beads and ceramics from Persia were being imported into eastern and southern Africa from the 9th century. Excavations at Mapungubwe in South Africa revealed Song porcelain, proving that there was trade with China at this time. The prevailing winds in the Indian Ocean made trade between Asia and the eastern coast of Africa fairly easy. The trade winds blow from the north-east from December to February, and the monsoon winds blow from the south-west between April and September, allowing the traders to cross the Indian Ocean, with the wind behind them, both ways in one year. To the south of Kilwa in Tanzania wind directions are unpredictable and often run against the ocean currents building up large, dangerous seas, but huge profits could be made exchanging beads for gold found inland of Sofala in Mozambique. Trade goods entered many ports on the coast, Mogadishu, Pemba, Zanzibar Islands, Kilwa and Sofala were the largest. The local inhabitants acted as middlemen and traded the items far inland.

## THE BEGINNINGS OF BEADWORK

FROM the mid-11th century glass beads were imported into the north of present-day South Africa and Zimbabwe. Excavations of the lowest levels have revealed beads roughly chopped from glass canes, dating from AD 1000, which was known as the Zhizo phase. Mapungubwe and K2 are best known for gold, but the volume of beads at these sites points to the creation of wealth through the bead trade. These beads were cut and heat-treated, but the sizes and shapes vary. Before European contact, beads were blue, green, yellow, Indian (brick) red and black. Indo-Pacific beads have been found along the east coast, and after 1200 Kilwa became the main distribution point for beads entering the southern Africa region. By 1250 drawn-glass beads were uniform and well made with heat-rounded ends. Large glass beads known as 'garden rollers' were made at these sites from imported smaller glass beads which were melted down. The origin of garden rollers remained a mystery until small clay moulds were found.

ABOVE, LEFT: *A young Maasai girl wearing strings of glass beads given by admirers.*

ABOVE, MIDDLE: *Unmarried Ovambo woman with ostrich eggshell girdle, strings of beads and disc ornaments.*

ABOVE, RIGHT: *Ndebele woman with coin headdress. Around her neck are coils of grass covered with strings of glass beads.*

BELOW, LEFT: *Netted collar worn by Xhosa men and women. The small red beads have a white core and are known as white hearts.*

RIGHT: *South Sotho fertility figure. Attention has been given to details, such as the hair, and small arms have been added to the basic shape.*

Beads found at excavations in southern Africa are smaller than those found on the coast further north. This may be because these traders were the last to buy the beads and only small ones were left, but it may also have been a preference as there is early evidence of beadworking – beads sewn to a surface or worked into a freestanding fabric.

When the Portuguese started trading in this area they brought large Venetian chevron and *millefiori* beads which they had traded with the West Africans, but they were forced to buy Indian beads from the south of India – the local preference. These were copied by the Europeans – the first, made in Venice (1600 to 1836), were opaque red on a dark green core (see p. 9, right). The green was then replaced with white to make white hearts, which were sold in America as well. By the early 19th century tons of beads of different colours and styles were imported into Africa from Venice, Holland, Germany and Bohemia. These small seed beads, used on articles of ceremonial importance and apparel, were one of the trade items most coveted by the African people. In different areas they had a different significance to the people who used them.

# SAN AND OVAMBO

**F**OR THOUSANDS OF years before the colonial period small groups of San hunter-gatherers led a nomadic existence within defined territories throughout southern Africa. By the end of the 20th century conflict and cultural assimilation had reduced them to a few groups in the Kalahari region. Ovambo people have lived on the vast sandy plain of northern Namibia and southern Angola for 400 years. There were several autonomous matrilineal chiefdoms. As sedentary agriculturalists with some livestock, the majority lived in small palisaded villages amid fields of millet and grain sorghum. In the 20th century most domestic income was earned by the men on labour contracts elsewhere in Namibia.

### San techniques

**N**EARLY all San groups are known to have used ostrich-eggshell beads for personal adornment, decoration of clothing, trade and gifts. Women made these beads in great quantities. They bit fragments of eggshell into a rough shape and drilled a hole through the centre of each piece using a metal- or stone-tipped wooden drill. They then strung the rough beads tightly on a fibre cord and smoothed the jagged edges with a stone. Bead ornaments were used by both sexes at all stages of life. Ostrich-eggshell beads

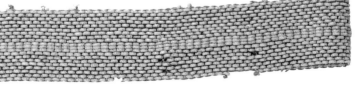

ABOVE: *Precious Venetian trade beads have been strung together with found organic objects to make a necklace.*

FAR LEFT: *This San woman is wearing an ostrich-eggshell headband.*

LEFT: *When glass beads were available the San women constructed headbands using the same technique they used with ostrich eggshells. The headband below is just like the one in the photograph taken by Alfred Duggan Cronin (far left) at the beginning of the 20th century.*

BELOW: *Beadwork belt made by the San.*

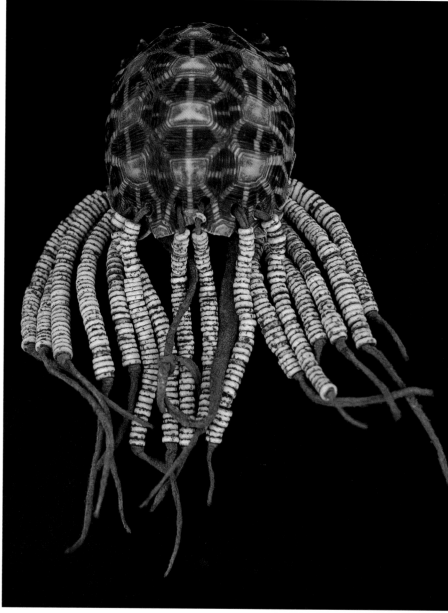

were strung into necklaces, armbands, waistbands and legbands, or threaded into headbands. They were also sewn onto aprons, cloaks, loincloths and skin bags. Most women wore a string of beads around the waist to carry a tortoise-shell cosmetic container decorated with beads. Iron and copper beads were obtained from neighbouring metal-working people, while European glass beads became available through trade from the beginning of the 18th century. In the 20th century San people in the Kalahari worked glass beads of all colours into brightly patterned

ornaments, including pendants which were often fastened to the hair.

San adornment was important for communicating group and individual identities. Today, San women in the Kalahari continue to work ostrich-eggshell beads into traditional ornaments, but they also use glass beads in innovative designs and complex colour patterns. The latter may reflect personal choice, but as an art form it may also communicate spiritual concepts that were formerly revealed by healers through dance, music and sacred imagery.

TOP LEFT: *A San tortoise-shell container – one aperture has been closed with gum and it has been filled with fragrant herbs. Jackal fur is used to apply the scent to the hair and body. The top two rows of 'beads' are twigs cut to the same length and drilled lengthwise; below is a row of porcupine quills.*

ABOVE, LEFT: *The Herero, neighbours of the San, use beaten metal beads to decorate their clothing and baskets.*

ABOVE, RIGHT: *A small container used by the San, made from a tortoise shell and decorated with strings of ostrich eggshells.*

**SAN AND OVAMBO**

RIGHT: *This belt with six attachments, each of a different design, was worn over a leather skirt by the Mbukushu (or Yei) people, who live in the Okavango region of Botswana.*

BELOW, LEFT: *Herero metal headband with hand-beaten metal beads; collected in 1922 in Namibia.*

BELOW, MIDDLE: *Neck ornament, with small beads sewn onto shaped leather, made by the Mbukushu, who live near the Okavango river in Namibia and Botswana.*

BELOW, RIGHT: *Ostrich-eggshell girdle worn by Himba women, a Herero subgroup, in Namibia.*

BOTTOM RIGHT: *Married Ovambo woman (left) wearing an organically shaped leather hat and unmarried Ovambo woman (right) with an ostrich-eggshell girdle over a leather skirt; her hair is shaped using mud and has shells pressed into it.*

## Ovambo techniques

BEADS have always been desired for working into a range of personal adornments or into decorations on domestic utensils. Metal beads were made by smiths using iron from Angola and copper from near Grootfontein. Beads were also manufactured from scented woods and roots, seeds and shells. Great quantities of ostrich-eggshell beads were obtained from San hunter-gatherers, and valuable strings measured over fifteen metres (50 ft). Glass beads were traded, the most favoured being large blue rod-shaped beads, as well as smaller red, black, blue and green ones. Beads were not worked into fabrics, but threaded into strings for armbands, waistbands, legbands and necklaces, while strings were also fastened together into panels or garments.

Most adornments are now store-bought, but strings of ostrich-eggshell and glass beads are sometimes worn over European-style clothing. Despite missionary influence since the 1870s, beaded dress, such as the back apron of ostrich-eggshell beads worn by Kwanyama women, may still be donned for festivals. From the age of eight to twelve, Ovambo girls started wearing a girdle of many strings of ostrich-eggshell beads. Though functionally decorative, it symbolized growth, virginity and potential fecundity, the beads linking it to valued fertility dolls which were also richly decorated with ostrich-eggshell beads.

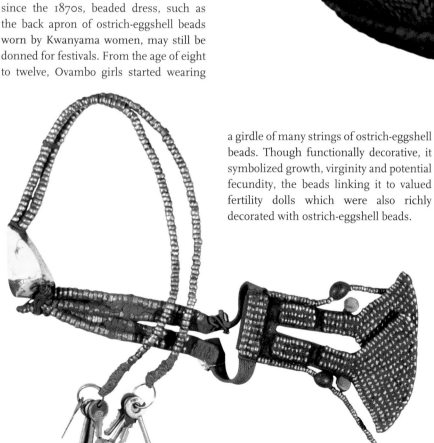

ABOVE: *Rare example of a Himba basket. It is tightly woven from a hard fibrous material; both the metal beads and the basketry on the outer surface are covered with ochre. It was collected in Namibia in the 1960s when they were still used to carry liquids. (Afri-Karner Collection)*

ABOVE, INSET: *Woman from the Kwanyama, one of the Ovambo groups. The circular discs are made from elephant ivory and were used to decorate the ceremonial dress of the women.*

LEFT: *Ovahimba neck piece made from hand-beaten metal beads – a rectangle of metal is beaten into a ring to form each bead. Ochre is rubbed into the beadwork and metal keys are added as a decorative element.*

37

# XHOSA

**T**HE MAJOR artistic expression of the Xhosa speakers of the Eastern Cape, South Africa, is exhibited in their clothing and beadwork. Their main creative focus was directed towards their personal adornment and regalia. From the 1830s onwards small glass beads were available in increasing numbers from Europe, and became the defining feature of the Xhosa's traditional apparel.

**T**HE Cape Nguni have inhabited the area from west of the Fish River in the south to KwaZulu Natal in the north for hundreds of years. There are many chiefdoms in the area, Gcaleka, Rharabe, Thembu and Mpondo being the largest. As the Xhosa were the most southerly group they were the first to come in contact with the white missionaries, traders and settlers from the Cape Colony, and theirs was the first language to be written down and translated. From this time on, all the Cape Nguni groups and their language were referred to as Xhosa. The language and culture of the Cape Nguni differ from those of the Nguni groups further north – the Zulu, Ndebele and Swazi. However, throughout the

ABOVE: *Xesibe bride, Eastern Cape. Small circles embroidered with white beads decorate this blanket.*

LEFT: *An apron made up of strips of beadwork worn by an igqira or healer.*

OPPOSITE, ABOVE, LEFT: *The top necklace is made from herbivore teeth and glass beads threaded on to animal hair; collected in 1871 from Mpumalanga, formerly the Eastern Transvaal, and is possibly Sotho. The middle one is made from sweet-smelling tamboti wood and is used by people in the Eastern Cape; collected in the Herschell District in 1907. The bottom one has hand-rolled and fired clay beads mixed in with the glass beads; collected in the Eastern Cape in 1939. Very similar beads are still made in Lesotho.*

OPPOSITE, MIDDLE: *Detail of a neckpiece made in the second half of the 20th century.*

OPPOSITE, BELOW, LEFT: *Xhosa youth with beaded blanket. Both the cloth and the beads were imported – the cloth from Manchester and the beads were probably made in Venice, but brought in by traders from England and Lithuania.*

OPPOSITE, TOP RIGHT: *Detail of ochre-dyed blanket. The cotton cloth was imported from England, and beads and thin strips of cloth or braid, in contrasting colours, were applied to the surface to form patterns.*

OPPOSITE, RIGHT: *This rare blanket from the Eastern Cape is decorated with an abstract pattern of white beads and buttons. Ochre could be bought from trading stores, or found locally. The shade varied in the different districts from a yellow ochre through terracotta to a deep maroon.*

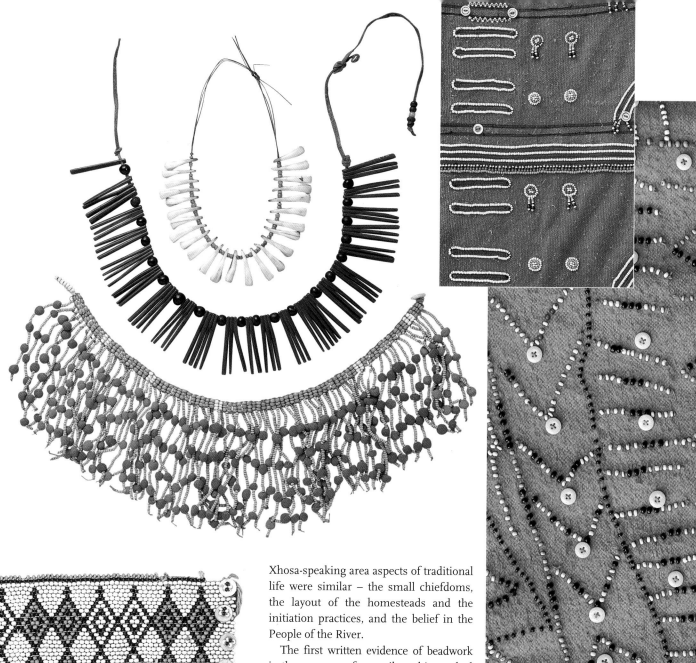

Xhosa-speaking area aspects of traditional life were similar – the small chiefdoms, the layout of the homesteads and the initiation practices, and the belief in the People of the River.

The first written evidence of beadwork in the area came from sailors shipwrecked during the 16th century. They reported the use of red beads of the kind being imported by the Portuguese from India and sold at Delagoa Bay in Mozambique. The same type of bead may well have been available even earlier through the Arab trade that entered Mozambique at Sofala. Beads at this time were rare and highly prized items only used by powerful chiefs and their family. Ornamentation for most came from natural sources – sun-fired clay beads, fragrant woods, seeds and shells. Up to the end of the 18th century travellers reported that strings of beads were worn around the neck and waist with metal arm and leg-bands originating from Phalaborwa and Messina in the Northern Province.

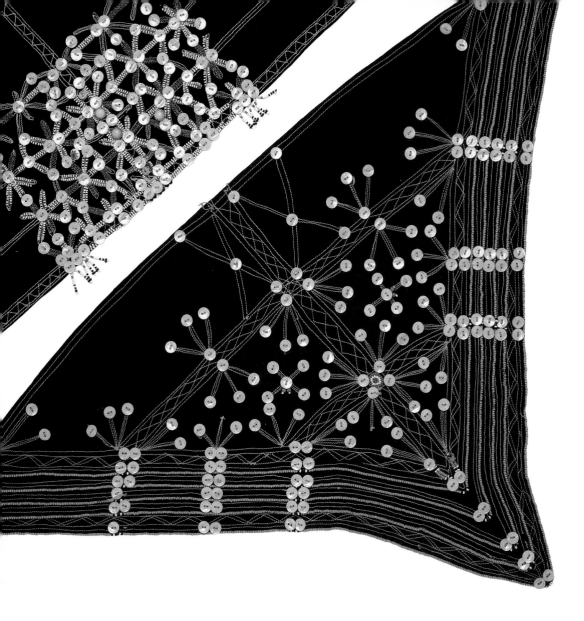

whole community. The converted turned their backs on many of the old traditions, including the wearing of beads, and embraced Western education and culture. The Red People, *amaqaba*, rejected the new teachings and continued to practise ancestral worship. Today, Christianity has reached most people, even the traditional healers, but the practice of venerating the ancestors and other traditional practices, such as the use of white clay during the seclusion of initiates, have continued.

## Trade

UP TO the beginning of the 19th century the trade of imported goods was controlled by the African chiefs. Small amounts of goods were bartered and it was reasonably easy to control. A few beads were traded from Sofala and Delagoa Bay. Metal was mined in the Northern Provinces and traded for skins and hides. Dagga, iron and copper were exchanged for goats from the Khoi pastoralists. The San hunter-gatherers killed elephants for meat, and traded the ivory for Xhosa dagga and cattle.

Trade between the colonists and the Xhosa was banned by the Dutch East India Company government at the Cape Colony, but the colonial settlers traded illegally with the neighbouring Xhosa, exchanging copper, iron and beads for cattle and ivory. This trade was profitable to both sides. In 1806 the British took control of the Cape Colony from the Batavian Republic

There has always been a belief in ancestral spirits. The ancestors, *izinyanya*, are the spirits of deceased men related through the male line. The male head of the household is the link between the living and the dead. Red ochre was rubbed onto their bodies and textiles as the colour red was an outward sign that the individual was partaking in the everyday life of the community. Those temporarily outside tribal activities – women who had just given birth and were breastfeeding their babies, or youths in seclusion during initiation – used white clay to cover their bodies. The significance of these colours was reflected in the colour of beads worn – red was chosen by chiefs and white was traditionally used by diviners and healers.

When missionaries moved into the area and established hospitals and schools, the conversion to Christianity divided the

ABOVE: *Triangular headscarves,* iqhiya. *Mother-of-pearl buttons and embroidery decorate the scarves with symmetrical designs. They were worn by newly married women in the Eastern Cape; late 20th century.*

LEFT: *Detail of a cotton skirt with tassels. Braid or thin strips of black cloth form decorative bands around the bottom of the skirt. Mother-of-pearl buttons add emphasis to the patterns.*

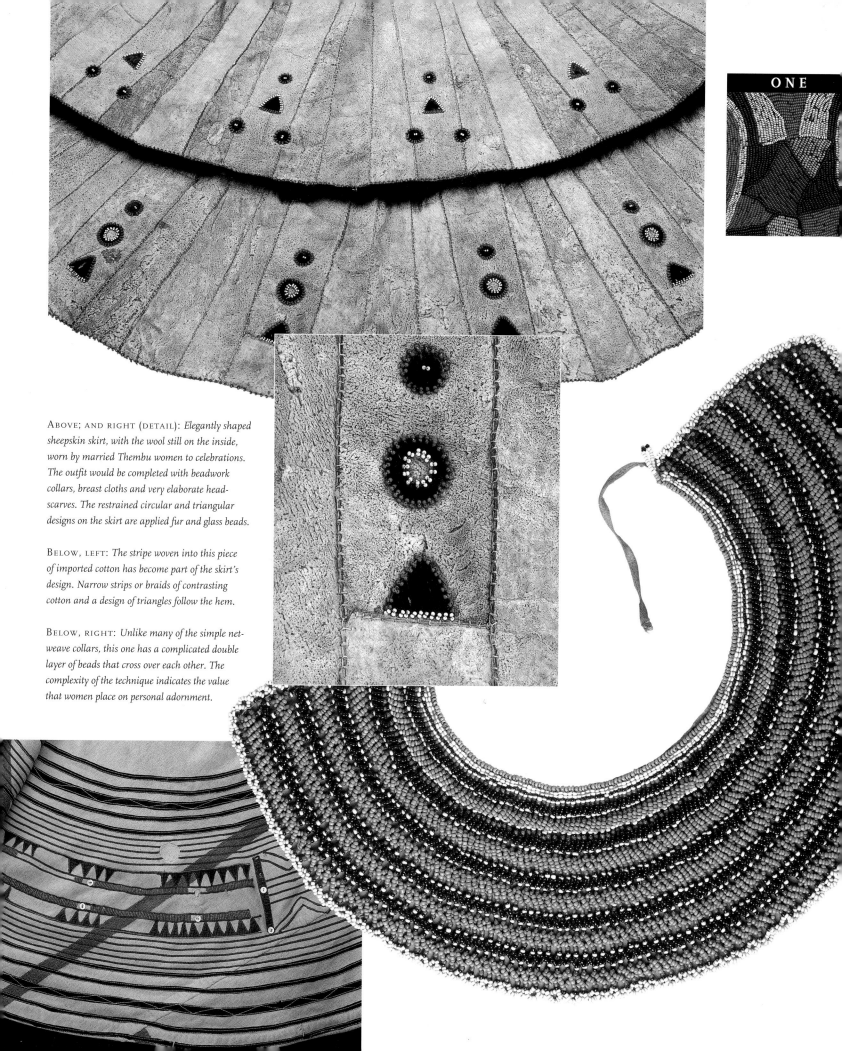

ABOVE; AND RIGHT (DETAIL): *Elegantly shaped sheepskin skirt, with the wool still on the inside, worn by married Thembu women to celebrations. The outfit would be completed with beadwork collars, breast cloths and very elaborate headscarves. The restrained circular and triangular designs on the skirt are applied fur and glass beads.*

BELOW, LEFT: *The stripe woven into this piece of imported cotton has become part of the skirt's design. Narrow strips or braids of contrasting cotton and a design of triangles follow the hem.*

BELOW, RIGHT: *Unlike many of the simple netweave collars, this one has a complicated double layer of beads that cross over each other. The complexity of the technique indicates the value that women place on personal adornment.*

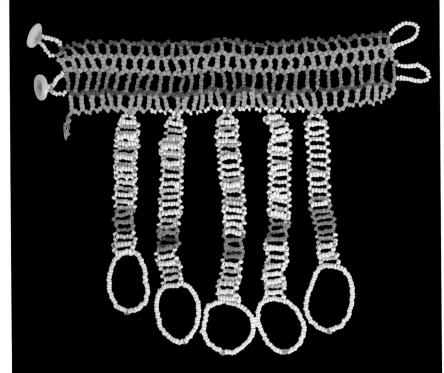

(as the Netherlands were referred to between 1795 and 1806), and in 1820 the first permanent British settlers arrived in the Grahamstown area. The illegal trading escalated, and, in an attempt to control it, official fairs were arranged. At the first fair only red ochre from pits that had been confiscated from the Xhosa was available for barter. The fair was a failure as the one commodity the Xhosa clamoured for was beads, but the second Clay Pits Fair was a resounding success as permission was granted for the trading of beads and buttons. The Xhosa brought 434 pounds of ivory to barter.

The Xhosa did not seem to be looking for essential items such as salt and the ochre they used to decorate their bodies, they wanted beads as they could be traded for profit. The beads moved through the country via small transactions. The value was directly influenced by the number of beads available. Fortunes could be made trading on the frontier, but it was a precarious business. As fashions changed those caught with unwanted colours and sizes went bankrupt.

In 1824 the first regular fair was held at Fort Willshire. No liquor or firearms could be traded. To boost the home industries, each transaction had to include an item of British manufacture such as iron pots, blankets or cloth. The most desirable trade item, the beads, had to be imported by

the British from Venice. Tons of ivory was sold at these fairs over the next few years and supplies became depleted. The fairs were no longer commercially viable for the Xhosa as cartels developed among the colonists, pushing down the price of cattle to unacceptable values. By 1830 the fairs were discontinued and traders were allowed to enter Xhosa territory and set up

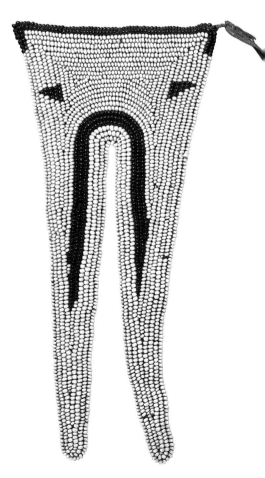

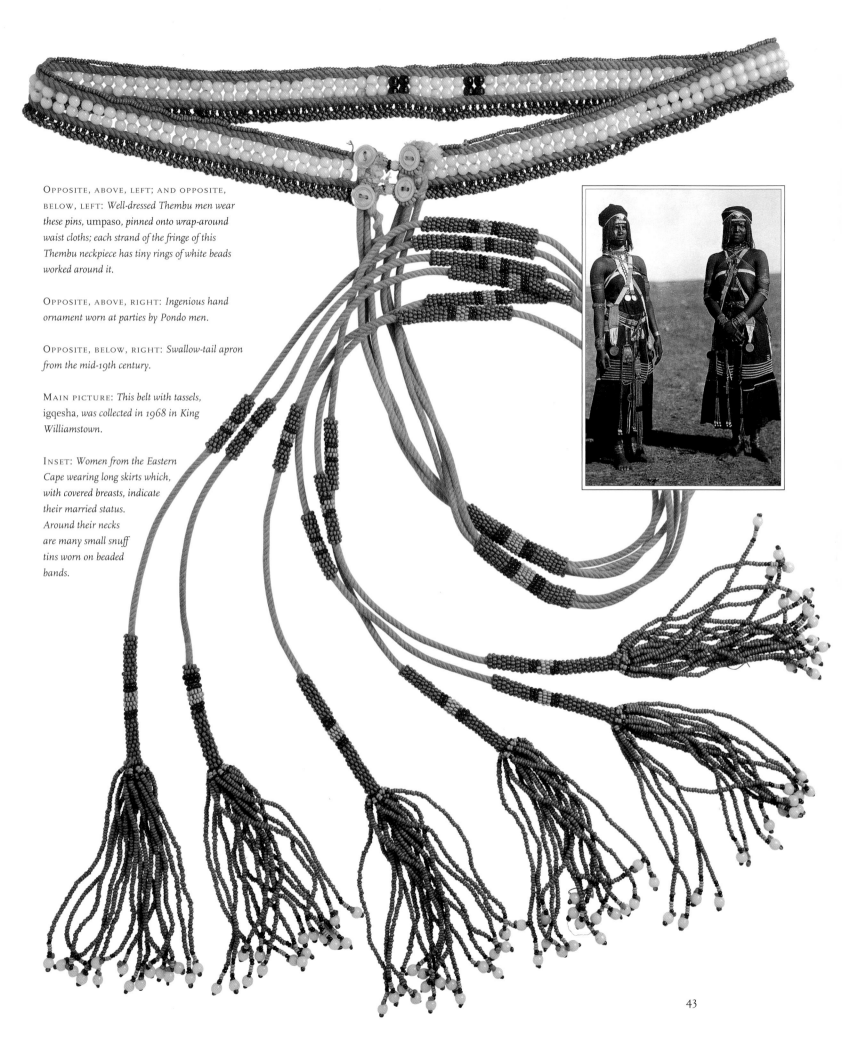

Opposite, above, left; and opposite,
below, left: *Well-dressed Thembu men wear
these pins,* umpaso, *pinned onto wrap-around
waist cloths; each strand of the fringe of this
Thembu neckpiece has tiny rings of white beads
worked around it.*

Opposite, above, right: *Ingenious hand
ornament worn at parties by Pondo men.*

Opposite, below, right: *Swallow-tail apron
from the mid-19th century.*

Main picture: *This belt with tassels,*
igqesha, *was collected in 1968 in King
Williamstown.*

Inset: *Women from the Eastern
Cape wearing long skirts which,
with covered breasts, indicate
their married status.
Around their necks
are many small snuff
tins worn on beaded
bands.*

43

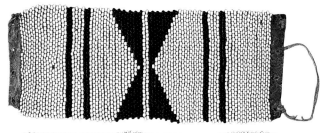

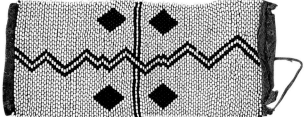

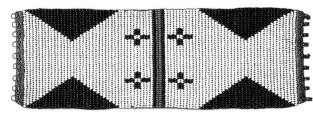

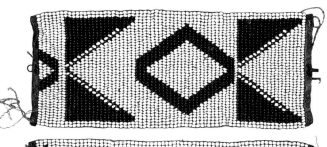

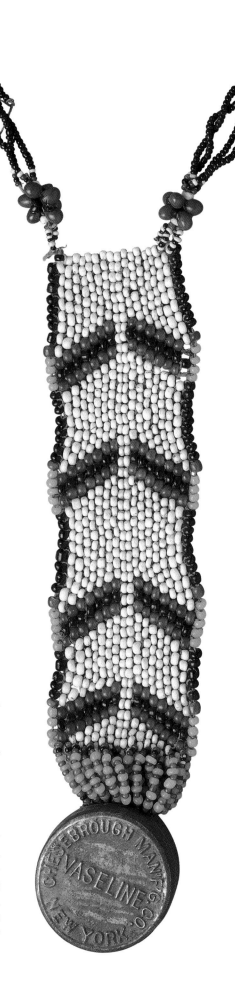

RIGHT: *An imported Vaseline tin used as a snuff container. The Xhosa in the Eastern Cape lived near the Southern Sothos, and the beadwork looks Sotho; collected in the Herschell district in 1908.*

trading stations. This meant that there was no longer a place in the trading chain for the Xhosa speculators. This and the over supply of beads caused their value to plummet.

Up until fairly recently glass beads could still be purchased at local trading stores. Women were very particular about the beads they selected – they had to be bright and clear, of an even size, and with a hole big enough to take their needle and thread or sinew. At the trading stores the hanks of beads hung from nails under each of which was an enamel basin to catch the beads from broken strings. Generally, the beads were sold by the string, but those from the enamel basins were sold by the spoonful. The beads used for beadwork, *intsimbi yesiXhosa*, are small and delicate compared to contemporary Ndebele beads, and require very fine needles to string them together.

Before cotton became available at the trading store sinew from the shoulders of goats and cows was used. A vegetable fibre was also freely available, the aloes (*A. arborescens*) which are planted around the cattle enclosures and have strong fibre in their fleshy leaves. These were beaten and washed, and, after drying, the fibres were twisted together for strength. Both the sinew and plant fibre are stiff enough not to need a needle. The preferred colours were pink, carnelian, various shades of blue and white. Within the traditional formats, there was always freedom to introduce new designs. Different forms of beadwork defined a person's age group, marital status and place of birth.

## Threading beads

BEADS were an important part of every stage and transition in a traditional Xhosa's life. The first ritual was the introduction of the baby to the ancestors. During this ceremony the baby's father gave each of the guests two white beads, which were then given to the mother who immediately made them into a necklace for the child.

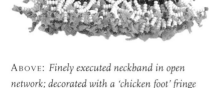

The young men, especially if they had been working in the mines, had enough money to buy beads to be made up into articles to adorn themselves. These were made by their girlfriends. The young men would wear numerous headbands, neckpieces with long flowing tassels, body harnesses and any accessory, such as glasses or tin cans, would be covered with beads.

During their period of seclusion, the youths undergoing initiation removed all their beadwork and rubbed white clay over their bodies. After circumcision the youth could be married. These young men were called *abafana*. The South African football team has taken the name Bafana bafana as their nick name.

A girl's initiation occurred when she first started menstruating. She was secluded behind a grass mat curtain in a hut. During this time she made a beaded fringe apron, *inkciyo*, which she would wear for the rest of her life. This is mainly made from white beads. During her time

ABOVE: *Finely executed neckband in open network; decorated with a 'chicken foot' fringe where each strand splits into three.*

OPPOSITE, LEFT; AND RIGHT: *Boldly designed anklets, isitsaba, worn by men at traditional ceremonies and meetings. Each anklet in a pair is different. They were collected in the second half of the 20th century, but because they are an important item of Xhosa formal dress, their shape and design have remained constant for over a hundred years.*

BELOW, LEFT: *Neck ornament representing a formal bow tie and tie which would have been worn mainly by men on special occasions.*

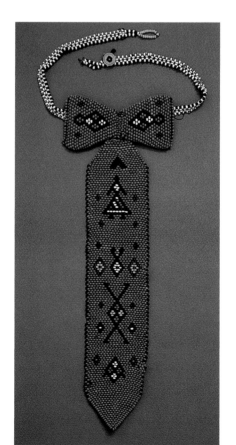

in isolation she received a fertility figure. As an *intombi*, she could attend the dances held for the young people. She wore many beaded decorations, but never as many as the *abafana*.

Among the various groups there were different traditions, but a man's first gift to the woman he intended to marry was a string of beads, or an *assegai* (spear), which was left outside her hut.

During the bride's seclusion before marriage, she and her retinue worked on their beadwork. At their formal reappearance elaborate beadwork was worn by both the men and the women. The bridegroom would wear headbands, long fringed necklaces, a body harness, armbands and neckbands. Everything he carried, including bags, umbrella and handkerchief, was also covered in beads.

White beads are associated with diviner's regalia. The older people remember the time when beadwork was the regular dress for special occasions.

The former president of South Africa, Nelson Mandela, is a Xhosa speaker from the Eastern Cape, as is the present president, Thabo Mbeki.

# ZULU AND SWAZI

I N THE 18TH CENTURY King Shaka's predecessors reorganized the traditional adolescent age-set into regiments as a response to cattle raiding. They helped to win the most desirable lands during the famine of the early 1800s and then under Shaka (r. 1816–28) to create a centralized state that became the Zulu Kingdom. To the south lived Xhosa-speaking peoples and, further south, the British, the Boers and the Xhoi, and to the north, Delagoa Bay in Mozambique was the closest major trade outpost. Today, KwaZulu Natal is made up of the former Zulu Kingdom and the Natal Colony.

## Glass bead trade

F OR centuries Arab traders bartered along the east coast of Africa as far south as Delagoa Bay. They brought glass beads, among other goods, by sea from India, Egypt and Syria, to exchange for ivory, gold and slaves. Overland routes were developed by the local inhabitants to distribute trade goods throughout Africa, so that for hundreds of years imported beads and other commodities had been available to the Nguni people.

The Portuguese arrived from the West at the beginning of the 16th century in search of a sea route to the spice trade in the East. They were soon followed by the Dutch and British, who exchanged beads and other goods for fresh provisions for their scurvy-blighted sailors.

When Henry Fynn sailed into Port Natal at the beginning of the 19th century to prepare for the arrival of the first settlers, he was summoned to the court of Shaka. The welcoming party included between 8,000 and 10,000 dancing girls dressed in beaded costume. All beads entering the Zulu kingdom had to be delivered to the king, who then distributed them, reserving certain colours for his favourite women. Others were given to soldiers for deeds of valour. Already a code was developing and the right to wear certain beads manifested a person's age group, sex, marital status and social standing.

## The art of beadwork

B EADWORKING skills were developed at court by the women and girls. Nguni society is exogenous – people only marry outside their clan – so the bride moved away from where she was born, and these skills spread over the whole Zulu kingdom.

Opposite, top: *Bhaca neck ornament from Richmond, Southern Natal, 1950–60. The fringe ends are decorated with Job's tears seeds.*

Opposite, middle: *Girdle from Sizanenjana, near Donnybrook, Southern Natal, 1910. Small triangles are joined to form a larger chevron design.*

Opposite, bottom: *Ricksha pullers still carry passengers on the Durban beachfront. Their costumes are made to attract customers, but the beadwork is in different regional styles.*

Above, left: *The provenance of early pieces is not always known. The fluted designs on this horn snuff box, 1871–86, are associated with Swazi carvings, and it is certainly of Northern Nguni origin.*

Above, right: *This simple fringed neckpiece, with colours arranged in horizontal bands, displays the colours popular in the Msinga area, 1981.*

Right, middle: *Neck ornament collected in Umginqo, Qudeni, in 1891, made in the Msinga colour scheme.*

Right, bottom: *Apron collected in the 1950s in the Nongoma/Ceza area.*

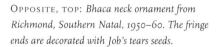

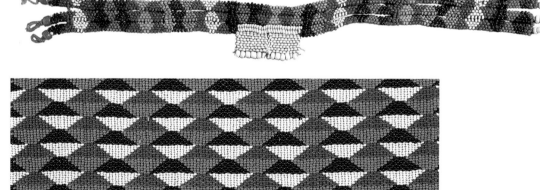

47

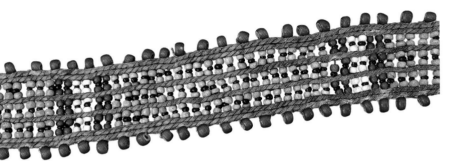

TOP: *Apron collected in 1950 in the Nongoma area.*

ABOVE: *Bead and grass belt collected in 1910 in Sizanenjana, near Donnybrook, Southern Natal.*

BELOW: *Bandolier band from the Nongoma area.*

ABOVE, RIGHT; AND INSET: *Bamboo snuff box or medicine holder covered with brick-stitch beadwork; the Zulu sangoma has several around her neck. (Both Afri-Karner Collection)*

As more white settlers arrived in the Natal Colony and the independence of the Zulu kings waned, more regional variety developed in beadwork styles; the king no longer had the prerogative of commandeering all new bead colours and styles. The beads that traders were bringing into the country were from Venice, Bohemia and the Netherlands – southern Africa was their biggest market, and distributors made up special sample cards for the different areas.

## Traditional use of beadwork

ONLY after Zulu girls reached marrying age would they progress from the teenage *amatshitshi* to courting age, and to the status *iqhikiza* when they could become engaged, and produce beadwork tokens for their lovers. The boy would present the girl's age-mates with loose beads, and the final ornament comprised a message to the recipient coded in the sequencing of colours and bead types, each having its agreed local connotation. Meaning was sometimes not specific, so the boy would call upon his sisters to divine what his lover was saying. In this way, by the mid-19th century Zulu beadwork became primarily a convention for communication between courting youths. With techniques for production of bead textiles (solid panels) appearing towards the end of the century, more complex meanings became possible, by the coding and juxtaposing of motifs.

Beadwork is now worn in KwaZulu Natal and Swaziland largely at recently revived ceremonies and celebrations. With the high price of glass beads, still only imported, much of the new work is made with plastic beads.

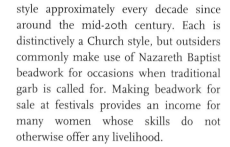

LEFT: *Elaborate headdress of a married Zulu woman.*

RIGHT: *An early 20th-century example of a simple chevron design in brick stitch. As beads became available from white traders in greater numbers, beadwork became more complex, and many regional styles developed.*

BELOW: *Man's formal jacket decorated with bands of beadwork of different designs, both front and back.*

## Sacred ornament

ONE OF the enduring sites of beadworking skills and use in KwaZulu Natal province today is the independent black church of the Nazareth Baptists. Founded in 1910, this blend of an unorthodox charismatic/messianic Christianity with Zulu dance, custom and dress has appeal far beyond KwaZulu Natal. Part of this may be due to its preservation of forms of expressive culture such as the dance uniforms of the four major age/sex groups, each with its ensemble of beadwork forms (headbands, hatbands, wristbands and anklets, blouse-hems and lap-covers) that have changed style approximately every decade since around the mid-20th century. Each is distinctively a Church style, but outsiders commonly make use of Nazareth Baptist beadwork for occasions when traditional garb is called for. Making beadwork for sale at festivals provides an income for many women whose skills do not otherwise offer any livelihood.

# NDEBELE

THE NDEBELE comprise two groups, the Nzundza and the Manala, each with their own individual characteristics and dialects. The Nzundza were defeated by the Boers in the Mapoch War of 1883 and thereafter were taken virtually as slaves to work on farms and their lands were confiscated. The customs of the Nzundza were regarded as a unifying factor for the scattered nation and the reconstruction of traditional family life, together with other traditions such as male initiation, were used to reinforce social and cultural unity. Beadwork was a visible means of emphasizing group values and identity as well as communicating status and the passing of rites of passage to the community.

## Traditional beadwork

THE indigenous culture of the Ndebele of Mpumalanga in South Africa – their traditional beadwork adornments, dress and unique wall paintings – is among the most internationally documented and well known of the southern African indigenous cultures. Their trademark bold wall decorations and geometrically designed beadwork are traditions which are linked both formally and culturally to their sense of identity. The social functions and status of the Ndebele are reflected in the types of beadwork they produce.

Traditional older pieces of Ndebele beadwork are characterized by large areas of white beads interspersed with small geometric designs in colour. This is probably due to the limited availability of coloured beads. These pieces are closely worked and highly prized among collectors of beadwork.

Ndebele contemporary beadwork is identified by symmetrical abstract geometric designs and later pieces include references to everyday life – such as licence plates, razor blades, pitched-roof houses, telephone poles and aeroplanes. Today, the availability of a greater variety of colours, the demands of the commercial market and the economic considerations of the Ndebele beadworkers are more likely to dictate the form and pattern of the beadwork.

ABOVE, LEFT: *'Telephone-pole' dancing stick.*

LEFT: *At the beginning of the 20th century white beads were almost exclusively used by the Ndebele.*

ABOVE, RIGHT: *Leg and arm rings made from strings of beads wound around grass coils.*

RIGHT: *Child figure covered with bead-covered rolls.*

OPPOSITE, ABOVE, LEFT: *Fringe of white beads used as a veil for a back apron.*

OPPOSITE, ABOVE, RIGHT: *Beaded blanket,* irari.

OPPOSITE, BELOW, LEFT: *A bride's cape,* linaga.

INSET: *Openwork design with tabs hanging down.*

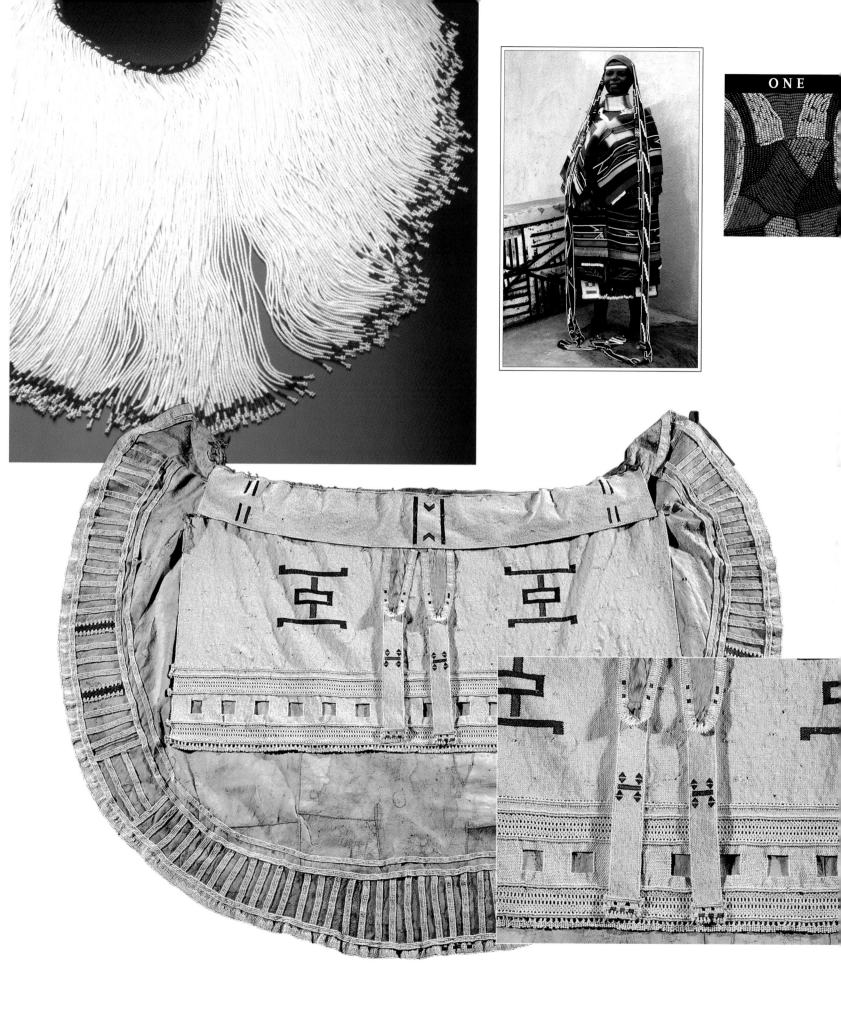

One of the main functions of Ndebele beadwork is of social significance. Distinctive types of beadwork, and the way it is worn, mark the various stages of a woman's life in Ndebele society. A beaded fringed apron, *lighabi*, worn around the hips, identifies a very young girl. An older pubescent girl wears an *isiphephethu*, a rectangular-shaped apron panel made of hide or canvas, which is decorated with geometric beaded patterns. The *isiphephethu* is usually made by a girl's mother or grandmother and symbolizes her passage from youth to adulthood, with the implicit prospect of marriage. The aprons worn by married women are called *liphotho* and have a fringe in the centre and rectangles at the sides.

For important ceremonies, such as female initiations, young women wear *isigolwane*, wide beaded arm and leg rings which, in an attempt to attract offers of marriage, accentuate their beauty and charms to the men who are watching. Ndebele brides wear a formal five-fingered apron, *ijogolo*. The most dramatic item of the bride's attire is the wedding cape, *linaga*, worn across her shoulders and back, which is often fully beaded. She would also wear an *inyoka*, a beaded veil attached to the back of her head which trails to the ground.

Another traditional Ndebele dress element, worn by mature women, is the *isithimba*, a back apron made from a semi-circular piece of hide which hangs from a thick roll of coiled grass covered with beads. Below this is a horizontal panel

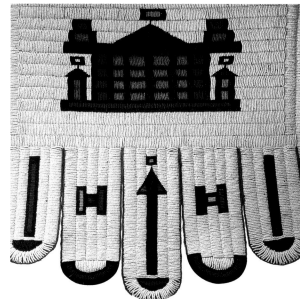

of beads. Ndebele women celebrate the return of their sons from initation by wearing long narrow strips of beadwork, *linga koba* (long tears), on each side of the head to show the change of their status to maturity.

## Fertility dolls

ANOTHER use for beadwork is the fertility doll. The Ndebele have traditionally made fertility dolls for marriages to symbolize the continuation of Ndebele traditional values. A fertility doll, *umndwana* (which means child), is a conical shape composed of a series of concentric beaded rings, which evoke ceremonial female dress, the *isigolwane* discussed above. The shape has evolved to include legs with leg rings and more human features.

## Collecting Ndebele beadwork

NDEBELE material culture has been a rich source for collectors of traditional 'African art' for many years. Ndebele beadwork can be found in museums such as the British Museum

OPPOSITE, ABOVE, LEFT: *Child figure.*

OPPOSITE, ABOVE, RIGHT: *This Ndebele man is dressed for a special occasion; his wife would have made the large, thin neck rings.*

OPPOSITE, BELOW: Lighabi, *a front apron worn by a very young girl.*

ABOVE, LEFT: *Striped woollen blanket decorated with two strips of dense beadwork.*

LEFT: *Gourd bowl decorated with beadwork.*

ABOVE, RIGHT: Ijogolo, *a marriage or ceremonial apron, with distinctive fingers hanging down.*

RIGHT: Liphotho, *a married woman's apron.*

BELOW, RIGHT: Isiphephethu, *a pubescent girl's apron, made by a mother for her daughter when she is old enough to invite proposals of marriage.*

in London and the Metropolitan Museum of Art in New York. Southern African beadwork is mostly represented internationally by Ndebele styles. These designs are also finding their way into contemporary branding and packaging designs of South African products and export items. Ndebele design has provoked international interest in sectors such as the fashion industry, particularly in the Paris fashion houses. Traditional designs are constantly finding their way into a post-apartheid mosaic of what is 'South African'.

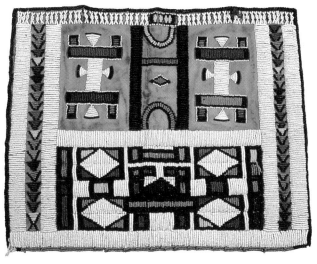

# TSONGA

TSONGA SPEAKERS live in three countries, South Africa, Zimbabwe and Mozambique, but the beadwork from the former is distinctly different. The Swiss anthropologist H. P. Junod suggested this was because they live close to the Ndebele and Sotho who had rich and well-established beadwork traditions. The name Shangaan is sometimes used interchangeably or in combination with Tsonga, which speaks to the history of the domination of the Tsonga in Mozambique. In the late 1820s the Zulu General Soshangane established himself and his army in the region around Delagoa Bay which led to the first in a series of mass migrations of Tsonga westwards into South Africa.

ABOVE, LEFT: *Loin cloth,* siyandhana, *worn by traditional healers.*

ABOVE, RIGHT: *Tsonga child figure,* nwana. *The wooden core is covered with a chevron pattern constructed using brick stitch. The skirt, made from salempore, has white beads sewn around the hem; a piece of netting is tied in a sash around the figure.*

## The uses of beadwork

TSONGA beadwork illustrated here was made by women who live in the Northern Province of South Africa and dates from the mid to late 20th century. Men wear some beadwork items for festive occasions, but it is worn primarily by women. Beadwork is incorporated into the regalia of *tinanga* (traditional healers) and pieces are made for specific rituals and age groups. The *nxanga*, associated with female puberty, is a long wide belt made entirely from beads. Though arrangements differ, the belt usually has a white ground with solid coloured (green, red, blue, orange or occasionally pink) geometric shapes, such as diamonds, triangles and chevrons, arranged in a continuous and repeating pattern. The whole is enhanced with folds and fringes and with metal ornaments such as small silver or brass circular discs.

In form and technique the *nxanga* is similar to some necklaces and body ornaments, but in function it is linked to two articles of dress used in rituals, the *titho* and *siyandhana*. The *titho* is made for the initiation school. The base is salempore which is decorated with horizontal rows of white beads in geometric patterns. The *siyandhana* is not a specifically female item of dress as it is worn as part of the costume of diviners, male and female. It, too, consists of horizontal registers of white beads on a plain fabric, usually red or black and more recently blue and green. The use of white beads on all these items may be linked to liminal periods when

girls move into womanhood and diviners call on their ancestral spirit to assist with the healing process. White beads are also used exclusively on the large skirt *xibelani* or *xitlhrkutana* worn by adult women. The skirt is made from a complete bolt (approximately 18 metres, 60 ft) of salempore, nowadays sold as Shangaan in downtown Johannesburg. It gives the wearer a rounded silhouette.

## Tsonga dolls

THE *xibelani* or *xitlhrkutana* skirt has become a characteristic feature, a marker of identity, among Tsonga-speaking women in the Northern

ABOVE: *Ndau apron from Zimbabwe.*

RIGHT: *Belt with chevron designs, and mother-of-pearl buttons.*

FAR RIGHT: *A beaded marriage basket. Asymmetry is a feature of Tsonga beadwork and can be seen in the completely different designs used on the basket and the lid. Strings of beads have been woven into an open fabric on the base.*

OPPOSITE, RIGHT, BELOW: *Tsonga medicine gourd with carved wooden stopper in a bead-covered basket.*

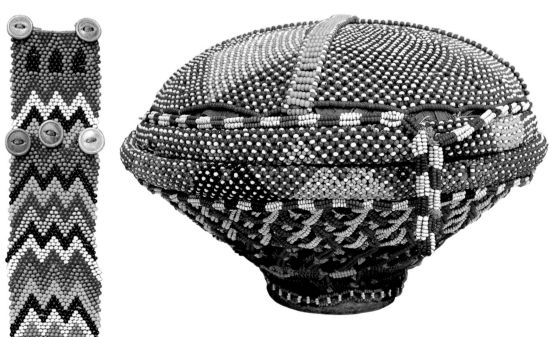

ONE

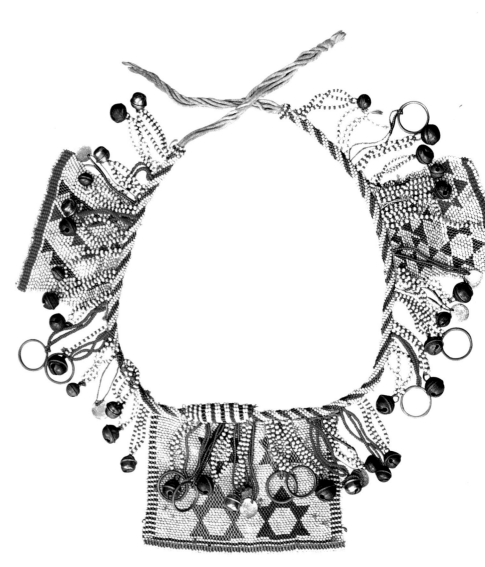

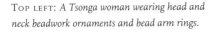

TOP LEFT: *A Tsonga woman wearing head and neck beadwork ornaments and bead arm rings.*

ABOVE, RIGHT: *Beaded belt associated with female puberty; the Tsonga often use star designs.*

ABOVE, LEFT: *Detail of a wrap-around cloth,* nceka, *which is worn over one shoulder.*

RIGHT: *Tsonga (Shangaan) front apron made from discarded items. Traditionally they are made from beads, but beads are very expensive.*

OPPOSITE, ABOVE: Nceka *with simple geometric designs and lettering which creates a visual impact.*

OPPOSITE, BELOW: *This waistcoat is constructed from beads alone, and is not attached to fabric.*

56

Province, and, as a sign of the female, has been incorporated into the small figures, more commonly known as dolls, but more correctly described as child figures, which are called *nwana* in Tsonga. The figure consists of two parts – a simple cylinder completely covered with beads and a fabric skirt, and these basic components have remained the same for the last forty years. An explanation for the constituent elements is that the cylinder is male and the skirt female, the two factors that make the child. There are no legs or arms or separate head with distinguishing features. The figures are decorated with beaded panels, plastic hair clips and necklaces.

Since the figure is called *nwana* this seems at one level to link it to the idea of fertility, like the *nxanga* which is taken to the husband's house after marriage, but they seem more like objects encompassing a wish for the child to come. Linked symbolically to female maturation and marriage, they can also be seen as a means of linking female generations. After the birth of the first daughter, the beads can be unpicked and used as ornaments for the child.

Tsonga women tie two cloths over their shoulders to cover their upper bodies. Named *minceka* these reveal the wearer's identity. They are not ritual garments, nor are they bound by conventions or the controls of ritual, and can be used to show initiative, both in subject and techniques. Beaded *minceka* are made from dark-toned fabric, which sets up a strong contrast with the beads, and have become virtual fantastic landscapes; some more recent ones record a history of the region.

Tsonga beadwork covers a range from the ritual to the everyday, from the spectacular to the ordinary. At a formal level there is an interplay between a coded form of abstraction and recognizable imagery. At another, beadwork reflects a life concerned with continuity, festivity, display and decoration of self. It tells essentially of the concerns of women.

# SOTHO

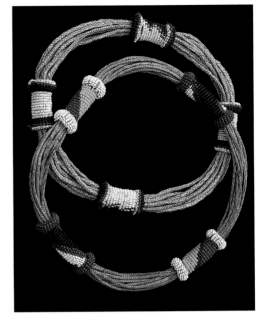

## THE BASOTHO AND THE BATLOKWA

THE Sotho-Tswana people inhabit the central plateau of southern Africa. Other than their language, their chief point of difference from the Nguni is their belief in totems. Descent is patrilineal, each clan member bearing the name of their ancestral totem. There are three divisions within the Sotho group, the Southern Sotho, including the Batlokwa, live mainly in Lesotho, a small independent country within the borders of South Africa, and small groups live in the Eastern Cape, Natal and the Free State; the Tswana or Western Sotho live in Botswana and the North-West Province; and the Northern Sotho cover a large area of Mpumalanga and the Northern Province. There are many subgroups, the Pedi is one of the largest. There are pockets of Sotho-Tswana people living in urban areas where, from 1870 onwards, many of the men went to work in the diamond and gold mines in South Africa. The Basotho nation developed during the early 19th century. This was a time of terrible upheaval and war in southern Africa.

## Initiation ceremonies

IN LESOTHO the young people associate beads with initiation and diviners. Both girls and boys attend initiation schools where, after a physically gruelling period, they are welcomed back into the community as adults. At this celebration the young men and women wear beadwork. Initiation, opposed by the missionaries, is once again becoming more sought after as a means of emphasizing their identity as Basotho.

Of all the Sotho people, the Batlokwa use the most beadwork in their attire. During the Difaqane the Batlokwa were defeated and lost their land. Some were granted land in the Eastern Cape by the

ABOVE, LEFT: *The Batlokwa have made a feature of larger beads in these tassels.*

ABOVE, RIGHT: *Neck ornaments made from plaited grass; decorated with rings of beadwork.*

BELOW, LEFT: *The fringe at the bottom is a complicated series of loops.*

BELOW, RIGHT: *The chevron design symbolizes the opposing forces of life – good and bad, day and night.*

ABOVE: *Child figures,* ngoana seho, *were carried by barren women in the hope that they would bear children. They were made from gourds, like this one, or bottles, reeds and beads; late 19th century.*

ABOVE, RIGHT: *Collar of netted beadwork with a bold chevron design.*

BELOW: *Lovedu waist ornament,* zwibebedana. *The Lovedu came from north of the Limpopo River.*

British, and others settled in Natal. At different times beads have had different meanings and values to the Sotho. The few beads that trickled through from the Arab trade on the east coast were rare and very valuable. They were used as currency, and could even be used as a bride-price in the place of cattle. 'In short, if cattle were not available for requesting a virgin from her elders, then she was requested by means of a hoe for cultivating sorgum, or else by means of a necklace.' (A. Sekese, 1892, translated by Heinz J. Kuckertz)

Later the beads were used as decoration, but only for the chief's headdress as they were still very expensive items. King Moshoeshoe I wore a simplified form of the headdress as a beaded headband or *setaka.* When beads became available in larger quantities they were incorporated into their existing apparel, especially for the newly initiated, to decorate and beautify their costume.

Originally, the South Sothos were known as the people of the blanket, *batho*

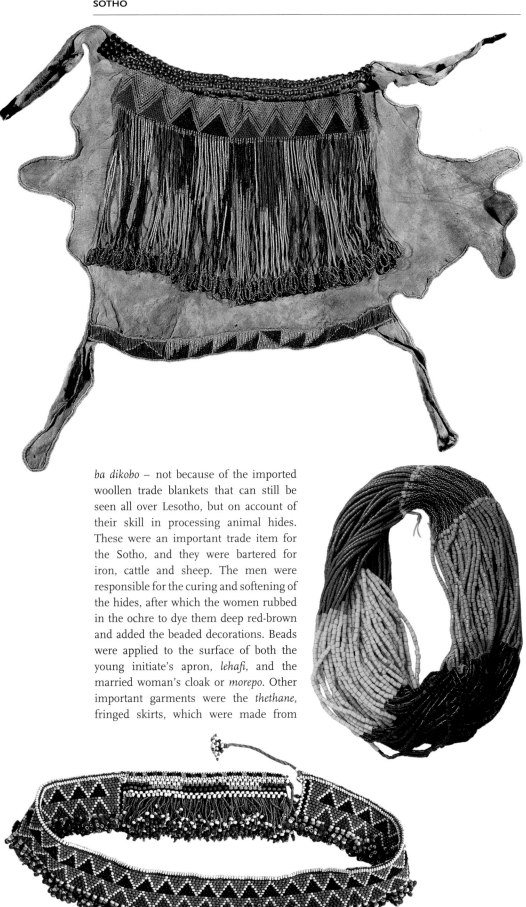

LEFT: *The whole goatskin has been left intact and decorated with beadwork and a long fringe to make this cape; South Sotho, probably Batlokwa.*

ABOVE, RIGHT: *The skin in this piece has been textured during curing, and sparse rectangular beaded tabs have been added.*

BELOW, MIDDLE: *A Lovedu necklace, made up of many strands, worn by a bride when she first arrived at her husband's home. It is usually strung so that each strand has four colours, and each is fixed so that blocks of colour are created.*

BOTTOM: *Beaded girdle, with a fringe in the front; late 19th century.*

*ba dikobo* – not because of the imported woollen trade blankets that can still be seen all over Lesotho, but on account of their skill in processing animal hides. These were an important trade item for the Sotho, and they were bartered for iron, cattle and sheep. The men were responsible for the curing and softening of the hides, after which the women rubbed in the ochre to dye them deep red-brown and added the beaded decorations. Beads were applied to the surface of both the young initiate's apron, *lehafi*, and the married woman's cloak or *morepo*. Other important garments were the *thethane*, fringed skirts, which were made from natural fibres, the leaf of the indigenous gazania, *tsikitlane*. The leather band holding the fringe was covered with beads. The only tool needed for making this was a sharp awl without an eye.

After the initiation ceremonies a necklace of suet from an animal ritually slaughtered for the ancestors is burnt and replaced with glass beads, *salebere*, symbolizing the end of a woman's childhood and her acceptance as an adult.

## PEDI

THE Pedi are a sub-group of the Northern Sotho. The boys undergo harsh initiation rites and at the celebrations to welcome them home after their seclusion red, white and blue or black bead-covered grass hoops are worn around the hips. Wide arm decorations, made up of numerous strands of beads held in place by spacers, display bold geometric designs.

Girl initiates wear bead-covered grass rolls around their waists at their home-coming ceremony and string aprons on a beaded band. Married women wear an

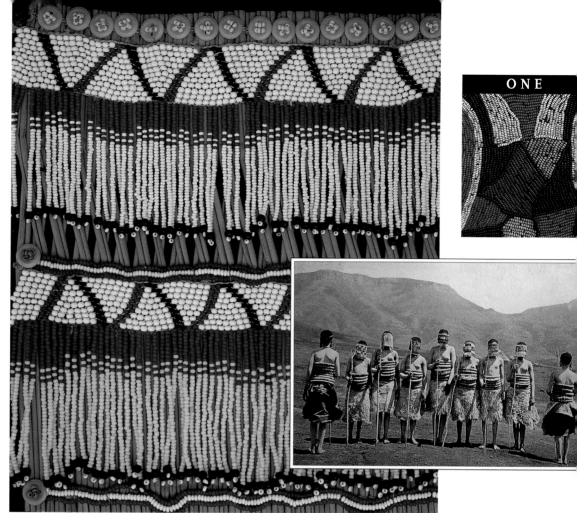

apron made from leather and decorated with small pieces of beadwork. A large smock, originally introduced by the missionaries, covers their upper body, and a headscarf is normally worn, often decorated with discs of beadwork.

## THE NTWANE

THE Ntwane live in Kwarrielaagte in Mpumalanga. Historically they have been closely associated with the Pedi, although they are of Tswana origin; they have links through intermarriage with the Ndebele, who wear the same beaded neck bands; they also decorate the walls of their dwellings with geometric designs.

During a girl's initiation the sides and back of her head are shaved, and the top is shaped into a 'bicycle seat' hairstyle and decorated with discs of beadwork called 'squirrel's tails'. Multiple grass bracelets are worn around the arms, resembling the fertility figures the girls make during their seclusion as initiates.

Many men leave the rural homesteads to work in the city or in the mines, and it is the women who preserve the Sotho traditions and customs.

ABOVE, LEFT: *Two half circles make up this Pedi decoration, which was attached to a headscarf.*

ABOVE, RIGHT: *Mask, made from reeds and glass beads, used by girls of the Balé initiation school.*

INSET: *Girl initiates in Lesotho wearing masks.*

RIGHT: *Ntwane child figure,* gimwane. *The Ntwane are a small group of North Sothos living near Loskop Dam.*

FAR RIGHT: *Fringed skirt,* thethane, *South Sotho; end of the 19th century. Many hours are spent making these skirts for newly initiated girls.*

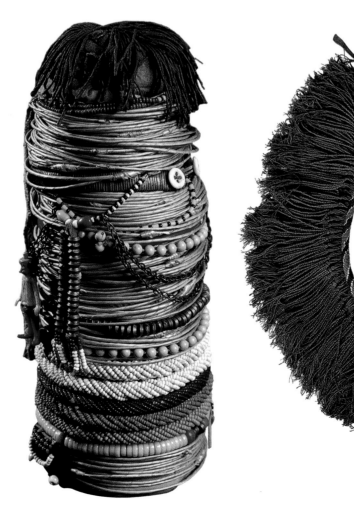

61

# EAST AFRICA

THIS AREA lies in the tropics and stretches from the south of Sudan, through Kenya, Uganda and Tanganyika, and includes Mozambique. To the west, the great Rift Valley runs where the oldest hominid – the precursor of the human race – remains were found near Lake Turkana in Kenya, and to the east lies the Indian Ocean, which provided access to influences and goods from the Indo-Pacific region.

## THE COASTAL PEOPLE

FROM the 9th century on beads from Persia, China and the Indo-Pacific area have been traded along the low-lying, hot and humid coastal belt of East Africa. With the spread of Islam, trade increased and Muslims from the Arabian peninsular, Shirazis from Iran and Indian traders brought beads, Indian fabrics, Persian ceramics and brass to trade for ivory, gold, slaves and rhinoceros horn. European beads became available, though in small quantities, in the late 15th century when the Portuguese battled for trading supremacy along this coast. Some of the most popular glass beads in the area were a brick red colour, known to the Portuguese as *barros miudas,* or beads of clay. These were made in India, but were quite soon copied by

European beadmakers in Venice, Bohemia and Amsterdam. By 1720 Arabs again controlled trade on the East African coast.

Weaving techniques, learned from the Arabs and Indians, were used to construct some of the beadwork, either using finger weaving, or a loom. Items of beadwork, worn as aprons, attest to the wealth built up by the coastal people acting as middlemen in trading transactions. All the way down the coast, especially in Mozambique, very beautifully designed, unique pieces, using interesting and varied colours, were made.

## PASTORALISTS

THE central area of East Africa is a highland plateau, some of it rolling grasslands and scattered bush, and some semi-desert. Cattle, sheep, goats and, in the dry north, camels were central to the economy of the Maasai, Samburu, Dinka, Pokot and Turkana pastoralists. For millennia, waves of migrators moved south through the country.

A few precious heirloom beads reached this inland area from both the west and east coasts of Africa along established internal trade routes, but it was not until 1900 that many seed beads of European manufacture were available, and never in as great a number as in southern Africa.

OPPOSITE, LEFT: *Apron originally from the highlands of Mozambique. (Afri-Karner Collection)*

OPPOSITE, ABOVE: *Comb from Mozambique. (Afri-Karner Collection)*

OPPOSITE, BELOW, RIGHT: *Shona knife from Mozambique. (Afri-Karner Collection)*

ABOVE, LEFT: *Snuff container, 19th century, possibly Zulu. (Afri-Karner Collection)*

ABOVE, RIGHT: *Maasai wedding top.*

RIGHT: *Turkana woman's beaded apron.*

Before then natural materials – seeds, bones, claws, teeth, sweet-smelling leaves, rolled and threaded – were used for adornment and to ornament their clothing. Ostrich eggshells were used to decorate their leather cloaks and skirts. Iron, both bought from the Swahili on the coast and smelted locally, was made into beads by bending a strip of metal into a ring and butting the joints. When aluminium pots were brought into the area about fifty years ago, they were cut up and made into beads by the Gabbra, perhaps imitating the imported faceted glass beads.

The pastoralists' beadwork from this area is distinctive, as narrow strips of stiff

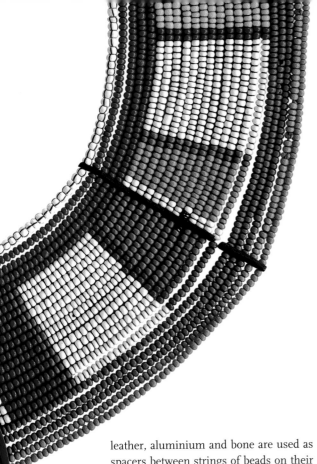

leather, aluminium and bone are used as spacers between strings of beads on their disc neck ornaments and gourd covers. In the earliest beadwork the colours favoured were white, black, green, navy, royal and pale blue, red and scarlet. Later yellow and orange were introduced.

Both men and women wore clothes that indicated their position in society. From puberty, girls started accumulating beaded neck and head ornaments – the greater the number, the higher the status. Much time was devoted to decorating their leather skirts and pubic aprons with ostrich eggshells, cowrie shells, an indicator of fertility and wealth since they were imported from the Indian Ocean. The Iraqw of Tanzania wear the most splendid leather skirts for ceremonies and weddings, using lazy stitch to apply large quantities of glass seed beads. Young Samburu girls wear numerous strings of beads around their necks, all gifts from admirers, and bands of beads around their heads with small bird-shaped pieces of metal hanging on the ends of a fringe of beads. The Turkana are proud, aggressive nomads, and their beadwork is bold. Beaded circles on a girl's cloak signify that she is not yet married, and their skirts are decorated with ostrich eggshells and glass beads. Bodices made up of beaded strings were worn by Dinka women, made in the

same way as the men's corsets, but loose and worn over the shoulders, more like a cape.

The men went through defined stages of transition according to their age – the main stages were childhood, warrior and elder. The most elaborate adornments and hairstyles were worn by the warriors. The Samburu (which means butterfly) warriors spend their leisure time creating very elaborate hairstyles. The rituals associated with transitions were most elaborate among the Maasai and Samburu who had settled in more fertile pastures. The warriors carefree life of raiding and courting came to an end at the Eunoto festival where they discarded their beaded ornaments and their fine hairstyles were shaved off, and, wrapped in a leather cloak, they became respectable elders.

## THE DINKA

THE Dinka, who live in the swamplands of the Sudd in southern Sudan, believe that their enormous herds of cattle are their link to the spirit world, and at a boy's initiation horn shapes are cut into his forehead to create a raised scar. The men wear tight corsets made up of many strings of small glass beads attached to two vertical

ABOVE, LEFT: *Beaded neck disc worn by Maasai women in southern Kenya and northern Tanzania.*

ABOVE, RIGHT: *Maasai gourd hollowed out to store honey and cow's milk. The detail shows how it was repaired after cracking with age.*

LEFT: *Small Maasai beaded wrist band.*

RIGHT: *Carved figure with beadwork apron made in Nairobi. (Afri-Karner Collection)*

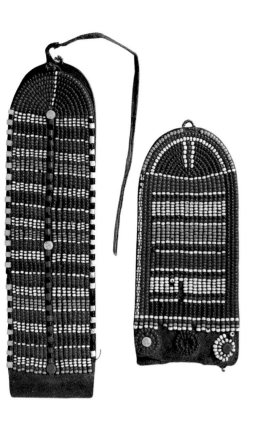

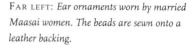

FAR LEFT: *Ear ornaments worn by married Maasai women. The beads are sewn onto a leather backing.*

LEFT: *This small finely constructed basket was made by the Tutsi. It is covered in a fabric of beadwork created using brick stitch. (Afri-Karner Collection)*

BELOW: *Ethiopian war cape.*

wires that run down the back. They are only removed when he moves on to another age set, when different colours are worn.

With colonization, and the establishment of large national parks, many of the grazing lands of the pastoralists have disappeared. Beadwork is one of the means of earning a living, so much of it for sale now is made specifically for the tourist market.

## INTERLACUSTRINE BANTU

THIS well-watered, fertile region lies to the west and north of Lake Victoria. Twa pygmies, who were the original inhabitants of this area, were replaced by the Hutu agriculturalists, and from the 16th century, by waves of pastoral Tutsi, who subjugated the Hutu. A feudal system developed, with the wealth held by the Tutsis. The king, *mwami*, held great power. Very beautiful coiled baskets with pointed lids were made by the women of the royal households, some covered with beads using patterns of triangles that were used in their basketry techniques. They covered musical instruments and weapons with beadwork, and made headbands and face veils. Elaborate headdresses fringed with colobus monkey fur were worn by the Himba royal dancers.

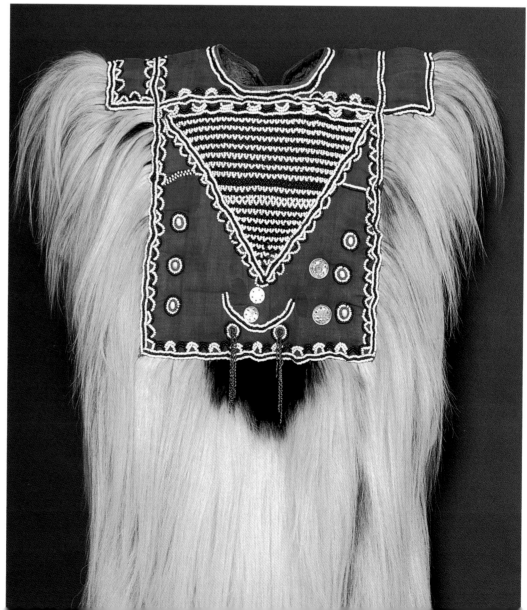

# Kuba

THE KUBA people are known for their beautiful woven and embroidered raphia cloths. They live in the southern Democratic Republic of the Congo, previously known as Zaire. The mountains of the Rift Valley form the eastern border of the enormous basin drained by the Congo, Kasai and Oubangui rivers. Most of the area is covered in dense tropical rainforest. Migrations of Bantu and Nilotic speakers from the north displaced and assimilated the hunter-gatherers who had formed settlements along the rivers on the forest edges. The first Kingdom to flourish was the Kongo on the coast, where the influence of the Portuguese was felt from the end of the 15th century. Following wars with the Portuguese in 1660 over their excessive demand for slaves for the Brazilian plantations, the economy of the kingdom of Kongo declined. The kingdoms that developed in the south were the Luba, who built their wealth on the copper ore found in the Shaba (Katanga) Province, the Luanda and the Kuba.

The Kuba, or Bushoong, live south of the rainforests where the wooded savannahs are drained by large tributaries of the Congo River. The dynasty was established in 1625, and the different groups within the kingdom owe allegiance to a king or Nyim. Because of its position on ancient trade routes between the east and west coasts of Africa, trade items, from very early on, became symbols of prestige and power. Only in the 19th century did the Kuba come in direct contact with Europeans. Ivory and raphia were the two main local products that were exchanged for manufactured goods, which included beads.

## Knot designs

THE interlocking geometric motifs of the Kuba culture, known as *imbol*, are used on their raphia-cloth embroideries, wooden carvings, tattoos, cicatrization and beadwork. Their masks, which often incorporated panels of interlaced patterns made in beads, were frequently used at initiation ceremonies. Many vocations, including chiefs, smiths, potters, singers and dancers, had long initiation periods where the values and secrets of their trades and vocations were learned.

LEFT, FROM TOP TO BOTTOM: *Most of the cowries used to embellish clothing were from the Indian Ocean, but this one is only found in the Red Sea; lion's tooth with bead decorations which enhance its power, worn as a charm around the neck; Songye headdress. (All Afri-Karner Collection)*

## Clothing denoting rank

THE Nyim, as the most important person, has to wear clothes that denote his rank and function as ruler, warrior or as a link with the ancestors. At his investiture his clothes are so heavily decorated with cowries and beads that he cannot walk unsupported.

Most men hold a title, and wear clothing to exhibit their rank. The hat is an essential requirement for any ceremonial occasion. The basic hat, *laket*, is a rimless crown made from coiled raphia. Embellishments of shells, beads and metal ornaments applied to the surface have different meanings and associations.

OPPOSITE, ABOVE, RIGHT: *Wooden mask with cowrie-embellished beard. On the nose and down the back are the distinctive interlocking designs of the Kuba worked in beads.*

ABOVE, LEFT; AND ABOVE, RIGHT: *Cut-pile raphia cloths woven and embroidered with the interlocking designs that are found in all Kuba art.*

NEAR RIGHT: *Carved wooden figure, from the Democratic Republic of the Congo, covered with strings of small beads. A small amulet bag hangs around the waist.*

FAR RIGHT: *Belt with an assortment of beaded amulets hanging from it. A belt as splendid as this could only have been made for a king, or a member of the royal family or court.*

# CAMEROON

ABOVE; AND BELOW: *Details of leg and head of a leopard-skin messenger's cape belonging to the Banjoun people who live in the Grassfields of Cameroon; thought to be early 20th century.*

CAMEROON LIES on the west coast of Africa in the Gulf of Guinea, bordering Nigeria to the north-west, and Chad, Central African Republic, Gabon and Equatorial Guinea to the east and south. The country is a microcosm of the whole of Africa, with semi-desert in the north, savannah running through to equatorial rainforest in the south and west, and a range of volcanic mountains, recently active, to the west of the country. The port city of Douala was established on the Wouri River. After Congo, Cameroon is the richest of the central African states – oil is the largest export, followed by agricultural produce, including coffee, cocoa and palm oil. All sorts of crafts have been practised for centuries, including wood carving, lost-wax bronze casting, cotton and raphia weaving, resist dyeing in indigo and beadwork.

## Grassfields

TO THE west of the country the plateau that rises from the lowlands is cooler and the volcanic soil very fertile, so it is the most densely populated area in Cameroon. Here, traditional chiefdoms, large and small, each headed by a fon, a hereditary title, grew wealthy as agriculturalists and pastoralists. The regions of Bafoussam, Bamenda and Foumbam were among the largest.

Bafoussam is the administrative capital of the western province, and home of the bantu-speaking Bamileke people. The most beautiful chief's compound, or *chefferie*, in this francophone area is at Banjoun. Secret societies, such as the fuosi, wear wonderful beaded elephant masks and waistcoats and indigo-dyed clothes at some celebrations.

Foumbam, an empire founded in the 14th century, is the capital of the Bamoun people. Thrones and masks decorated with beadwork can still be found in the treasury of the Royal Palace.

## Beads as a mark of status

BEADS and beadwork were used to add glory and status to the fon, and were lent or given to men who had performed particular services to him. The first beads to arrive in the area would have come from Egypt and the Middle East via the Trans-Saharan trade routes. Around Lake Chad to the north, the powerful Bornem-Kanu Empire peaked during the 16th century, their wealth had been built on trading with North African countries. Their main exports were ostrich feathers, slaves and ivory. When the Portuguese started trading in West Africa and the main commercial centres moved to the coast, large quantities

ABOVE, LEFT: *Bamileke elephant mask, Cameroon. It would have been worn by men belonging to elite societies such as the Kuosi during elephant masquerades at annual festivals and at funerals of chiefs and important men. On top is a soft sculpture covered with designs made with beads.*

ABOVE, RIGHT: *Handle of royal fly whisk with two carved male figures on the end representing king's retainers. Bamum kings used the fly whisk on ceremonial occasions and at festivals.*

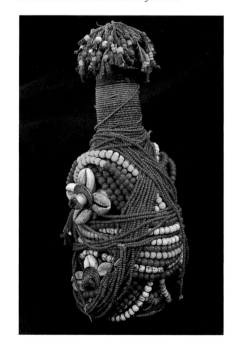

of beads became available. The large fancy Venetian beads, such as the chevrons, were much loved by all West African people, but the smaller glass seed, bugle and coral beads were used extensively by some, especially the Bamileke in the Grassfields, to cover thrones, palm-wine containers, drinking horns and ceremonial garments such as the elephant masks. The use of beads was controlled by the fons, and used to add value and status to certain articles related to power.

Further north in the lowlands that drain into Lake Chad the Kirdi, or unbelievers, have settled. They resisted conversion by both Christians and Muslims and retained their traditional beliefs. They withdrew into these rather inhospitable, but spectacular Mandara Mountains, made up of volcanic plugs which have been eroded by the Harmattan winds, to escape the Fulani slave raiders. In the small inaccessible villages such as Rhumsiki, Mabas, Oudjilla and Kosa beadwork is used to adorn personal items – bags, fertility figures, aprons and, for special occasions, for instance, harvest festivals, beautiful beaded hats are worn.

LEFT; AND ABOVE: *Fertility figures made and used by the Kirdi people from northern Cameroon. They are used at girls' initiation ceremonies, and to promote fertility. The multiple strings of beads wrapped around the body are not only decorative, but add status and power.*

**ONE**

# YORUBA

**W**EST AFRICA, land of the ancient kingdoms of Ghana, Mali and Benin, is overwhelmingly rich in every facet of artistic endeavour. The long tradition dates back to 6,000 BC when the earliest known pottery was made.

LEFT; ABOVE; AND BELOW, RIGHT: *The spirit of the king was believed to be in his head, which had to be covered at all times. For very formal occasions the fringed crown was worn, but at all other times the king wore the smaller* orikogbofo. *The* orikogbofo *is often four sided and has medicines in its peak to protect the head of the king. Every surface is covered with beads and decorated with three-dimensional shapes, also covered with beads. The shape of the one on the left represents a European crown – a symbol of power and status.*

BELOW, LEFT: *Sculptural knot in a Yoruba belt. The rest of the belt is decorated with cowries,* mbuum, *which were also used as currency.*

## History of trade

**E**VIDENCE of early trade is found in cave paintings of horse-drawn chariots along routes through the desert linking West Africa with the Mediterranean. African gold and Indian spices, especially pepper, encouraged the Portuguese to go on extended voyages from the 15th century onwards to find the source of these riches. Their arrival in West Africa shifted the main areas of trade from inland, the southern end of the old Trans-Saharan trade routes, to the coast where the Portuguese and, later, other European powers, established trading forts. Manufactured

European goods, including beads and brass, were traded for gold, slaves and ivory. West Africa was Europe's main source of gold until it was discovered in America.

## Beads in Nigeria

**I**FE in south-western Nigeria was a city-state that became wealthy through trade with forest products and goods brought south on the Trans-Saharan trade routes. A glass-making industry flourished there from the 11th century. Wound-glass beads are still made in Nigeria. When the Portuguese arrived with Venetian beads, it was the large, fancy ones –

*millefiori* (which means thousands of flowers) and chevrons – that were most coveted. These wonderful old beads are now being bought up in West Africa and resold to collectors all over the world, even in Venice, where they were originally made.

Evidence of early beadwork in Nigeria, in the form of netted coral headdresses, is found on cast bronze portraits from the old Benin kingdom. Coral from the western Mediterranean probably came overland to West Africa, and later in ships around the coast. Tubular coral beads that have been made up using a netted structure into hats and waistcoats and to cover royal regalia can be seen in old photographs and in museum collections. The Yoruba believe that both coral and beads are gifts from the god of the sea,

Olokun, who protects them when they wear them.

There are two areas in West Africa where small glass beads were embraced as part of the ceremonial culture – Nigeria and Cameroon. In south-western Nigeria and adjacent areas in Benin, the Yoruba invested the use of glass beads with a spirituality, using them as a link with higher forces. They decorate clothing and articles used by kings, priests and diviners.

The traditional kings, or *obas*, claim descent from a common ancestor, Odudua. Only they are privileged enough to wear the elaborate beaded and veiled crowns that represent the office of the *oba* and link the wearer to previous rulers, ancestors of the spirit world. The beads on these crowns invest the *oba* with power,

TOP: *This chair, from Nigeria, is impressive because of its sheer size, and the number of beads used. It was made for the tourist market, but familiar Yoruba imagery can be seen in the face masks representing Odudua, birds and crowns. Elephants represent power. Lazy stitch has been used to attach strings of beads to a cloth covering on the chair.*

INSET: *Detail of the chair. Birds are frequently represented in Yoruba beadwork, most often in three-dimensional forms.*

71

and, together with secret ingredients wrapped in the crown, help to protect him. Three-dimensional birds are often used on crowns and refer to the power of women who create new life. Bead-covered shoes, boots and other ceremonial regalia complete the splendid shimmering aspect of royalty.

Specialized workshops create these wonderful beaded articles, the famous Adesina family in Efon-Alaye receives commissions from many wealthy patrons throughout Nigeria. Colours symbolizing different Yoruba gods, and designs with different meanings are worked to represent character attributes of the wearer. It is one of the only places in

ABOVE, LEFT: *This could be the face of Odudua, the legendary founder of the Yoruba, which has been worked with beads onto this diviner's bag.*

BELOW, LEFT: *This little bird made of tiny beads sits on top of a hat. Birds are the link between the everyday world and the world of the spirits.*

OPPOSITE, ABOVE, LEFT: *Bag belonging to a diviner,* babalawo – *'father of ancient wisdom'. The surface has been decorated with small cowrie shells. The diviner looks in the mirror in the centre to see into the future.*

OPPOSITE, ABOVE, RIGHT: *Reverse of diviner's bag (above, left). The whole surface, both the flower and the background, has been covered with beads using couching stitch.*

OPPOSITE, BELOW, LEFT: *Hats protected the head of the king and dignitaries. This was made in the shape of a British judge's wig. The accumulation and distribution of beads and cowries was the prerogative of the ruling powers, so not only the shape of this hat, but the fact that it was completely covered with beads, displayed enormous wealth and power.*

OPPOSITE, BELOW, RIGHT: *Eshu shrine in Nigeria.*

Africa where beadwork is done by men. The intricate sculptural work on these objects illustrates the reverence with which they regard the power of beads.

### Beadwork traditions today

Masses of beadwork is still being produced in Nigeria, much of it for export. Wonderful three-dimensional belts and sculptural crowns are finding their way into curio shops all over the world. Many of the slaves that were transported to the Americas were of Yoruba descent, and they have carried on the traditions of beadwork in North America, Cuba and Brazil.

# NORTH AFRICA

Some of the earliest mass-produced beads made from faience were made in Ancient Egypt and some of the oldest examples of constructed beadwork have been found there, but beadwork using small glass beads was not an important technique in either Egypt or the rest of North Africa until the end of the 19th century.

## MOROCCO

The Berber women of Morocco have traditionally used silver, copal and coral for their jewelry, and sequins for embellishing tassels, but in the Ante Atlas beadwork is now produced using both a variation of one-bead netting and loom weaving. The beads are small glass seed beads from the Czech Republic, and the work is constructed using a stiff nylon thread so the beads can be strung without using a needle. The beadwork is made into large breast ornaments and belts, the patterns often imitating the patterns seen in the woven textiles of this region.

## ALGERIA

Beadwork is also used in Algeria, though, as in Tunisia, embroidery and the use of metallic thread and sequins are much more frequent, and important, embellishments.

## THE RASHAIDA

In the early 19th century, the Rashaida migrated to southern Egypt and the Sudan from western Saudi Arabia. It is not known if beadwork was a skill carried with them or if it is from a later date, learned after the migration, but today they make fine beadwork edgings and fringes to decorate household items.

## EGYPT

The phenomenal increase in interest in Arabian dance in Europe and North America has meant that Egypt, like Turkey, is now a major importer of beads from the Czech Republic, and produces, for export, vast quantities of

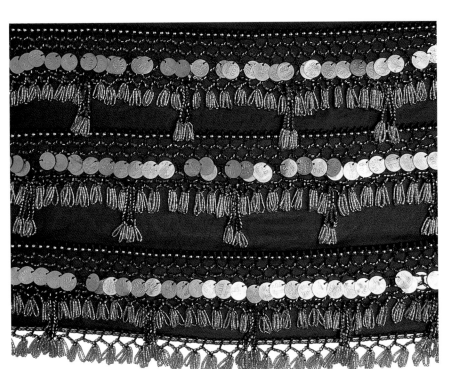

FAR LEFT; AND TOP RIGHT (DETAIL): *Loom-woven belt from Taroudant, Morocco.*

ABOVE, LEFT: *Contemporary 'belly dance' costume, made in Egypt. The beads and smaller beaded motifs are made in the Czech Republic.*

NEAR LEFT: *Hip 'scarf', of crocheted beadwork and coins, made in Egypt for Arabic dance.*

OPPOSITE, LEFT: *Breast ornament of beads threaded on nylon thread, from Taroudant, Morocco.*

OPPOSITE, ABOVE, RIGHT: *Detail of a woman's belt from the Ida ou Nadif tribe in the Ante Atlas, Morocco.*

OPPOSITE, RIGHT, BELOW: *Dance costume, from Egypt, with sequin and bead decoration.*

beaded costume and accessories. These can be bought ready made, or made to meet a dancer's particular requirements. The more elaborate costumes are frequently constructed of beadwork components – fringe and motifs – made in the Czech Republic, and then assembled in Egypt. Small beadwork items also find a ready market with tourists, though the styles of beadwork are not indigenous, and could be found in any of the countries where low labour costs make beadwork a viable means of earning a living.

LEFT: *Lane stitching on a Plains Sioux pipe bag (detail).*
RIGHT: *Iroquois 'Glengarry' cap, Woodlands.*
BELOW, LEFT: *Athabaskan wall pouch.*
BELOW, CENTRE: *Iroquois sash and bag, of floral beadwork on cloth, Woodlands.*
BELOW, RIGHT: *Small bag, of extremely fine multi-coloured knitting, from Peru. Very small white glass beads have been sewn to the edges of the flap.*

# THE AMERICAS

TWO

# THE HISTORY OF BEADWORK IN THE AMERICAS

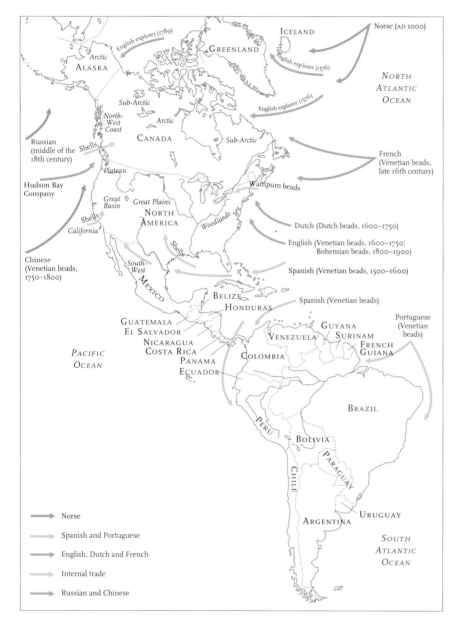

ABOVE: *Small pouch made to be attached to a belt, from the Plateau region.*

BELOW: *Man wearing a Woodlands-style fine beadwork panel, as well as a beaded belt, probably loom woven, and beaded bag.*

THE EARLIEST beads were, of necessity, made from natural materials – silver, gold, copper, semi-precious stones and freshwater pearls are all found in the Americas and can be fashioned into beads. Most early beadwork, however, was made from humbler materials – shells, bird or animal bones, stones and seeds. In equatorial South America brightly coloured seeds were used; and in California and New Mexico juniper seeds and silver berries.

## THE MANUFACTURE OF BEADS

VERY SMALL disc-like beads were made from olivella shells, and the whole shells were either constructed into a piece of beadwork or stitched onto hide. Vast quantities of these loose beads have been found at ancient burial sites, but intact examples of beadwork are extremely rare. The most important shell beads are known as wampum. They are blueish purple or white beads, cylindrical in shape. The white beads were made from the central whorl of the whelk *Busycon canaliculatum*, and the purple ones, considered more desirable, were from the Atlantic Ocean clam shell, *Mercenaria mercenaria*. The wampum beads were woven into ceremonial strips or belts, used to record the history of a tribe, or to ratify a treaty between tribes. Strings of wampum were an item of trade and exchange throughout most of North America. They were so valuable that by the mid-18th century white settlers were manufacturing them, referring to them as 'Indian money'.

Beads of bird bone were made in the south-west, animal-bone beads in Alaska; and very small stone beads were produced in North America in what is now California and New Mexico, and in Ecuador and Peru. The latter could be constructed into complex pieces of beadwork, and, if combined with shell beads, a range of colours enabled figurative patterns to be worked into the item. The actual size of some of these beads is just 2 mm in diameter. Minute, ancient beads of gold have been found throughout Central and South America, and are small and even enough to have been used for beadwork.

LEFT: *Umbilical cord holder, western Plains. A newborn baby's umbilical cord would be stitched into an amuletic figure, which was then hung on a tree near the home. This ensured the well being of the child.*

BELOW: *Plains Sioux female doll, in tribal dress, wearing earrings of dentalium shell.*

When Columbus landed in northern America in 1492 this marked the arrival of glass beads manufactured in Europe. Two brief, early attempts were made to produce glass beads in North America. In 1606 a large company of artisans arrived in the, then, English colonies, and one of the trades represented was glassmaking. The venture failed within a few years. Later, in 1621, six Italian glassmakers and their families arrived in Virginia with the express purpose of manufacturing glass and beads. This venture, too, failed within a few years.

European glass beads were brought to the indigenous population primarily by traders, but also by missionaries. The new, small glass beads were quickly adopted by the Native Americans into existing decorative crafts, using hide and sinew, and later cloth and thread to construct beadwork; eventually the glass beads all but replaced the pre-contact shell, seed and quill work. In Central and South America, and the Caribbean, glass beads were initially introduced by Spanish explorers, though the beads were never as important to the indigenous population as they were in North America.

TWO

**TWO**

Initially, the imported beads were of Venetian manufacture, but by the early 19th century Bohemian glass beads, with their brighter colours and glossy finish, were imported. Bohemian cut-glass beads became especially popular for some styles of work. To generalize somewhat, older pieces of beadwork can be identified by the softer colours and very small size of the Venetian beads. An exception to this, however, are the pieces dating from the 17th century when the fur trade began and larger beads were imported prior to the smaller 'seed' beads.

White and blue were favoured colours from the beginning, perhaps reflecting the colours of the shell beads then in use; a dull semi-translucent yellow and green, soft pinks and lavenders, and a particular type of bead known as rose or 'red-under-white' or 'rose-white-inside' (a more accurate description) were also popular. The 'rose-white-inside' was made of a transparent deep rose pink or red glass covering a white glass core.

ABOVE: *Woman, possibly Blackfoot or Kiowa, with heavily beaded baby carrier.*

NEAR RIGHT: *Tanaina Second Chief. This Athabaskan family's hide clothes are trimmed with beadwork in the floral style of the Sub-Arctic.*

FAR RIGHT: *Moccasins, probably Gros Ventre tribe of Montana.*

BOTTOM RIGHT: *Arucanian woman, from southern Chile, wearing shell and bead ornaments.*

OPPOSITE, BELOW: *Billy Bowlegs, Seminole tribe, wearing a wide, loom-woven belt.*

## TECHNIQUES

ONE OF THE main methods of construction used throughout the Americas is weaving on a loom, with or without a heddle, and a variation from the Woodlands region known as bias or diagonal weave, related to the technique of finger weaving. Beads could be incorporated into a woven fabric, or the fabric formed almost entirely of beads, a technique related both to wampum belts and woven quillwork. Other methods of construction include brick stitch, sometimes known as Comanche stitch, and one-bead netting, or gourd stitch. Spot stitch and lazy, or lane, stitch was used for stitching beads onto hide or cloth. Beaded fringes were a frequent and attractive addition to garments and bags. Beads were also combined with basketry in the south-west, and ceremonial bowls made from gourds were decorated with beads. Variations of netting were employed, particularly in the south-west.

ABOVE, LEFT: *Typical Plains war bonnet of eagle feathers, with band of beadwork.*

ABOVE, RIGHT: *Plains Sioux male doll.*

## THE NATIVE AMERICAN WAY OF LIFE

As the 19th century progressed, the traditional way of life for the North American Native Americans was fast disappearing – lands were seized, game depleted, and they were forced to live on reservations. The enforced idleness of reservation life led to a marked increase in beadwork, both as an occupation, and as a means of achieving status within the community. All craftwork, including beadwork, was retained out of a desire to express identity, and to retain some part of the traditional lifestyle. The participation of Native Americans in stage shows and 'Wild West' entertainments also gave rise to an increase in elaborate beaded costumes. Furthermore, beaded articles, once an item of trade, now drew the Native Americans into the cash economy, making them dependent on the production of these 'knick-knacks' or 'native curios' for their livelihood. Today, there is a great deal of interest in the collecting of authentic, old North American beadwork, and the production, using traditional methods, of new pieces; the craft is undergoing something of a revival.

The history of white (non-Native American) beadwork in North America parallels that of Western Europe, and was subject to the same changes of fashion both in female dress and the popularity of pastimes.

81

# ARCTIC

THE ARCTIC region has permanently frozen soil, permafrost, and no trees grow there. The land is not suitable for agriculture, so the only means of survival is hunting, both land and sea mammals, and fishing. During the long harsh winters extended family groups eke out stored foods and hold festivals to honour the spirits who will help them with their hunting in the following season.

## THE ESKIMO-ALEUTS

THE Eskimo-Aleuts sailed from Siberia across the Bering Strait 2,500 years ago and settled all the way from the Aleutian Islands in the Pacific Ocean, through the Alaskan mainland along the Arctic coast to the shores of Hudson Bay and Labrador in Canada, displacing the original inhabitants.

## THE ALEUTS, YUP'IK AND INUPIAT-INUIT

TODAY, the descendants of the original Eskimo-Aleut settlers are divided into three separate linguistic groups, Aleutian, Yup'ik and Inupiat-Inuit.

The Aleuts lived on the islands of the Aleutian archipelago that stretches 1,000 miles west from Alaska. Russian fur traders, *promyshlenniki*, brought Chinese and European glass beads to Alaska to trade with the Aleuts.

The Yup'ik-speaking people lived on the coast of the Bering Sea and on the off-shore islands. There was abundant sea and land wildlife, especially around the Yukon-Kuskokwim delta. This meant that they could establish permanent villages, only leaving during the migrations to hunt caribou. All the men and boys over six years old lived in the communal men's house, *qasgiq*, while the women lived in their own houses where they raised the children, sewed and cooked, and taught these skills to their daughters.

The first glass beads available to the Yup'ik would have come from the Russian traders in the 18th century. The beautiful blue Chinese wound-glass beads were used to decorate hunting equipment, labrets (or lip plugs) and clothes. Small European glass beads, probably Venetian,

BELOW: *Woman's inner parka, Iglulingmiut, Canada, heavily embellished with seed beads. In the severe climate of the Arctic, the family's survival depended on the skill of the woman to make clothing that protected her family from both the harsh elements and supernatural forces.*

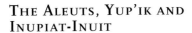

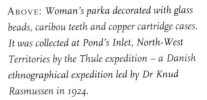

ABOVE: *Woman's parka decorated with glass beads, caribou teeth and copper cartridge cases. It was collected at Pond's Inlet, North-West Territories by the Thule expedition – a Danish ethnographical expedition led by Dr Knud Rasmussen in 1924.*

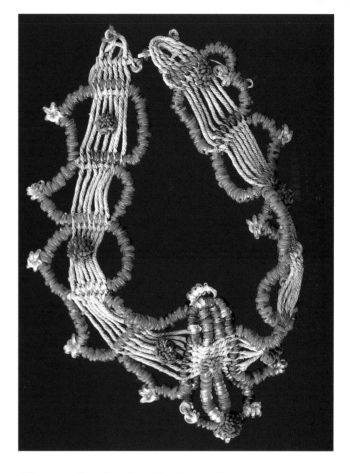

LEFT: *A young girl's* amautik, *Caribou Inuit or Igloolik Inuit, c. 1930. Made from plain hide with fur on the inside. The square of red wool on the chest and the red and black wool around the sleeves and hood are decorated with bead embroidery. The bead fringes across the front, sleeves and hood have small ivory points on the ends.*

ABOVE: *Dancing cap from Nunivak Island, collected by the explorer Dr Knud Rasmussen. Small glass beads have been sewn into circular rosettes – the circle represents the sun, the moon and the seasons. Larger glass beads have been sewn in horizontal rows.*

RIGHT: *Dog harness, of dentalium shells and beads, from the Labrador coast in Canada.*

were also available. They could have travelled overland on the Silk Route, or by sea. Some families became dependant on the trade goods imported by the Alaska Commercial Company, but many others continued to live a traditional life of hunting.

The Inupiat-Inuit people who lived in northern Alaska, Arctic Canada and Greenland shared a common language and customs. During the long dark winter months they built snow houses to live in, and a very large one for social gatherings which were an important part of their calendar.

In the 1570s British explorers were searching for the north-west passage to the Far East by following the coast of North America. A hundred years later the British crown gave a trading monopoly to the Hudson Bay Company. In return for pelts, they provided iron knives, copper

kettles, cloth and glass beads. But it was not until the late 19th century that large numbers of beads became available.

## Clothing

THE main purpose of clothing among the peoples of the Arctic was to provide protection against the cold. The secondary purpose of the outer parka was to identify the wearer's gender, and place of birth. The woman's outer parka, *amautik*, made from seal or caribou skin had a pouch on the back to carry a baby, and on the front, an inset of pale fur in the shape of an oval representing the womb. These features emphasized the woman's main role in Arctic society.

The man's role as hunter was also very evident in his parka. The shape of the back flap resembles a caribou's tail, and sometimes ears were added to the hood, giving him a very animal-like

silhouette when hunting. Amulets and beads were attached to the woman's inner parka for safety and protection. After the missionaries had discouraged tattooing, similar designs were applied to their inner parkas with imported glass beads and embroidery.

## Dolls

FOR hundreds of years dolls have been made by the people of the Arctic. They were used as playthings, but were also educational, as the girls were taught by their mothers to make the clothing.

# SUB-ARCTIC

T HE SUB-ARCTIC stretches from Alaska in the west to the Atlantic Ocean in the east, and is immediately south of the Arctic area, which occupies most of the coastal areas of the Arctic Ocean. There were two main language groups in this area. The Athabaskans lived in the west in the Yukon and Mackenzie river basins, and the Algonquins to the east of the Churchill River which flows into Hudson Bay. Similar lifestyles were imposed by the harsh climate and because they lived a mostly nomadic lifestyle their decorated artifacts are small and portable.

ABOVE, LEFT: *Athabaskan family; jackets like this one belonging to a Tanaina man were worn by native and non-native men involved in the fur trade at the beginning of the 20th century.*

ABOVE, RIGHT: *Woman's hood, 1875–1900, with floral beadwork typical of the James Bay Cree. This one was probably kept for special occasions.*

## Early trade contacts

T HE Athabaskans living in Alaska would have had contact with the *promyshlenniki*, Russian fur traders, from the middle of the 18th century. Glass beads, being highly valued but small and easy to transport, were important trade items. Cobalt blue wound-glass beads from China were imported from the end of the 18th century. European beads, which probably arrived in Russia overland across the Silk Route, were also traded. These beads and other trade goods would slowly have been traded west over old intertribal barter networks, mainly along waterways. Various tribes, such as the Tanainas, were middlemen in this fur trade. Copper ingots and arrowheads from the Copper River and dentalium shells from Vancouver Island would have been found throughout the Sub-Arctic region.

From the late 1500s European trade goods started entering North America. The French established a commercial base in Quebec, and in 1670 the English set up trading posts at Charles Fort in Hudson Bay. The tradition of gift giving that is so much a part of Native American tradition made bartering an extension of this practice. Dentalium shells had always been a status symbol to the Athabaskans, so when glass beads were traded into their area they naturally became indicators of wealth.

It was not only the beads, steel needles, embroidery silks, silk ribbon and brightly coloured fabrics which they could acquire,

through trade, that influenced their designs, it was the contact with European dress, ecclesiastical designs and mission school education. Teaching orders, such as the French Ursulines in 1639, founded mission schools in north-eastern Quebec where needlework, using printed floral European patterns, was an important part of the syllabus for girls. Precursors of curvilinear motifs can be found in the hand-painted Naskapi ceremonial robes.

## Beadwork

IN NEWFOUNDLAND graves dating back to 3,000 BC with large quantities of shell beads, probably originally attached to clothing, have been found. Later wolf teeth, seal claws, bills of loons, dentalium shells, bone and seeds were worn.

The first smallish glass beads available from traders were 3 to 4 mm in diameter and were used in addition to the ornaments made of natural materials. Glass beads were believed to have magical properties. By the mid-19th century seed beads with a smaller diameter were being imported from Europe. Their size made them very versatile ornaments in maintaining their tradition of decorating their clothing. The geometric designs and techniques used in their quillwork, an ancient indigenous art form, could easily be adapted when working with beads, and the quill-wrapped leather fringes translated easily into bead fringes. The colour of the dyed quills and shells were the colours they first used in their beadwork.

More curvilinear motifs became possible with the availability of sharp metal needles and fine thread. The threaded beads were caught with a stitch every two or three beads onto a base, of leather and later fabric, with another threaded needle. A precursor for these curved motifs can be found on the painted coats of the Montagnais and Naskapi from Quebec and Labrador. These beautiful designs were painted by the women, with instructions from the men, who saw their new designs in a dream.

By the end of the 19th century a new style had evolved, created by the Metis who were the result of intermarriage between the traders and local people and exhibit the perfect marriage between the traditional styles of the Native Americans and the new European trade goods and styles. Floral motifs in curvilinear beadwork decorate smoked moose or caribou hide coats made in European styles.

Beadwork is still practised in the Sub-Arctic region. The tradition of beauty to please both the spirit and human world persists.

ABOVE: *Valance in an elaborate floral design, Sub-Arctic region.*

RIGHT: *Headband of loomed beadwork, made by the Naskapi from Labrador in Canada, c. 1900.*

OPPOSITE, BELOW, LEFT: *Valance of floral beadwork on velvet, Sub-Arctic region.*

OPPOSITE, BELOW, RIGHT: *Athabaskan dog blanket, 1875–1900, made in the Mackenzie River region of the North-West Territories. The practise of decorating sledge dogs with embroidered blankets or tapis (which became known as tuppies) originated with the Red River Metis during the first half of the 19th century.*

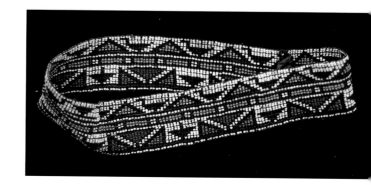

# WOODLANDS

**T**HE WOODLANDS area, including the north-east, Great Lakes and south-east, covers the deciduous and evergreen forests of the east coast of North America from the Great Lakes area to Florida, a central plain between the coast and the Appalachian mountains. The area is drained by the Mississippi, Ohio and Illinois rivers. The main language families of these regions were Algonquian, Iroquoian and Siouan.

**T**HE peoples of this region led a predominantly hunter-gatherer/horti-culturalist way of life. The area provided the inhabitants with all the materials they needed for their daily life and for the decoration of their clothing and artefacts – wood and bark, reeds, porcupine and bird quills, shell, bone, copper, animal skins and sinew.

## The arrival of the Europeans

**T**HE east coast of the Woodlands region saw some of the earliest contact with Europeans – sailors and explorers arrived at the end of the 16th century, soon to be followed by French fur traders. By the end of the next century, silver, brass, wool, cloth, ribbons and beads were all traded for furs and hides.

ABOVE, RIGHT: *Early 19th-century 'tourist' work bag of exceptionally small beads, probably Venetian, on velvet, made by the Malacite or Abenaki tribe.*

RIGHT: *Chippewa cradle board, from the Great Lakes region, made between 1900 and 1910.*

BELOW, LEFT: *Late 19th-century cloth waistcoat, from the Chippewa tribe, decorated in typical Woodlands floral style in spot or appliqué stitch.*

BELOW, CENTRE: *Moccasins made by the Malacite tribe, mid-19th century.*

OPPOSITE, ABOVE; AND BELOW, LEFT: *Hide jacket made by Canadian Cree or Ojibwe; and gauntlets almost certainly made by the same person.*

OPPOSITE, INSET: *Iroquois chief, wearing epaulettes and cuffs of beadwork on cloth in typical Woodlands style.*

OPPOSITE, BELOW, RIGHT: *Beaded belt with cloth backing, from the Ojibwe tribe, late 19th century.*

## Techniques

**T**HERE is a very wide diversity of beadwork in the Woodlands area from the Micmac in the north to the Seminoles in the south. The making and decorating of items of clothing for the family was almost exclusively done by women, who were taught the many and varied skills from early childhood, learning from older female relatives. A woman's social status was directly related to her creativity and aptitude for various skills, including preparing animal skins, weaving, finger weaving, quillwork and beadwork. A talented woman would perhaps be asked by other women to make things for them, or could trade her work, thus enriching her

TWO

family; inter-tribal trade was already well established before the Europeans came.

Even though beads were introduced to the area as a trade article, beadwork skills were built on existing techniques. Glass beads were available in a range of colours, and could be used to decorate clothing more easily than quills, and were more readily obtained than the handmade shell beads that preceded them. In finger braiding the method of intertwining the threads results in diagonal lines, and the beads threaded onto selected threads accentuates these, making diamond- and arrow-shaped designs. Finger-braided sashes were worn by the Metis in the north-east, and bags and sashes were made and worn by the Seminoles in the south-

east. In finger braiding and in loom-woven beadwork the beads are part of the structure and construction of the bead textile, unlike spot and lazy stitch which are applied to a hide or cloth backing as decoration.

Loom-woven beadwork is based on one of the techniques of quillwork. Porcupine quills were coloured with natural dyes, and decorative strips were woven on a bow loom of flexible wood, with sinew warps. These were attached to garments, or made into belts, headbands or garters. Not only the technique, but the designs, too, could be used for beadwork. For longer, wider pieces of beadwork a box loom was used, where a continuous thread was wound around a frame of four pieces of wood to form the warp. The large, decorative

Opposite, above, left: *Small 'tourist' bag, made by the Iroquois, late 1880s. The white 'zipper' edging and rather coarse beadwork in floral style are typical of this genre of work.*

Opposite, above, right: *Bag, from the Great Lakes region, made in c. 1840. The top half has fine bead embroidery, the lower portion is a loom-woven beaded panel with a beaded fringe.*

Opposite, below, far left: *Cree 'strike a light', or tobacco, bag, with a beaded panel and quillwork fringe.*

Opposite, below, near left: *Ojibwe bandoleer bag, c. 1880. These large, ornate bags were also known as 'gift' bags.*

Top left: *Algonquin man in tribal dress.*

Above, left: *A small Micmac purse, with pleated cloth edging and beadwork in spot or appliqué stitch.*

Above, right: *Wool cloth leggings in 'regimental' colours, from the Great Lakes region, c. 1880. The leggings are ornamented with panels of beadwork, and brass bells and thimbles have been strung as bells to make a pleasing sound.*

Below, left: *Finished, but otherwise unused, bead embroidered panel from the Great Lakes region, possibly intended as a baby blanket.*

Below, right: *Detail of Athabaskan beadwork on a shelf valance, late 19th century.*

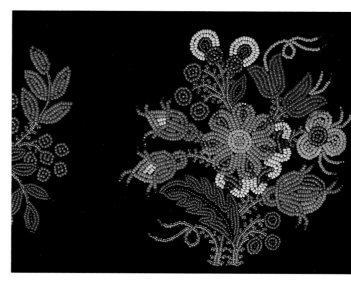

89

**TWO**

bandolier bags were woven on this type of loom. The designs of loom-woven beadwork, like those of quillwork, were imposed by the technique. The rigid warp-weft framework created geometric designs.

Even the spot-stitch technique, which was used for floral curvilinear designs, had an indigenous equivalent. Small bundles of dyed moosehair were attached to hide garments with a second thread. With the introduction of steel needles, floral designs, inspired by the French Renaissance designs introduced by the mission schools, became a part of their repertoire.

BELOW, LEFT: *Iroquois bag with bird motifs.*

BELOW, RIGHT: *A 'Glengarry' cap in typical Woodlands style. These caps, first made in imitation of regimental caps, became part of the traditional dress.*

BOTTOM RIGHT: *Iroquois bag made for the tourist trade, c. 1880. Two shades of one colour are typical of such work.*

LEFT: *Iroquois bag with the typical 'zipper' edging. Although these are often referred to as 'tourist work', they were also made for personal use.*

RIGHT: *Small wall pocket, from the Great Lakes area, with beadwork in appliqué stitch.*

BELOW, LEFT: *Detail of the beaded decoration on an Athabaskan shot pouch, with a quillwork fringe.*

BELOW, RIGHT: *Child's moccasins, probably made as tourist souvenirs by the Iroquois.*

The women soon adapted their wares to trade with the European fur traders. This began as early as the mid-18th century. This trade expanded throughout the 19th century, though increasingly the sales were to the new class of wealthy white tourists – the beginning and increase in tourism coincided with the erosion of the traditional way of life. This 'native' craftwork, designed to appeal to non-Native Americans, gradually came to have a recognizable style of its own, and has recently become very collectible.

# THE GREAT PLAINS

THE ARID grasslands bordered by the Saskatchewan River in the north, the Mississippi and Missouri valleys in the east, the Rio Grande in the south and the Rocky Mountains in the west are the traditional lands of the Plains and Prairie tribes, who are some of the most widely known of all the tribal groups – the Kiowa, Cheyenne, Comanche, Blackfoot, Sioux, Crow and Cree, among others. As with other regions in North America, the climate and vegetation impose a certain lifestyle, which in its turn has defined the material culture of the people in the area.

## PRAIRIES

PRAIRIE culture, in the east, characterized by semi-settled farming and seasonal hunting, predates Plains culture, and is considered to have developed from Mississippian and Mexican influences. The settled tribes – Sauk, Fox, Omaha, Mandan, Arikara – farmed in the river systems of the Mississippi and Missouri, but later the

pottery they produced was replaced by hand-painted leather parfleches which could easily be transported by horse. The speed and freedom of movement provided by horses meant that they could move over large areas in search of herds of buffalo which became the centre of their economy. Besides being a source of food, household articles, clothing and dwellings were made from skilfully prepared hides.

## PLAINS

IN THE western Plains the short grass could only support a nomadic hunting community so they were dependant upon the buffalo (bison) and put every part of the animal to good use. The nomadic way of life now considered typical of Plains culture developed comparatively late, and was largely shaped by the introduction of horses, through contact with Spanish settlers. Horses soon replaced dogs as a means of transporting loads, allowing these tribes to spread widely over the Plains region. The horse became as central to the Plains way of life as the bison. Much

ABOVE, LEFT: *Detail of beadwork in floral style, Crow tribe, c. 1880.*

FAR LEFT: *Medicine Crow, Apsaroke, Montana, wearing a beaded scalp shirt, a hawk-hide headdress, earrings, disc ornaments and shell beads, 1908.*

NEAR LEFT: *Hidatsa woman, from present-day north Dakota, in a dress decorated with dentalium shells, 1908.*

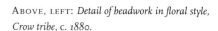

OPPOSITE, RIGHT: *Small bag of skin and cloth, made by the Santee Sioux, 1880s.*

ABOVE: *Child's jacket, Crow, c. 1880.*

LEFT: *Heavily beaded waistcoat in appliqué stitch.*

BELOW: *Beaded blanket strips made by the Plains Cree, which have been re-made into a waistcoat back.*

of what is now considered typical of Native American culture – the tepee, the use of hide and buckskin, geometric painted and beaded patterns, beaded horse trappings, feathered 'war bonnets' – have their origins in Plains culture.

## Quillwork to beadwork

THE Plains tribes excelled at quillwork, and later the beadwork that superseded it. The quills of a porcupine found on the northern and central Plains have been used for centuries as a means of decorating hides. The quills are white hollow tubes about 13 cm (5 in.) long and 2 mm (¹⁄₁₆ in.) in diameter. They were originally dyed soft colours with organic dyes made from berries, mosses and bark, but brighter colours were achieved when trade cloth became available. When the cloth was boiled with quills the extra dye that had not been properly washed out coloured the quills. Later aniline dyes were available as trade goods.

The Cheyenne and Arapaho controlled quillwork through guilds, where only initiated women could make certain sacred designs. There were sixteen different quillwork techniques used to decorate clothing, including wrapping

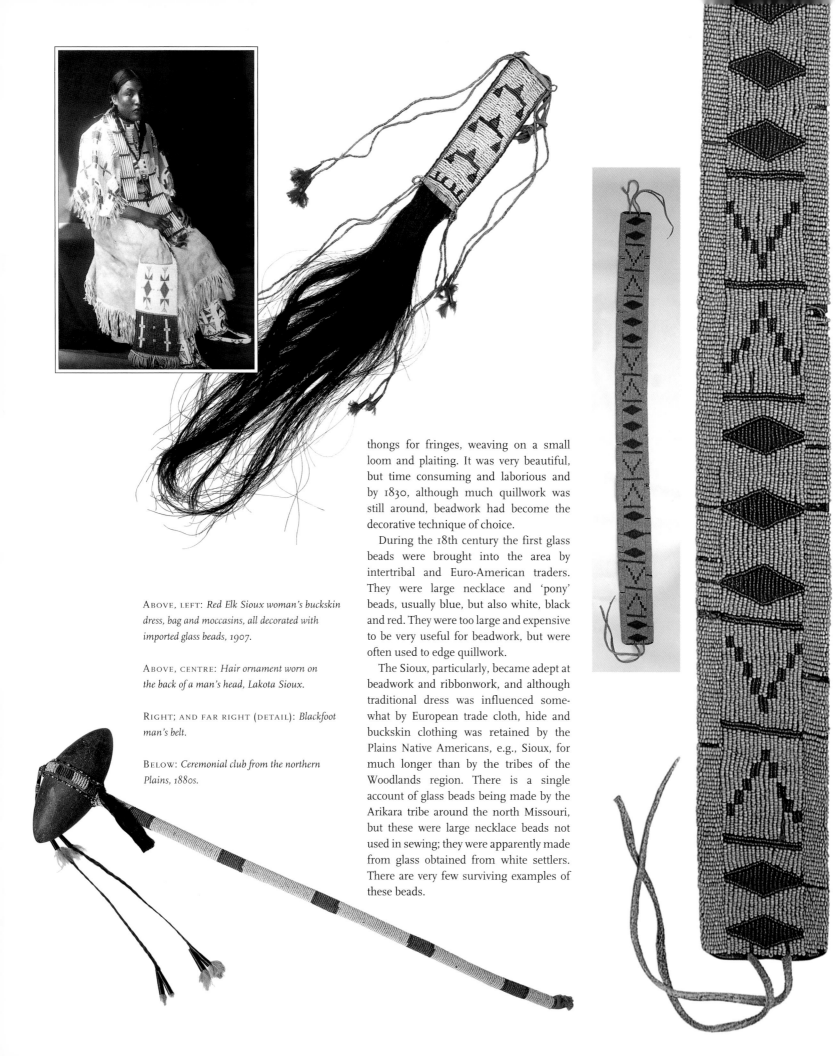

thongs for fringes, weaving on a small loom and plaiting. It was very beautiful, but time consuming and laborious and by 1830, although much quillwork was still around, beadwork had become the decorative technique of choice.

During the 18th century the first glass beads were brought into the area by intertribal and Euro-American traders. They were large necklace and 'pony' beads, usually blue, but also white, black and red. They were too large and expensive to be very useful for beadwork, but were often used to edge quillwork.

The Sioux, particularly, became adept at beadwork and ribbonwork, and although traditional dress was influenced somewhat by European trade cloth, hide and buckskin clothing was retained by the Plains Native Americans, e.g., Sioux, for much longer than by the tribes of the Woodlands region. There is a single account of glass beads being made by the Arikara tribe around the north Missouri, but these were large necklace beads not used in sewing; they were apparently made from glass obtained from white settlers. There are very few surviving examples of these beads.

ABOVE, LEFT: *Red Elk Sioux woman's buckskin dress, bag and moccasins, all decorated with imported glass beads, 1907.*

ABOVE, CENTRE: *Hair ornament worn on the back of a man's head, Lakota Sioux.*

RIGHT; AND FAR RIGHT (DETAIL): *Blackfoot man's belt.*

BELOW: *Ceremonial club from the northern Plains, 1880s.*

By early in the 19th century small seed beads in an array of bright colours started arriving in North America. They were made in Venice and Bohemia, and were evidence of the improved techniques for mass producing these small drawn-glass beads. Quillworking methods and designs were adapted to beadwork designs and developed into an artform that characterizes the Plains Native Americans.

## Techniques

THE different methods of construction – which impose various designs – can be used to identify the origin of some of the pieces of beadwork. In the northern Plains overlaid or spot stitch were mostly used. The beads were threaded onto a piece of sinew which was caught by another thread, every two or three beads, onto the base

cloth or hide. Geometric designs were common, but the technique made it easy to produce curving lines and floral motifs, and by the late 19th century some moccasins and horse gear of the Blackfoot Native Americans were decorated with these motifs.

Further south, lazy stitch was used. The thread is anchored to the fabric base, then a certain number of beads threaded on, and a small stitch is taken, and the same number of beads added before another stitch is taken close to the starting point. In this way large areas can be covered with beads. Geometric designs are the most natural development of Sioux designs. The Crow people used this technique as well, but their geometric shapes were bigger, and many were outlined in white, the motifs perhaps

ABOVE: *Hail-stone, a Dakota, wearing a breast ornament of shell discs.*

BELOW, LEFT: *Pair of armbands worn by men around each upper arm; probably Blackfoot. While the beading covers the entire article, it is appliqué rather than lane stitch.*

BELOW, RIGHT: *Moccasins with stylized floral motifs, Blackfoot.*

TWO

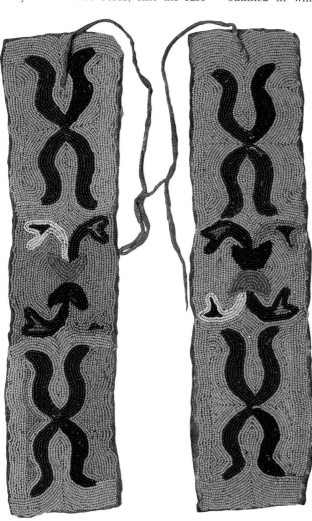

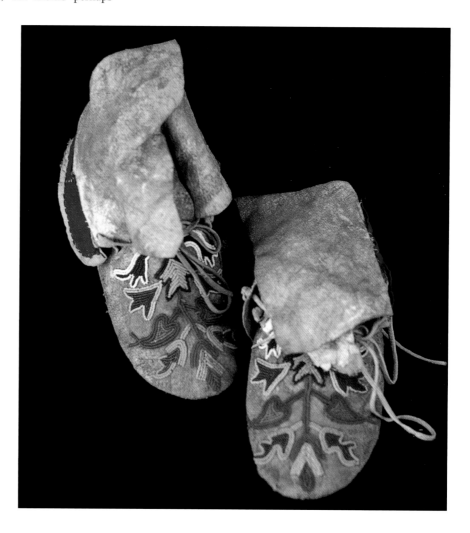

LEFT: *Sioux belt of loom-woven beadwork, mounted on leather.*

ABOVE: *Girl's leggings, made by the Lakota Sioux, 1880s.*

RIGHT: *Two young men, one wearing a breastplate of shell pipe beads.*

OPPOSITE, BELOW, RIGHT: *This small piece of beading would have been one of four corners of a pad saddle. It is in appliqué stitch, but the background has been worked in straight lines rather than following the contours of the design like the piece on page 95.*

**TWO**

ABOVE, LEFT: *Ration ticket holder – an object born out of the enforced dependency of reservation life.*

ABOVE, RIGHT: *Pair of gauntlets, Blackfoot. These and the ration ticket holder (above) were almost certainly made by the same person.*

reflecting the bold geometric designs painted on their parfleches.

The Cree adapted quillworking looms for the small seed beads. Long narrow strips were woven and attached to clothing.

## Trading networks

THE way of life of the Plains Native Americans was a result of European trade. Horses had long been extinct in the area, and their re-introduction by the Spanish from the south-west meant they could follow the herds of buffalo further into the drier areas of grassland. The introduction of guns by the French traders in the north-east made it easier to hunt. Other trade goods arrived – including red and blue cloth, coloured glass beads and metal bells. During the 18th century glass necklace beads and pony beads were traded, later the first seed beads arrived in large quantities. In the 1890s greasy yellow and red-under-whites were popular, and in the 1920s cut glass and metallic beads. Intertribal exchange involved the barter of products from the hunt with excess agricultural products.

## The beadworkers

WHILE the men were the hunters and warriors, the women reared the children, and were the craftworkers and traders. Status was acquired through excellence. Their designs were symbolic of their belief in the three worlds of the sky, this world and the underwater world.

# THE PLATEAU AND THE GREAT BASIN

THE COLUMBIA River flows through the Plateau cultural region, which lies between the Rocky Mountains to the east and the Cascades to the west. The Fraser River marks the northern boundary, and the Great Basin area lies to the south. The Great Plains stretch from the Plateau south into increasingly arid regions, with the Sierra Nevada to the west and the Rocky Mountains to the east. In the north and east the cultures adopted a nomadic, equestrian lifestyle, hunting buffalo and big game, like the Plains people. Further south in the desert regions, the traditional lifestyle of hunters and gatherers continued.

## Quillwork, hide painting and basketmaking

BONE beads, needles, awls and basketwork have been found dating back at least 9,000 years, evidence of an ancient tradition of craft work, but beadwork was a comparatively late development in the material culture of the Plateau Native Americans. When glass beads became available through the intertribal networks in the 18th century the designs traditionally used by women in porcupine quillwork, hide painting and basketmaking were transferred to beadwork.

Two interesting techniques of quillwork were used extensively by Plateau Native Americans and others – small bunches of horsehair were bound with quills which had been dyed in different colours, then sewn onto a hide or cloth backing material. The ridges formed, and the changing colours would easily have translated into beadwork designs. Multi-strand braiding was also used in quillwork, and the geometric designs which are imposed by this technique were used in the early days of beadwork. The hand-painted rawhide storage bags, parfleches, were decorated with bold-coloured, geometric designs with a strong similarity to the early geometric beadwork. Being semi-nomadic hunter-gatherers, there was no pottery tradition, so their baskets, with the parfleches, were used for storage, carrying and cooking (they put hot rocks into the closely woven baskets to cook food). But their baskets were not only functional, they were beautifully made, and decorated with geometric designs – the beadwork designs grew out of this strong tradition of geometric design.

## Beadwork

THE first beads that appeared in the trading network were fairly large, and known as 'pony beads' because they arrived on pack horses. They were about 4 mm (1/8 in.) in diameter, made in Venice, and available in a limited colour range. They were sewn onto hide backing using sinew in simple geometric shapes, often with strong tonal contrasts, making a bold statement. Clothing for men and women, horse equipment and baby cradles all had beads sewn on. The first beads available were extremely expensive, but were the most sought after and prized.

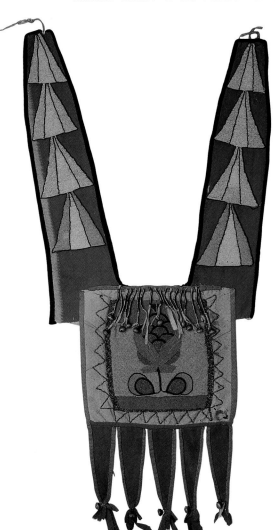

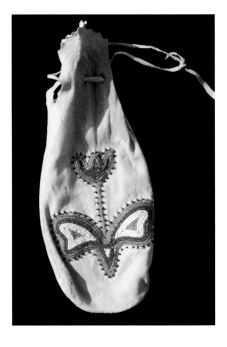

LEFT: *Horse martingale; horse trappings were very important for ceremonial occasions.*

ABOVE, CENTRE: *Small pouch, possibly Kutenai.*

By the mid-19th century smaller seed beads had arrived in the area, also of Venetian origin. They had a great impact on design, partly because of the increased number of colours available, but particularly because the smaller size (1–2 mm) made it possible to create more intricate designs. The curvilinear designs that had been attempted with the pony beads now flourished. A special feature of Plateau beadwork is the fully beaded backgrounds that echo the shape of the motifs, contour style, accentuating the often bi-symmetrical floral forms and creating a wonderfully lively background. 'Contour beadwork' is thought to have developed from a basket-weaving tradition where the design grows from a central point. In later years horizontal beading was used to fill in the backgrounds.

On the dress yokes lane or lazy stitch was used, either in a single colour, or in geometric designs, as in the Plains. Curvilinear designs were also applied to a hide or cloth background with the two-

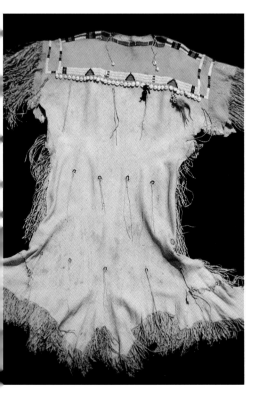

OPPOSITE, TOP RIGHT: *Cayuse woman, Oregon, on horseback wearing a buckskin dress. Her horse's trappings are decorated with beadwork and beaded fringes for a festive occasion, 1910.*

ABOVE: *Beaded child's dress. Made in 1989 by James Lavadour, Umatilla/Cayuse. (Courtesy of the Heard Museum, Phoenix, Arizona)*

LEFT: *Woman's dress, possibly Ute, c. 1870.*

RIGHT: *Cayuse chief David Young, c. 1900. The horse regalia is typical of the Plateau region with a mask and matching martingale.*

99

# TWO

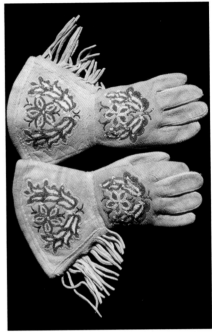

ABOVE, LEFT: *Moccasins in typical Ute style.*

ABOVE, RIGHT: *Plateau region gauntlets.*

BELOW, LEFT: *Sash, possibly Nez Perce; the design is a variation of the stars and stripes of the American flag.*

OPPOSITE, INSET: *Tlakluit/Wishram bride, 1910, wearing a beaded buckskin dress and a dentalium shell and coin headdress which indicates her elite status.*

thread couching method, sometimes called spot stitch or appliqué. The floral motifs could have been influenced by beadwork worn by Arctic and Sub-Arctic tribes involved in the fur trade in the Plateau region. A third method of attaching beads to hide was used, it was a technique shared with the Crow on the other side of the Rocky Mountains. Sometimes called 'crow stitch', the beads were secured in a ladder formation, then a thread running at right angles to the bars secured the thread every few beads.

The Transmontaine style of beadwork is common to tribes on both sides of the Rocky Mountains – the Nez Perce and Flathead on the Plateau and the Crow and Blackfoot on the Plains. It was a form of design used in the second half of the 19th century and is distinctive because the motifs are beaded in a similar tone to the background, so it is not clear which is the positive and which is the negative space.

Beautifully beaded bags, usually filled with food, were given as wedding presents, 'first food', and at other ceremonies, and were part of the generosity that helped people to survive during difficult times.

Without a history of quillwork in the south of the Great Basin, beadwork never became important. However, the Ute in the east, and to a lesser extent the Shoshoni and Bannock, who had contact with the Plains and the Plateau Native Americans, have a long history of beadworking.

From the late 18th century bold, geometric designs using 'pony' beads were used as decoration. These larger beads (4 mm) were available in a limited range of colours – black and white were the most frequently used.

Both lazy and spot stitch were employed to decorate men's and women's shirts, leggings and tobacco bags. The people in this area used pony beads much later than the neighbouring Plains tribes.

Today, some of the best contemporary beadwork is made by the Shoshone and the Bannock.

ABOVE: *Densely beaded bag, Plateau region.*

RIGHT: *Mirror bag, Plateau region, with American flag motifs and brass bells.*

## Trade networks

THE geographical position of the people of the Plateau and the Great Basin and their large river system used for transport and travel led them to be traders and middlemen. There is evidence that in 1000 BC dentalium shells were already being traded from Vancouver Island on the Pacific coast across the Plateau area to the Plains and Prairies. Trading centres grew up at the major waterfalls at Kettle, Okanagan and Dalles-Celilo. Dalles was an important trade centre all year round, and in the autumn a great fair took place, the Dalles Rondezvous. Initially it was an intertribal market where buffalo hides and leather goods, beaded clothing, shells, dried salmon, edible camas bulbs, baskets, canoes and many other specialities of the different groups of Native Americans were traded. European goods reached the Plateau area by 1700 when glass beads, cloth, copper pots and mirrors appeared in Dalles and in the trading networks. The acquisition of horses increased the scope of their trade on overland routes such as the Lolo trail, and increased their contact with the Plains tribes, and their lifestyle.

# THE NORTH-WEST COAST

IN CONTRAST with the Arctic and Sub-Arctic regions, the north-west coast has a moderate climate and a sufficient supply of food has meant that permanent villages have been established. It also meant that part of the community was released from the acquisition of food and so they could develop specialist creative skills.

The area extends 2,000 miles from southern Alaska along the narrow coastal strip, never more than 150 miles wide, through British Columbia, Washington and Oregon to the northern tip of California.

## Trade connections

THERE was a long-established pattern of trade in the area long before the Russians and Europeans arrived. Products from the sea, such as salmon and abalone and dentalium shells, and manufactured goods – canoes and baskets – were traded with the Plateau tribes, who, in turn, traded with the Plains people. In return they bought mountain goat wool and yellow lichen dye to make their Chilkat robes, quilled and beaded clothing, beaded cloth bags and black spruce chewing gum!

The wealth accrued by their activities as middlemen in the trade between the Russians, Europeans and Americans and the Native Americans further inland led to a blossoming of all their art forms. Starting with the explorers Vitus Bering and Aleksei Chirikov in 1741, the export of sea otter pelts to the Chinese, via the Russians, began. Some of the goods

RIGHT: *Small wall pocket, for holding 'spills', used to take a light from an open fire.*

BELOW: *Dentalium-shell and imported glass-bead headdress. The tip of the shell was snapped off and strung into standard lengths, hy-kwa, and traded through most of western North America.*

exchanged were the larger blue wound glass beads and coins from China. The arrival of Captain Cook in 1778 at Nootka Sound on Vancouver Island was the start of trade with the English. Copper and brass pots, glass beads, coins and mother-of-pearl buttons were among the articles traded for furs.

## Material culture

THE material culture of the north-west coast was moulded by its position on the coast and the easy access to

enormous trees. The specialist crafts, practised by men, of carving crest poles (totems) and sea-going canoes from the trunk of a tree, which were steamed and bent to the final shape, and the construction of monumental homes positioned along the beaches, which accommodated many families, define the culture.

The women's work, making baskets and weaving, also relied on products from the forests. The famous Chilkat robes are woven on a warp of the inner bark of the giant cedar tree, and a weft of natural and dyed wool from mountain goats.

## Beadwork

AFTER Russian and European traders entered the area the woven and painted cedar bark and hide ceremonial blankets started to be replaced with 'button blankets'. These were blue, red or black blankets bought from the Hudson Bay Company, and decorated with a central crest which identified the clan of the wearer. The bold central motif,

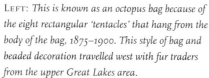

LEFT: *This is known as an octopus bag because of the eight rectangular 'tentacles' that hang from the body of the bag, 1875–1900. This style of bag and beaded decoration travelled west with fur traders from the upper Great Lakes area.*

RIGHT: *Tlingits at Sitka potlatch in dance regalia. The two outer figures are wearing bead-embroidered octopus bags across their shoulders.*

BELOW, LEFT: *Chilkat chiefs wearing their woven dancing costumes and beaded leggings.*

BELOW, RIGHT: *Beaded shirt, Tlingit, 1924. The bead embroidery on this shirt resembles the designs woven into the Chilkat dancing shirts which traditionally showed the Raven, Thunderbird and Lightning Snake spirit beings.*

often in red, was appliquéd onto the blanket and outlined in shell or mother-of-pearl buttons. The dance shirts, previously woven, like the Chilkat blankets, or painted on leather, were replaced with trade cloth shirts decorated with small glass beads in a set of formalized shapes which depict human and animal representations.

Some of the beadwork designs on octopus bags, which can be seen in early 20th-century photographs, resemble floral motifs from the Sub-Arctic.

# SOUTH-WEST AND CALIFORNIA

T HE SOUTH-WEST culture area is found in Arizona, New Mexico and adjacent states and large areas of northern Mexico. The whole area experiences low rainfall, and much is desert. In the north the flat-topped mesas and steep canyons are cut by the Colorado River, the most famous is the Grand Canyon.

The California cultural area spreads south into the California peninsular which is part of Mexico. The high Sierras Nevada mountain range forms a natural barrier to the east, and the Pacific Ocean lies to the west.

*LEFT: Pomo feather basket, c. 1900. The beads are made from clam shells. (Courtesy of the Heard Museum, Phoenix, Arizona)*

*BELOW: 'Apache White lady' bag; these were made in imitation of the handbags carried by settlers.*

## PUEBLO TRIBES

A MONG the Pueblo tribes, shell beads are still made, and are regarded as being of greater value than imported glass beads, as the shell is thought to be sacred, symbolizing water and its life-giving properties. Necklaces are made of a mixture of glass and shell beads, some shell beads have been recovered from ancient sites. During the 19th century, glass beads gradually became popular – they were adopted much later by the Pueblo than by many other tribal groups and even now glass beads are mostly worn by children. Dentalium shells collected on the Pacific coast were traded extensively across North America to the Atlantic coast and used as currency, as well as stitched to clothing as decoration or threaded into necklaces. Several Spanish accounts from the 16th century mention the giving of glass beads to the Pueblo people.

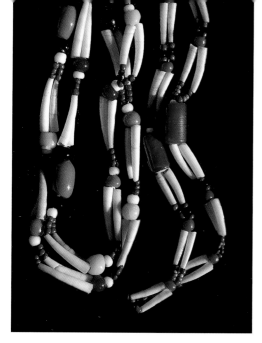

ABOVE, LEFT (DETAIL); AND RIGHT:
*Dentalium shell and bead necklace, probably
Calf tribe.*

ABOVE, FAR RIGHT: *Contemporary Huichol
ritual bowl made of the inside of a gourd decorated
with beads pressed into an adhesive substance.*

FAR RIGHT: *Bead-decorated gourd made by
Norma Jaichima, Huichol, in 1982. (Courtesy
of the Heard Museum, Phoenix, Arizona)*

BELOW: *Contemporary Huichol beaded
necklace (detail).*

## Techniques

VARIOUS related techniques were used
to 'weave' the shells, using thread or
sinew, into belts and choker-type neck
ornaments. The Zuni of New Mexico still
make small disc-shaped beads of shell,
the favoured shell is the *Olivella biplicata*
because of its purplish colour. The Zuni
also make beads of turquoise, a much
harder material – many tribal groups in
this region are well known for their skilled
work in silver and turquoise. In Ohio and
California freshwater pearls and beads of
bird bones are used. Juniper seeds, on
their own, or threaded with pine nuts
were made into fringes on ceremonial
garments. Also typical of this region were
very small white seeds, *Onosmodium
subsetosum*, giving the appearance of small
white glass beads.

The Astawaki of California produced
woven beadwork as well as twined baskets
decorated with woven beadwork attached
only at the top and bottom edges. Basketry
is a highly developed craft in this region,
and beadwork on basketry, using several
methods, is also common. The various
tribal groups use different techniques: the
Mono use beads woven with woollen
threads; the Washo of Nevada make netted
neck ornaments, a technique also used by
other tribal groups in this region; the Yuma
apply the netted construction to make bags;
and the Mohave make netted collars.

# SOUTH AMERICA

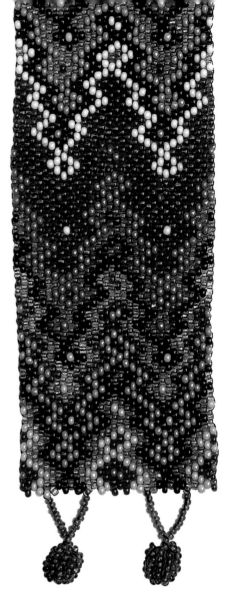

SOUTH AMERICA, stretching from Panama in the north to Cape Horn on the southernmost tip of the continent, includes dense rain forest in the Amazonian basin, the sub-tropical climate of central Argentina, as well as dry steppe, areas of desert and a high mountain range, which all influence the way of life of the inhabitants.

### Early evidence of beads

SHAPED bone beads have been found in Columbia, some with two perforations as though they were intended to be stitched onto a garment, or onto an article, and some drilled for threading. Finely worked stone beads, some smaller than the modern glass seed bead, about 2 mm in diameter and mostly made of black steatite, have been found in burial sites in Peru and Ecuador, and turquoise beads of equally fine workmanship have been discovered from Central America to Argentina. Similar-sized beads of rock crystal, and carnelian, from Columbia, and larger calcite beads found in Jamaica all testify to a long history of bead manufacture and use in Central and South America.

### Tribal groups

BANDOLIERS of strung seeds or small insect larvae were a symbol of shamanic power among Ecuadorean tribes. As many of the materials used in the making of beads were traded over long distances, a heavily ornamented article of dress conferred considerable status.

The Jivaro, a warlike tribe, from Ecuador and Peru made ceremonial breast ornaments of beaten bark, decorated with feathers, with beads of seeds and bird bones both stitched to the bark and threaded into decorative fringes.

Among the tribes of Amazonian Brazil, Guiana and Columbia, an apron-like garment worn by women is common. Originally made of small, hard, highly polished seeds, they are now made of glass beads obtained through trade.

### Beaded weaving

WEAVING using beads was practised before the arrival of glass beads from Europe. The types of looms used included the bow loom (also found in North America) and the backstrap loom which is still widely used in South America. The Tahltan of Columbia, the Patamona of Guyana and the Wai Wai from Brazil all weave beads. The weaving is done by women, and the apron is constructed upside down – that is, the weaving commences from the top (waist) edge of the apron, and proceeds upwards, away from the worker, to the bottom edge of the garment. The loose ends of the weaving are finished off at the lower edge.

Among the Guyami of Central Panama, the beaded weaving is carried out by men, and very bright colours of beads and metallic finishes are favoured. Yet another variant of beaded weaving is produced by Mosquito Native Americans of Nicaragua.

ABOVE: *Bracelet of contemporary beadwork from Guatemala which echoes the local weaving in colour and design.*

BELOW, LEFT: *Bracelet of glass beads, used as trade goods by the Piro people, Amazonian Peru.*

BELOW, RIGHT: *Tiny beads of stone and shell were drilled and then ground into discs used in assemblages of beadwork in the ancient kingdoms in the north of Peru – the Moche and Chimu.*

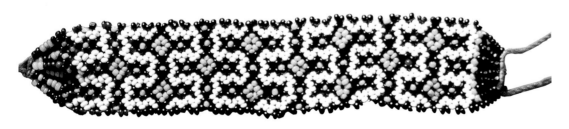

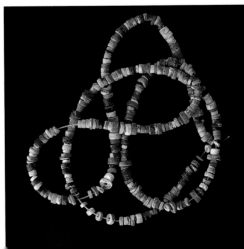

*ABOVE; AND CENTRE: Woman's 'apron', Wai Wai people, Guyana; and katami used only by the Wai Wai in the Esequibo-Maguera region.*

*BELOW, LEFT: Wai Wai girls dressed for dancing.*

*BELOW, RIGHT: Quechua woman from Paucartambo, in the Andean highlands of Peru.*

## Netted beadwork and decoration

NETTED beadwork is produced in Columbia, Nicaragua and Panama. Geometric designs are worked into the articles. Yet another variation is worked by the Chokoi Native Americans of Panama.

Brightly coloured beadwork is used in Peru on modern dance and carnival headdresses of beads and feathers in the 'Inca' style. The villagers of Peru, where each village has a different version of the felted 'bowler' hat, use white beads to decorate the chinstraps of their hats. The Voudou temples of Haiti and Cuba are decorated with flags covered with sequins, as are costumes of the performers affiliated to each temple.

# ASIA, OCEANIA
## AND THE
# ARABIAN GULF

FAR LEFT: *Beaded prayer mat, Afghanistan (detail).*
ABOVE, LEFT: *Head shawl from Kohistan (detail).*
ABOVE, RIGHT: *Animal trapping from Baluchistan, southern Pakistan.*
NEAR LEFT: *Contemporary beaded hair tassel from Pakistan.*
BELOW, RIGHT: *Ceremonial basket, from south Sumatra, used to hold gifts of textiles or food.*

# THE HISTORY OF BEADWORK IN ASIA, OCEANIA AND THE ARABIAN GULF

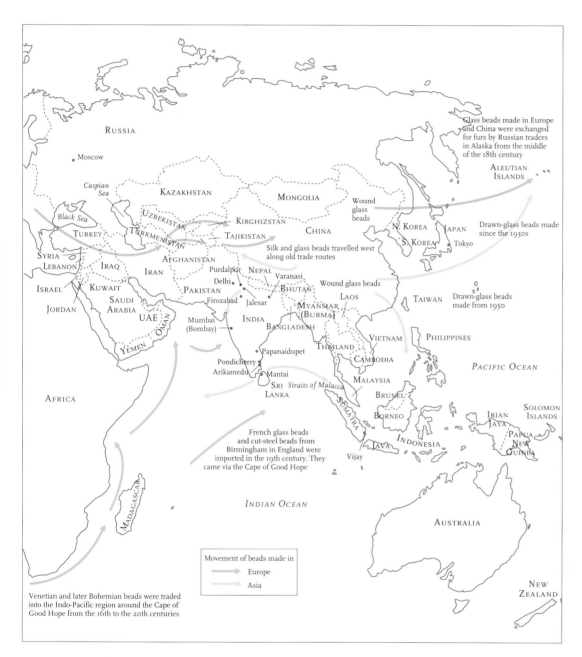

Glass beads made in Europe and China were exchanged for furs by Russian traders in Alaska from the middle of the 18th century

Drawn-glass beads made since the 1930s

Silk and glass beads travelled west along old trade routes

Wound glass beads

Drawn-glass beads made from 1950

French glass beads and cut-steel beads from Birmingham in England were imported in the 19th century. They came via the Cape of Good Hope

Movement of beads made in
→ Europe
→ Asia

Venetian and later Bohemian beads were traded into the Indo-Pacific region around the Cape of Good Hope from the 16th to the 20th centuries

ABOVE: *Young woman, from the Caucus Mountains, Georgia, wearing a beaded headdress.*

BELOW: *Miao girls, from Guangxi Province, southern China, in modern festival costume.*

OPPOSITE, BELOW, LEFT: *Woman's* jumlo *(traditional dress) from Kohistan.*

OPPOSITE, BELOW, RIGHT: *Two lamas from Tibet; the one on the left is wearing the traditional costume of the dancing lama.*

**A**SIA IS CRISS-CROSSED by some of the oldest trades routes in the world, though this is hardly surprising when one considers the long history of the manufacture of fine textiles, beads and other goods in this region.

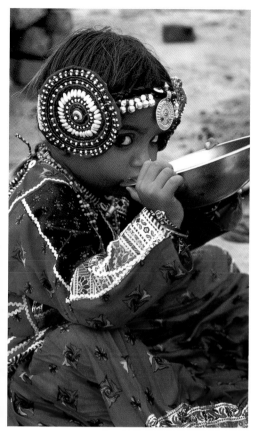

ABOVE, LEFT: *Rabari girl, from Gujarat in India, with beaded* dhabak, *amuletic discs worn on each temple.*

ABOVE, RIGHT: *A large, early 20th-century rectangle of netted beading in the style typical of beadwork from Kathiawar, Gujarat, India.*

## THE MANUFACTURE OF BEADS

BEADS OF semi-precious stone, shell or bone have been made on the Indian sub-continent for thousands of years – archaeological excavations have uncovered beads dating from 23,000 BC in Maharashtra, and beads made in the Indus Valley have been found dating from 7,000 BC. There is evidence to suggest that as early as 2,500 BC beads – and other goods – were traded over long distances, through Afghanistan to Iran, Iraq, Turkey, and so to the Mediterranean. Beads were also made, and traded from, Afghanistan until around 1600 BC. Glass beads were made in India from 1,000 BC on, and some of the oldest drawn-cane glass beads that have been discovered, dating from 200 BC, were made in southern India at Arikamedu. Glass beads were produced in several locations on the sub-continent and, for at least the next 1,500 years, were exported to East Africa and throughout Asia – beads of Indian manufacture have been found in Indonesia, Malaysia, Thailand and Korea. At one time referred to as 'trade wind beads', they were carried by Chinese, Indian and Arab traders, sailing the monsoon winds. The manufacture of beads continued in India until the 16th century, when European colonization, coinciding with the output of beads from Venice, and, later, Germany, sent the Indian bead industry into decline. By the late 19th century, India was importing large quantities of European beads; the very fine Murano beads from Venice travelled the trade routes around the Cape of Good Hope to East Africa and from there to the Arabian peninsula and on to western India, particularly Gujarat. As seed bead manufacture ceased in Venice, the resultant gap in the market was filled by beads imported from Bohemia and Japan until 1981 when small glass beads were produced in Varanasi, India, to supply the domestic market.

ABOVE: *Man, from Makasar Straits region, Indonesia, wearing ornaments of shells and shell beads.*

## TRADE ROUTES

THE ISLANDS of South-East Asia are at the point where the sea trading routes between Europe, western Asia, India and China meet; Arab and Chinese seafarers dominated the routes from the 10th to the 17th centuries. By the 16th century the Portuguese and Spanish began to explore and trade in this region, followed by the Dutch and the British in the 18th century. From ancient times traders plying these routes carried beads, and many types of bead are so widely distributed throughout this region that it is difficult to trace the history of their manufacture. There is some evidence that artisans from India migrated to various sites in South-East Asia during the 1st century AD, beginning the manufacture of beads in Thailand, Korea and possibly other sites. A bead particularly prized throughout this region was the *mutisalah*, an orange-red drawn-glass bead also known in East Africa as 'Indian reds'. These beads, made in southern India, were used as a wedding gift from a groom to his bride.

ABOVE, LEFT: *Man's cap from Persia (Iran); the appliqué patterns have been outlined with seed beads.*

LEFT: *Group of Angami Naga men, from north India, wearing typical shell and bead regalia.*

RIGHT: *Moti-wallah, or bead seller; interior of a shop in the bead bazaar, Kathmandu, Nepal.*

OPPOSITE, BELOW: *A group of chiefs from the island of Vella Lavella, Solomon Islands, wearing* tarkolas, *a chest ornament, made of clam shells, red, blue and white beads, and opossum teeth, which denotes rank.*

THREE

LEFT: *Mongolian woman, probably of the Khalka people, in the headdress worn by married women, decorated with beaded motifs and long strands of seed pearls. The large side pieces are said to represent cow's horns.*

RIGHT: *Adult woman's headdress from the Akha tribe, probably from Myanmar – the shape and decoration of the headdress varies slightly according to which sub group or region the woman belongs. The headdress is decorated with Job's tears seeds and other seed cases, and wool tassels and aluminium discs. It is supported on a bamboo frame.*

With the arrival of European traders, coinciding with the decline in bead manufacture in India, European glass beads from all the European manufacturing centres were widely traded in the area – French beads and cut steel beads from Birmingham, England, were particularly favoured by the Straits Chinese community, during the relatively brief period of British rule in the 19th century. Though the Silk Route had declined in importance following the discovery, by the Portuguese explorer Vasco da Gama, of a sea route to India in 1498, nevertheless trade still continued on the ancient route. With the mass production of glass seed beads in Bohemia from the 18th century, these were traded through Turkey and from there to the Middle East, or on to the Caspian Sea, and further to the oasis towns of Central Asia, and to Afghanistan and the northern Indus valleys. Today, beads are mass produced in northern India, Japan and Taiwan, and exported throughout the world.

Imported glass beads, whether from Asia or, later, from Europe, did not find equal acceptance everywhere; throughout the islands of Oceania locally made shell beads were regarded as superior to the imported glass beads. The shell beads had long been important, both as a means of exchange and also to facilitate friendly relations between the

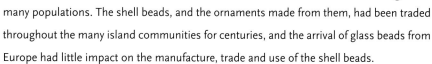

many populations. The shell beads, and the ornaments made from them, had been traded throughout the many island communities for centuries, and the arrival of glass beads from Europe had little impact on the manufacture, trade and use of the shell beads.

The Middle East and the Arabian Gulf were served by ancient trade routes and beads from Asia, particularly India, were probably traded throughout this region. According to the records of factories in Bohemia, European beads arrived in the Middle East via the major export market of Turkey. From Turkey, the beads travelled to Iran and Iraq to the south east, and to Syria, Jordan, Egypt and North Africa to the south and west. From Egypt, small glass beads were traded to Arabia; during the second half of the 19th century, Venetian beads traded through East Africa to Gujarat, in India, passing the Arabian peninsula.

# CHINA AND JAPAN

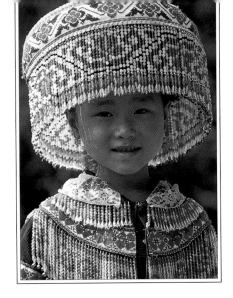

THE MAJORITY of the peoples of mainland China have not, historically, used small glass beads or beadwork in the decoration of their dress or household items. From ancient times fine beads of precious and semi-precious stones were made, and worn by those who could afford them, but even when seed beads arrived with European traders, there was little interest in their use. The same is not true, however, of the Chinese ethnic minorities.

## CHINESE ETHNIC MINORITIES

THE Chinese ethnic minorities, most of whom live in south-west China, each have their own distinctive dress and customs. As with the related groups spread through Myanmar, Laos and Thailand, the most elaborate decoration is reserved for the festival dress of young people of marriageable age. The New Year festivities are traditionally a time to seek a marriage partner, so the most eye-catching and colourful garments and jewelry are worn. The Dong people of Guizhou Province use white beads couched to fabric as well as the embroidery and appliqué common to nearly all the ethnic minorities. The designs, used to decorate garments and baby carriers, are intricate curvilinear patterns highlighted by the white beads. The Miao women and girls now use a great deal of beadwork in the form of patterned fringes on their headdresses and festival garments. The use

OPPOSITE, TOP: *Miao girl from Longlin Guangxi Province, southern China; the costume has become more elaborate in recent years.*

OPPOSITE, BELOW, LEFT: *Man's velvet cap with metallic bead embroidery, Guangzhou Province, China.*

OPPOSITE, BELOW, RIGHT: *Woman's chest and back ornament, Miao people, southern China; and woman's festival hat, Gejia people, southern China.*

of beads in this manner and the quantity is a comparatively recent innovation, and the amount of beading seems to be increasing year by year.

The Gaoshan people of Taiwan used to decorate garments with small white shell beads, stitched on in long, loose rows in a manner reminiscent of the 'lazy stitch' beadwork from North America.

## THE NEW TERRITORIES OF CHINA

IN THE New Territories of China, comprising Hong Kong and a small part of the mainland (formerly owned by Britain), beads and beadwork were used, both by the Punti (local Cantonese) population and the Hoklo, from Fujian. Married Punti women wore a *fa lap*, a headband densely embroidered with beads, and, if the owner's means permitted, with a jade or gold ornament at the centre. In the past this headband was one of the wedding garments, thereafter worn for festivals. The Hoklo women wore strings of beads to decorate their hair for festival occasions, and also made embroidered and beaded collars, with

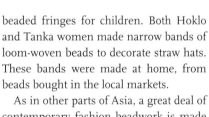

beaded fringes for children. Both Hoklo and Tanka women made narrow bands of loom-woven beads to decorate straw hats. These bands were made at home, from beads bought in the local markets.

As in other parts of Asia, a great deal of contemporary fashion beadwork is made in China today, for export. In particular, beadwork on leather, using Native American-style motifs, is made for export to the United States. Beadwork of this style was also made in Singapore during the 1950s, where it was briefly popular among the expatriate British community – every teenager had to have a 'Singapore belt'.

## JAPAN

DESPITE the fact that very good-quality seed beads are made in Japan, there is no history of beadwork or bead embroidery, though there is now some interest in contemporary beadwork.

ABOVE: Fa lap, *a headband, worn by the Punti women, Hong Kong, on their wedding day, and for festivals, mid-20th century.*

LEFT: *Late 20th-century pair of beaded slippers from the New Territories of China.*

BELOW, LEFT: *Ainu people, Japan; the woman is wearing a breast ornament decorated with small glass beads.*

BELOW, RIGHT: *Bag of Japanese silk in the traditional* kikko *pattern.*

# INDIAN SUB-CONTINENT

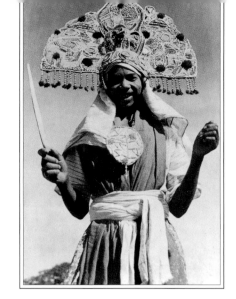

**B**EADWORK FROM the Indian sub-continent is as diverse in style as the many national and tribal groups that produce it. Though beads have been made on the Indian sub-continent since ancient times, the construction of beadwork, especially that using drawn-glass beads, is comparatively recent. While beadwork flourishes in some parts of the sub-continent, the traditional use of ornament and dress has all but vanished among some of the minor tribal groups.

## NAGALAND

**T**HE Nagas, from the north-eastern Indian state of Nagaland and northern Myanmar (formerly Burma), used shells, beetle wings and beads of shell, bone, semi-precious stones and glass to make ornaments. Not all Naga tribes wore such ornaments, but among those that did, the necklaces and belts were worn by both sexes. The best-known and most common Naga necklace is typically made of many strands of orange or red beads; the multiple ends of the fibre on which the beads are threaded are plaited or woven together at each end of the necklace. Some Naga tribal groups made more elaborate netted necklaces – which were *beadwork* rather than simply stranded beads – of shell and glass beads, with simple geometric patterning. In traditional Naga society, personal dress and adornment conveyed information about the wearer's accomplishments and social status, or in the case of women, of the accomplishments of her father or husband. Formerly much feared

head-hunters, the Naga man's cloak embroidered with cowrie shells proclaimed his prowess. Today, most of the Naga are Christian and no longer maintain many aspects of their traditional culture.

## ARUNACHAL PRADESH

**T**RIBAL groups from the north-eastern hill state of Arunachal Pradesh still wear a style of dress and ornament similar to those of Myanmar and Tibet, both of which border the state. Sherdukpen women wear Tibetan-style necklaces of seed pearls, silver, coral and turquoise, while Atapani women wear multi-stranded necklaces of black, yellow and red beads. Hill-Miri men's necklaces are made of large and small blue glass beads; all of these ornaments are stranded beads rather than beadwork. In the small Himalayan kingdom of Nepal, traditional beadwork is very much Tibetan in style, consisting of small coral beads, stitched to a black cloth base, and turquoise and cowrie shells.

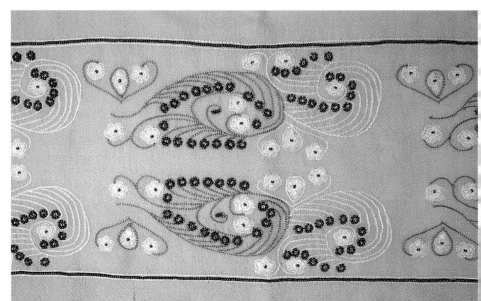

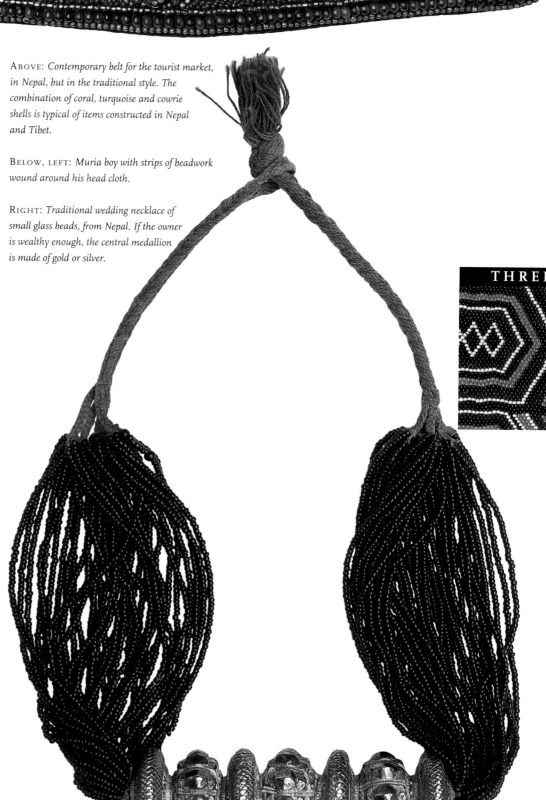

OPPOSITE, ABOVE: *Young dancer dressed for the annual Dussera festival, in eastern India, wearing a headdress of paper, mica and beads.*

OPPOSITE, BELOW, LEFT: *Two necklaces, made by the Nagas, incorporating glass and shell beads with central pendants of shell and cast metal. During the time of the British rule, the Nagas had to travel outside their own region to obtain shells and beads – trade within their area was prohibited.*

OPPOSITE, BELOW, RIGHT: *Detail of beadwork and embroidery on a cashmere shawl made in Nepal for the Western fashion market. The chain stitch appears on the same side as the beading which means the work was done using an ari hook.*

ABOVE: *Contemporary belt for the tourist market, in Nepal, but in the traditional style. The combination of coral, turquoise and cowrie shells is typical of items constructed in Nepal and Tibet.*

BELOW, LEFT: *Muria boy with strips of beadwork wound around his head cloth.*

RIGHT: *Traditional wedding necklace of small glass beads, from Nepal. If the owner is wealthy enough, the central medallion is made of gold or silver.*

THREE

## EASTERN INDIA

IN EASTERN India many tribal groups used beads and beadwork – the Gonds, Konds, the Saoras of Orissa and the Juang in Bengal all wore multiple strings of beads. In the past the women, in particular, would wear a great number of bead strands, partly to cover their (bare) breasts. The Muria made necklaces and earrings, the latter worn by men and women, of small glass beads and bells. The men also wore strands of netted beads around the neck and a turban-like headcloth, as did the Kond men. The

Saoras and Bhattras made and wore elaborate headdresses, decorated with coloured paper, mica, mirrors and beads, for use at the annual Dussera festival. The coloured paper and the mirrors were a fairly recent innovation in 1950, and an indication of assimilation into mainstream society, a process that by the end of the 20th century had all but obliterated these distinctive tribal cultures. Cowrie shells were used extensively by all these tribes.

## THE BANJARA

COWRIES are an important item of embellishment for the Banjara people; originally from Rajasthan in western India, the Banjara are now dispersed throughout most of India, though the greatest numbers live in central and southern India. Their textiles

and costume testify to their love of embellishment – metal beads (at one time made from recycled lead shot), cowrie shells, mirrors, embroidery, appliqué, tassels, and in some areas, small white beads are all lavishly used as decoration. Within the last decade, some Banjara groups from western central India have begun to use multi-coloured glass beads, embroidered onto the women's *pisar potyda* (money bags) and also to make small items of personal adornment. Lead beads and cowrie shells are the most important embellishments on *pachela*, though tassels

ABOVE, LEFT: *Cowrie shells often convey status or power. This tribal man from eastern India is wearing a cap, bag and belt all embellished with cowrie shells.*

ABOVE, RIGHT: *Woman's blouse from the Banjara tribe, with mirrors, embroidery and white beads in the typical quincunx pattern used on so many Banjara textiles.*

BELOW: *Narrow strip of embroidery and beadwork, made to be attached to the edge of a woman's head shawl, so that it would frame the face; Banjara tribe, central and southern India.*

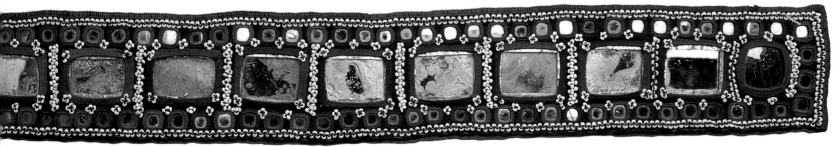

and glass seed beads are considered an acceptable substitute. The Banjara have retained much of their culture and though full traditional dress may only be worn for festival or ceremonial occasions, they continue to thrive as a distinctive people.

## GUJARAT

GUJARAT, in western India, is well known for the variety of skilled craftwork produced by its many different communities. Seed beads were imported into this region in the late 19th century and at that time beadwork was produced by professional embroiderers of the Mochi caste. By the beginning of the 20th century, women of the Kathi landowning class were producing beadwork as a home craft, in place of embroidery, by then mostly professionally made. Beadwork was adopted and copied by other caste groups, some of whom would have been employed by the Kathi landlords. Beadwork in the Kathi style invariably has a white background, with beads of clear primary-coloured glass, in motifs of peacocks, deities, elephants and flowers,

ABOVE: *A* pachela, *the arm decoration worn by married Banjara women. The metal beads, which in the past would have been made of recycled lead shot, are typical of Banjara ornaments.*

RIGHT: *Arm decoration, of netted glass beadwork, shells and tassels, formed over a ring of tightly packed straw, covered with cloth.*

BELOW: *Part of a* palli *(long frieze) from Gujarat. Usually embroidered, this example is made entirely of beadwork. The complex patterns seen here are difficult to achieve with this method of construction.*

all worked in a variation of three-bead netting. Older pieces have large and complex motifs – a testament to the skill of the worker, since this particular method of construction is one of the most difficult to use when depicting a figurative object. Many pieces are worked in such a way that the network of beads is attached to the backing fabric as it is made, while others are made more conventionally as a separate fabric of beads, which is then attached to a supporting fabric. Beadwork was used to decorate a great variety of small-to-medium-sized household objects such as *chakla* (square wall hangings), friezes (*palli*), bullock trappings, and items used in marriage ceremonies. Large pieces of beadwork were also constructed, among the surviving pieces is a cover for the framework of a bullock cart, used for ceremonial purposes. After the First World War the supply of good-quality beads declined, as did the quality of the

TOP: *Small* toran *(doorway hanging) of netted beadwork, with typical peacock and flower motifs.*

ABOVE: Chakla *(square wall hanging) of netted beadwork, only fastened to the backing at the edges.*

NEAR RIGHT: *Small plastic box, decorated with beadwork; sold very cheaply in Bombay.*

FAR RIGHT: *Pair of chapatti sticks, covered with beadwork – these are used in marriage rituals, symbolizing the desire for a plentiful food supply. Similarly, pairs of decorated sticks are used in the dandia ras dance.*

beadwork produced. While beadwork is produced extensively today, the beads used are often uneven in size, and may be plastic rather than glass. The women of the Meghwal leather-working caste continue to produce beadwork for their own use, making netted chokers of two rectangular sections linked at the centre by a shank of beads. In recent years beadwork has been used increasingly to decorate traditional Meghwal blouses – while a few years ago beadwork would have just formed the edging for the blouse, now wide bands of beadwork are attached to the body of the garment. A Meghwal bride-groom covers his face with a mask of many strands of beads and small white shells, or beads of similar shape and size in place of the shells, suspended from an embroidered strip across the forehead. These masks are made by a female member of the groom's family. The Ahir pastoralists also use seed bead fringes to decorate household items.

THREE

ABOVE, LEFT: Cloth 'parrot', decorated with old glass buttons, beadwork and embroidery, for hanging over a baby's cradle; typical of work from many of the tribal groups of Kutch, Gujarat.

ABOVE, RIGHT: Traditional chariot, from early to mid-20th century, with a fine beadwork canopy. The beads are almost certainly fine Venetian ones, and the beadwork is so well executed that it is probably the production of a professional workshop.

FAR LEFT: Mirrored and embroidered decoration for the head of a bullock, with beaded and tasselled edging; Ahir caste.

LEFT: Beadwork matchbox cover, from a Meghwal village north of Bhuj city, Gujarat.

## THE RABARI

THE Rabari, one of the largest groups of pastoralists, use beadwork to edge the small bags they make as part of a bride's dowry. Among some sub groups of Rabari, beadwork is used extensively to decorate bags and belts for the bridegroom, and the *indhoni* (woman's head ring), which is used during the wedding ceremony as a stand for a ceremonial vessel. Rabari beadwork is quite distinctive in style, and though predominantly white and primary colours, like Kathi-style beadwork, it is quite easily recognized as Rabari – small white shells and white buttons are often included, the latter in particular mark a piece as Rabari.

Traditional-style beadwork is made in many places in Gujarat, especially

around Rajkot and Bhavnagar. The bead-work is sold to visitors to the region, and further afield; trinkets decorated in Kathi style are sold in the markets of Bombay.

## SIND

SIND, in southern Pakistan, is home to a number of pastoral and artisan groups also found in Gujarat; Ahir, Rabari and Bhil are all found in this region as are other groups with a similar culture. Beadwork and tassel edgings are used on women's blouses, bags and animal trappings, and beads are used to decorate the elaborate tassels plaited into women's hair. A typically Sindhi style of decoration for a woman's blouse consists of many small pompoms interspersed with rosettes of glass seed beads.

Beadwork today is produced commercially throughout the sub-continent, much of it for export. The method of beading with a fine hook (the ari hook used by Mochi embroiderers) is used in professional workshops to produce beaded and embroidered garments and accessories. These may be somewhat traditional in design, as the beaded pashmina shawls from Kashmir and Nepal, or made to specific designs sent out by Western fashion houses. Beadwork is a time-consuming process, made by hand, so the low cost of labour in this region has ensured a flood of orders – as the small workshops of Europe fed the demands of the fashion industry during the 19th and early 20th centuries, so now the countless small workshops of the sub-continent feed the fashion industry of the 21st century.

OPPOSITE, FAR LEFT: *The beadwork of this money bag has been backed with metallic papers, to embellish the item further. Rabari bridegrooms wear a great deal of embroidery and beadwork, worked by the bride to be.*

OPPOSITE, CENTRE: *The colouring and pattern of the beadwork on this belt are typically Rabari – small oval white glass beads have replaced the small shells that would once have been used. The Rabari say they can no longer obtain the small shells, and even these glass beads have now been superseded by plastic beads.*

OPPOSITE, RIGHT: Indoni-i-choti *used during religious ceremonies. The object on the stand is a beadwork-covered coconut.*

ABOVE, LEFT: *Young Rabari girl waiting patiently while the older family members make ready for the migration; she wears a beaded headdress as well as a netted necklace.*

ABOVE, CENTRE: Chakla *(wall hanging) of traditional embroidery with beaded edging, from Sind, southern Pakistan. The floral motifs are typical of several caste groups from this area.*

ABOVE, RIGHT: *Support for a nose ring from Sind – the weight of the large, heavy nose ring would be supported by this decorated strip, attached to both the nose ring and the hair.*

BELOW: *Modern man's cap, from Pakistan, with metallic embroidery and white beads – the embroidery has almost certainly been worked with an ari hook.*

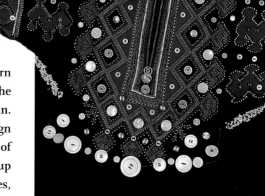

# CENTRAL ASIA

**THREE**

THE HEART of the great continent of Asia stretches from Iran in the west to western China in the east, encompassing northern Pakistan, Afghanistan and the republics of Uzbekistan, Tajikistan, Kazakhstan, Kirghizstan and Turkmenistan. The culture of this area has been shaped over the centuries by the many foreign influences travelling the ancient and legendary Silk Route, as well as the waves of migration and invasion by the tribal groups of Mongolia. The population is made up of the settled inhabitants of the once very wealthy oasis towns along the trade routes, and the nomadic or semi-nomadic herdsmen of the steppe. The nomadic rural people have retained, in the decoration of their textiles, many symbols from their pre-Islamic past – solar motifs, symbols of fertility and of the hunt. The textiles of this vast region reflect something of the history of the area and the diversity of the peoples and cultures contained within it. Embroidery is used extensively to decorate dress and household textiles, very often with the addition of fringes, tassels and beads.

## NORTHERN PAKISTAN

THE North-West Province of Pakistan – comprised of the Punjab, Waziristan, the Indus, Swat and Chitral valleys, and further north, the Gilgit and Hunza regions bordering Afghanistan – is home to several different tribal cultures. Throughout the province very fine embroidery and decoration is widely used on dress, not only for its aesthetic value, but also as a means of identifying the particular group or region to which the wearer belongs.

The Kalash people, an isolated non-Muslim, non-nomadic community, live in the Chitral Valley. The women wear necklaces made of numerous strings of beads – orange, red, yellow and white – brought from Peshawar. In addition, the traditional headdress, the *shushut*, has a long strip hanging at the back of the head decorated with wrapped tassels, buttons and beads. The larger festival headdress, only worn for special occasions, and worn on top of the *shushut*, is larger and

ABOVE, LEFT: Shushut, *the traditional head-dress of the women of the Chitral Valley, Pakistan.*

ABOVE, RIGHT: *Woman's dress from the Palas Valley, northern Pakistan.*

LEFT: *Child's waistcoat from Kohistan.*

OPPOSITE: *Extremely fine counted-thread embroidery on a woman's shawl from Kohistan.*

INSET: *Woman and child, from the Chitral Valley, wearing the* shushut.

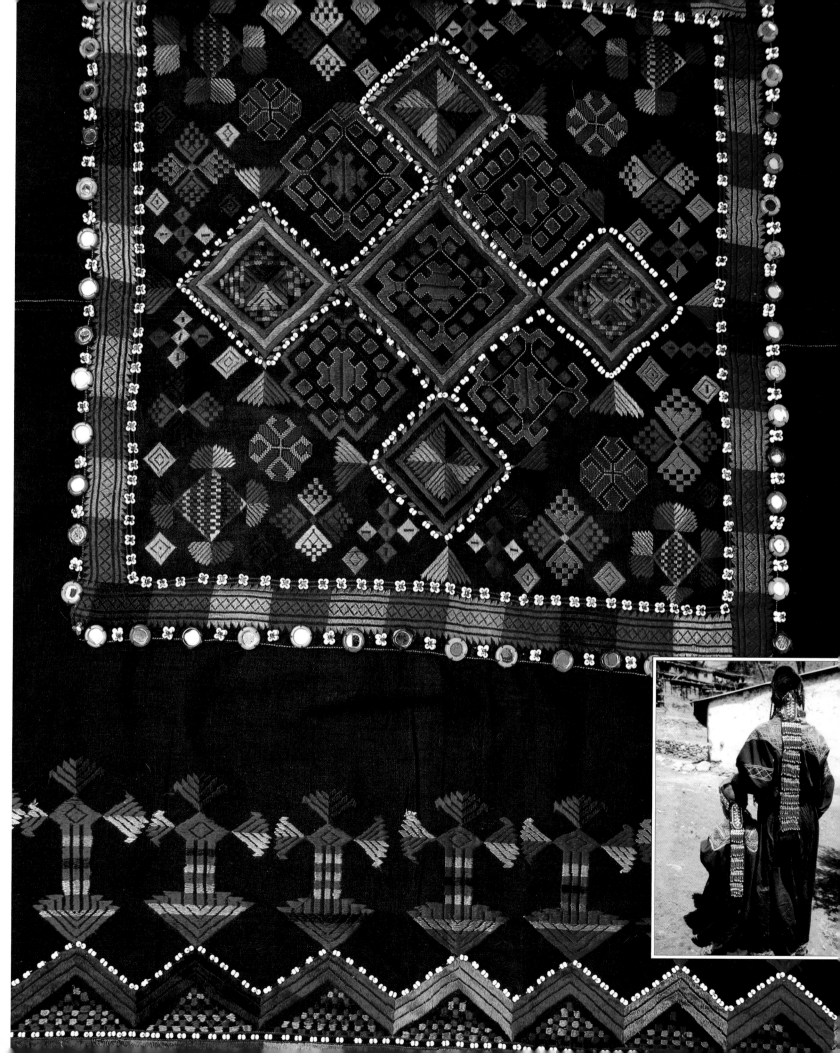

more elaborately decorated. In Kohistan (once known as Kafiristan, the land of unbelievers) traditional dress is decorated with extremely fine embroidery, the cherry red tree of life and solar motifs outlined with tiny white beads. Narrow strips of white beadwork and other amuletic objects such as buttons, pieces of zip fastener and small lengths of chain are frequently added to the embroidery to increase its 'protective' quality against evil. In an area of high infant mortality, children's clothes are often particularly elaborately decorated – strips of red, white and yellow beadwork, with a dense, looped fringe, are stitched to the garment in between the embroidered areas.

ABOVE: *A section of embroidery, possibly from a dress front, has been utilized by a Mangali (nomadic shepherd) family from Waziristan to make this small bag.*

OPPOSITE, ABOVE, LEFT: *Heavy tassels of wrapped beadwork and twisted beadwork fringe are plaited into women's hair, to sway with the movement of their walk. Thick, luxuriant hair is said to be a sign of good health, so girls plait extra wool into their hair.*

OPPOSITE, BELOW, LEFT: *Corner of a cushion cover embroidered with the fine chain-stitch embroidery typical of the Hazara. The fine fringe of silk thread has protective blue beads twisted into it.*

OPPOSITE, BELOW, RIGHT: *Hood, or helmet, decorated in typical Kohistani style. Said to be worn by children, they were also probably worn by women.*

## AFGHANISTAN AND THE CENTRAL ASIAN REPUBLICS

BEADWORK is used extensively in Afghanistan and the Central Asian Republics. Items decorated with the traditional fine chain-stitch embroidery are further embellished with the ubiquitous twisted thread and bead fringe that seems common to most of Central Asia. Constructed separately, then attached to the object, the fringe is almost invariably of deep maroon or purple thread with one or three beads, generally white, or the more protective blue, twisted into each strand. This fringe decorates many small bags and purses, and other

ABOVE, LEFT: *This entirely beaded, splendidly heavy motorcycle seat cover was made in Afghanistan, after a Central Asian tradition.*

TOP RIGHT: *Small bags and purses for personal items – such as this coin purse – are essential in Central Asia, and are often given as gifts.*

ABOVE: *This small, jewel-like container holds kohl used by women as a cosmetic. Here, the smallest of mirrors are set in metallic-thread embroidery.*

household items, which are traditional in this society. Instead of the fringe, an edging of – usually – blue beads may be stitched over the outer edges of the object. The protective, amuletic triangle with its dangling strands is common to all the different ethnic groups of Central Asia, regardless of their faith. It is worked in embroidery, made of cloth, or constructed of beads; a small beaded triangle is worn on the little finger of the left hand by bridegrooms as a symbol of fertility. Animal trappings and bags to transport

LEFT: *Uzbek tent decoration; and necklace, from Uzbekistan, mid-20th century.*

ABOVE: *Padded velvet amulet from Uzbekistan.*

BELOW: *Dress from Afghanistan, the embroidered bodice has several gul-i-peron (dress flowers).*

INSET: *Seller of embroidery and beadwork, Urout market, Uzbekistan.*

THREE

goods were essential to the nomadic way of life, and were part of every girl's dowry, produced by the bride-to-be to show her weaving and embroidery skills. These, too, would be embellished with tassels and beads that swayed with the movement of the animal. A woman, whether settled town dweller or nomad, would acquire status within her community according to her skill at needlework. Most everyday household cloths and bags – cushion covers, purses, cradle covers – are decorated. The desire to make decorated covering cloths is so much a part of Central Asian culture, even though nomadic life is fast disappearing, that today this finds expression in the making of coverings for possessions such as bicycle saddles, televisions, and, sadly, the kalashnikov rifle – a reminder of the conflict that all too often dominates life in parts of Central Asia. Beadwork pistol holsters are made and sold in quantity by Afghan refugees.

Beadwork is also used on dress – on trouser cuffs, sleeve cuffs, shawls, and as *gul-i-peron*, or dress flowers; these are discs of beadwork, sometimes including small shells or *shisha*, stitched to the bodice of a dress. Beads larger than those used on the Kohistani dress or the *gul-i-peron* are used for articles constructed entirely of beads; these may be as small as a coin purse, or as large as a prayer mat. Such a large object is made in sections which are then put together – the weight of the finished item is considerable. The patterns used reflect those woven into rugs.

ABOVE, LEFT: *Two* gul-i-peron, *with fringe and beadwork strip, to decorate the front of a dress.*

ABOVE, CENTRE: *Baby's rattle, which would be hung above the cradle, from Bukhara; the larger metal beads are hollow.*

ABOVE, RIGHT: *Dress amulet of fine Turkomen embroidery and tassels from Ashkabad.*

FAR LEFT: *Breast ornament, from Uzbekistan, with netted beads and twisted bead fringe.*

NEAR LEFT: *Cloth-lined small coin purse with 'clover leaf end' beaded fringes.*

# South-East Asia

Myanmar (Burma), Thailand, Laos, Kampuchea (Cambodia) and Vietnam make up mainland South-East Asia; the many islands form the countries of Malaysia, Indonesia and the Philippines. Beadwork from this region is as rich and varied as the many ethnic groups, with their diverse cultures, that inhabit it.

Embroidered *kalagas*, jewelled hangings originally for monasteries in Myanmar, are decorated with padded embroidery, sequins and glass 'beads' – these are not true beads, having no hole for threading, but are spheres of glass, fused to a square glass base. This base is used as an anchor to attach the 'beads' to the *kalaga*. Most *kalagas* are now produced for the tourist market.

Intricate beadwork, of small glass beads, was an important part of traditional dress in Indonesia, particularly in Borneo. The Chinese community of Malaysia and Indonesia used fine beadwork and embroidery to adorn the many hangings and other items that were required for the bridal chamber. Several of the tribal groups of the Philippines used small shell beads, embroidered onto clothing for men and women.

## THE MAINLAND

The hill tribes of Myanmar, Thailand and Laos use beadwork to decorate their festival costumes; the most elaborate dress is worn by young men and women of marriageable age, to attract a prospective partner. The amount of decoration on the costume declines with the wearer's age, until in old age the costume is quite plain, generally of indigo-dyed cloth.

The women of the Karen or Yang hill tribe, living in Myanmar and northern Thailand, decorate themselves and their clothing with small glass beads and the hard seeds of a tropical grass (*Coix lacryma-jobi*), known as Job's tears. These seeds are long, thin and soft when young, and become round when mature. Naturally greyish in colour, they can be whitened by heat. The elongated, immature seeds are used by married Karen women, stitched to their blouses in intricate patterns, further enhanced by embroidery. The women also wear a great number of strings of glass beads around the throat which are chest or even waist length, sometimes adding tassels of bright wool to the strands. Unmarried men occasionally wear beads

ABOVE: *Job's tears seeds used as beads, with embroidery, on a woman's blouse, Karen tribe, north Thailand.*

LEFT: *Late 20th-century* kalaga *from Myanmar. Though the round glass objects are called 'beads', they have no central hole, but are attached to the cloth by stitching over their square base. Each component of a* kalaga *is made by a different village – one will make the 'beads', another the sequins and so on.*

around the throat or as longer strands. Many of the glass beads worn by the Karen are of European manufacture, obtained through trade a century or more ago. The Karen also make very small beads from coconut shell.

The Akha, or Hani, live in Yunnan in southern China, Myanmar and northern Thailand. The Akha women also use both glass beads and Job's tear seeds abundantly, though the Akha generally prefer to use the mature, round seeds, which are then strung, like beads. Multiple strands of glass beads and Job's tear seeds are used to decorate a girl's or woman's headdress; adding the beads and seeds indicates that the wearer has reached another stage of maturity between adolescence and adulthood. A further stage of maturity is indicated by the wearing of a sash, also ornamented with beads and seeds. The girls and women wear belts, wide for unmarried girls and narrow for married women, decorated with cowrie shells, silver coins and red and white beads. If a girl is poor and unable to afford cowries or silver, she will decorate her belt entirely with seeds. Women's jackets and bags carried by both sexes are decorated with embroidery and appliqué as well as small white buttons, strands of beads and seeds, while the men's jackets are decorated with appliqué and embroidery only. Small bamboo baskets and containers, wound round with strands of mostly white beads,

are used by the women to hold their spindles and unspun cotton.

Of the other tribal groups of this region, the Lahu women wear multiple strands of glass beads, but do not use them on their clothing; the Lisu women decorate their festival turbans with beads, and use intricate, netted beadwork on the bags made for young, unmarried men. The 'bachelor's' or 'courting' bags are highly decorated with embroidery, silver and fringes as well as beadwork, and are intended to attract a prospective bride.

**THREE**

ABOVE, LEFT: *Akha woman, from Myanmar, wearing an earlier, less elaborate version of the headdress shown on page 113.*

ABOVE, CENTRE: *U Lo Akha girl's headdress, with gibbon fur and chicken feathers, dyed scarlet.*

ABOVE, RIGHT: *Cloth, from Laos, with strands of seeds and long 'bugles' of metal, reputedly made from sardine tins.*

RIGHT: *Woman's jacket, Akha tribe, showing the intricate appliqué and strands of Job's tears seeds with which the Akha women adorn their clothing.*

## MALAYSIA AND INDONESIA

THROUGHOUT the islands of South-East Asia, beaded textiles were highly regarded as objects conferring status on their owner. In contrast to the islands of Oceania, glass beads were especially favoured, for being more colourful and more durable than beads of natural materials. The islands of Indonesia have produced some of the most stunning beadwork in the world, worked in netting. Netting is one of the most difficult constructions in which to work a design, particularly any design using curves, but large and complex designs of convoluted

**THREE**

curves, ancestor figures, and dragon or monster motifs are worked into the beadwork. Ceremonial costume is very important to the tribal groups of Borneo; elaborate beadwork is considered to give strength and vitality to the wearer, and ensure fertility for crops. The costume consists of a knee-length straight skirt, jacket or sleeveless waistcoat, headcloth or headband. They are all, with the exception of the headcloth, covered with highly ornamental beadwork, in the favoured colours of predominantly yellow and black, or white and black. Baby carriers and bags are also ornamented with the

OPPOSITE, ABOVE, LEFT; AND ABOVE, RIGHT: *Batak cloth with beads; and betel-nut pouch of pandanus fibre, probably Batak, both from Sumatra.*

OPPOSITE, BELOW, LEFT: *Cloth made by the Batak people, Tapanuli district, north Sumatra.*

OPPOSITE, BELOW, RIGHT; AND DETAIL: *Iban man's jacket with curvilinear, sea-monster motifs, Malaysia.*

ABOVE, LEFT: *Small cloth bag, from Sulawesi, Indonesia, with coins attached.*

ABOVE, RIGHT: *Small pouch fringed with hair, beadwork and coins, probably from Borneo.*

NEAR RIGHT: *Hanging for the marriage bed, from the Chinese community in Indonesia.*

FAR RIGHT: *Woman's hat of woven palm leaf made by the Kayan people, Mukah, Sarawak.*

133

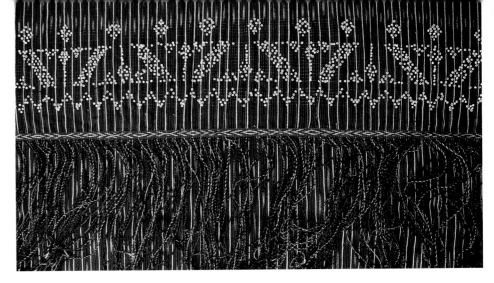

same elaborate beadwork. Woven cloths, with beads woven into the warp, are made in southern Sumatra, worn as a shoulder cloth by men on ceremonial occasions, or exchanged as ritual gifts at weddings, when the fabric is known as *tampan maju*. The Mentawi people of Siberut Island, off the western coast of Sumatra, use beaded bands to hold the wigs they wear for healing ceremonies in place. This is a recent development; the government of the islands has stipulated that the Mentawi must cut their hair, so a long wig is used as a substitute. On older pieces of beadwork from Sumatra, the beads are stitched to a cloth (usually velvet) base, to make dance belts. In Bali, large, delicate temple hangings are made of netted beadwork, mirrors and long beaded fringes.

## STRAITS CHINESE

THE Chinese community of the Malaccan Straits, known as the British Straits Settlements during the 19th century, used beadwork extensively, very probably influenced by the Malay community, as

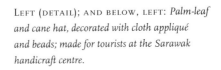

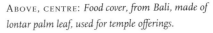

LEFT (DETAIL); AND BELOW, LEFT: *Palm-leaf and cane hat, decorated with cloth appliqué and beads; made for tourists at the Sarawak handicraft centre.*

ABOVE, CENTRE: *Food cover, from Bali, made of lontar palm leaf, used for temple offerings.*

OPPOSITE, TOP RIGHT: *Handwoven cloth made with machine-spun cotton; beads have been added to the weft. These ceremonial shoulder cloths were exchanged at weddings by the Karo Batak people in Sumatra.*

OPPOSITE, CENTRE, RIGHT: *Woman, from Borneo, wearing a cylindrical hat – the beadwork is very similar to the beaded panel on the jacket on page 132.*

OPPOSITE, BELOW, RIGHT: *Densely beaded hat from Indonesia, almost certainly made as a tourist item, since the weight of the beadwork would render it impracticable as a item of everyday wear.*

RIGHT: *Cigarette case, from the Perakanan Chinese community, finely worked with couched metallic thread and beads.*

BELOW: *Three long beaded bands, made by the Straits Chinese community, used to decorate the doorway of the marital bed chamber. Brilliantly coloured and patterned – the bottom one, in particular, has an elaborate, scalloped edge – they are a testament to the skill of the women who made them.*

**THREE**

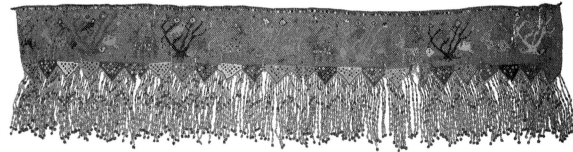

beadwork of this type is unknown in mainland China. The very distinctive style, characterized by glowing colours and ornately floral designs, was almost entirely for furnishings for the wedding chamber, using typically Chinese symbols – pairs of bats for conjugal happiness, or pairs of phoenixes to represent the married couple. Large hangings for the marriage bed, panels to hang over mirrors, and beaded panels for the pillows were some of the larger items made; small dress and ornamental items include slippers, spectacles cases and small vases. The technique predominantly used is a small form of netting; again, the very great skill of the Straits community women is shown in the use of complex floral designs worked

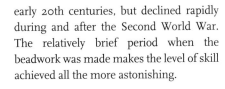

with this method. The beadwork was made entirely of rocaille beads of glass, or metal, bought from the *jarong* man, a travelling haberdasher who carried his wares on a tricycle. Beaded ornaments were not worn by the women (though some personal ornaments were made for the bride and groom) apart from a small pair of beaded slippers, worn in the house, and a small beaded headdress worn by older women. The shell beads, so popular in other areas of South-East Asia, were never used. This community flourished during the 19th and

early 20th centuries, but declined rapidly during and after the Second World War. The relatively brief period when the beadwork was made makes the level of skill achieved all the more astonishing.

## THE PHILIPPINES

THE Bagobo tribal group use beadwork extensively to decorate their costume – their ornate dress, which includes much beadwork, is very much admired. It would be unthinkable for men or women of any of the tribal groups to attend a festive occasion 'incompletely' dressed. The T'Boli and Tagakaolo also use glass and shell-bead beading. There are similarities between the costume of the groups – sometimes clothing made by one tribal group was ornamented with shell beads by another. Traditional dress for women would consist of a straight skirt of ikat-patterned abaca cloth, and a jacket decorated with beadwork and embroidery. Men's costume would be knee-length trousers and jacket, of matching decoration, a beaded headcloth, and several small bags also covered with beadwork. Large bags, covered with beadwork, were an important part of a man's festive dress. Small shell discs, or white beads (imitating shell) were favoured, with other rather pastel colours, which give the beadwork a pleasing subtlety. Garments decorated with a large quantity of shell discs were regarded as particularly valuable. The beadwork of the men's costume depicted motifs very similar to those used on the *pelangi* (tie-dyed) cloths – stylized reptilian figures with geometric borders. All the tribal groups, particularly the T'boli, use cast brass bells as personal adornment. Unmarried T'Boli girls used to wear a belt of brass chain mail and bells to show they were eligible for marriage. More recent versions of the belt are made of beadwork, with fewer bells. The T'Boli also use long beaded fringes around the appliquéd cloth that covers women's sun hats. Old

ABOVE: *Pair of slippers from the Straits Chinese community – the slipper tops would have been embroidered at home and then taken to be made up at the local shoemakers.*

LEFT: *Straits Chinese hanging for the marriage bed – nearly all the beadwork produced by the Straits Chinese community was to furnish the bridal chamber.*

BELOW: *'Bachelor's' hat, Bontoc people, from Luzon, Philippines, decorated with hair, boar's teeth, and finely plaited strands with beads.*

OPPOSITE, LEFT: *Bag of banana-fibre ikat t'nalak cloth, with a hair tassel and cast metal bells, said to deter spirits, from Mindanao, Philippines.*

necklaces (and old cloths) are sometimes considered to have spiritual powers, so these items would never be sold.

Earlier dress for men would have been a loincloth; the adoption of trousers is very probably due to Islamic influence. Today, everyday wear is either 'Western' dress, or, among Islamic communities, a form of Middle Eastern dress. Traditional dress is worn for 'cultural' festivals, though not necessarily by members of the group to which the style of dress would originally have belonged. Elaborate, showy head-dresses of feathers, and beadwork neck-laces and earrings are also worn by participants at these festivals, though these items are often of fairly recent adoption.

**THREE**

ABOVE: *Jacket belonging to the Bagobo people, Philippines, decorated with small beads of shell.*

BELOW: *Group of Bagobo men, wearing traditional dress, including jackets ornamented with small, white, shell beads.*

# OCEANIA AND AUSTRALIA

OCEANIA COMPRISES a vast area, almost entirely ocean, stretching from the Hawaiian islands in the north, to the most easterly islands of Polynesia, New Zealand in the south, and Australia to the west. Beadwork in this region is entirely constructed of beads made from natural objects, of which shells, either entire or cut, are the most common. Though larger glass trade beads are found in some items from this region, they were never considered as precious as beads made of shell. With the exception of the Melanesian Islands, there is little constructed beadwork; the shell and other beads are mostly strung as necklaces, hung loosely from objects, or stitched to a woven or twined fibre textile.

*ABOVE, LEFT (DETAIL); AND LEFT: Skirt of bark cloth, with tassels of cloth and white beads, from Papua New Guinea.*

*LEFT (INSET): Soloman Islander wearing two ropes of small beads, as well as armlets, a belt and headdress of large cowries.*

*ABOVE, RIGHT: Man, from the Soloman Islands, dressed in regalia of shell beads and teeth.*

## PAPUA NEW GUINEA

IN PAPUA NEW GUINEA, small twined bags, used by men to hold personal items, are decorated with small, entire shells, and seeds, dotted over the surface of the bag. Women of Papua New Guinea wear multiple necklaces of modern, brightly coloured beads, as well as festival headdresses of cane, decorated with feathers, beetle wings and shell discs.

Discs cut from clam shells, made in the Solomon Islands, were traded throughout the islands to the east of Papua New Guinea and were an important part of ceremonial exchanges of gifts – wealth and status were acquired by the accumulation of shell beads. The shell discs were constructed, using a technique that is part netting, part weaving, into ceremonial loincloths, which were worn by men of status within the community. These loincloths had a beaded and tasselled fringe at the lower edge, and further embellishment of feathers. Belts netted with shell and coral beads were used as a medium of exchange, and could be loaned to family members wanting to marry, for the bride-price. Woven beadwork was used for bracelets, armbands and other items of personal adornment, worn by men at ceremonial feasts.

## TAHITI

AT THE extreme eastern edge of Oceania, in Tahiti, hundreds of pieces of mother-of-pearl shell were used to decorate mourners' costumes for the

funerals of prominent members of the community; the jingling of the loosely attached shell pieces was intended to frighten away spirits.

## AUSTRALIA

AMONG the tribal groups of Australian Aborigines, various seeds, shells and sections of reed were threaded into necklaces for personal decoration.

ABOVE, RIGHT: *Dyed seeds and beans, contemporary Australian aboriginal work from Central Australia.*

RIGHT: *Necklace of dentalium shells from north-western Australia.*

BELOW, LEFT: *Necklace of threaded seeds worn by young girls of the Ingibandi tribe, Australia.*

BELOW, RIGHT: *Sections of reeds, threaded into strands, from north-western Australia.*

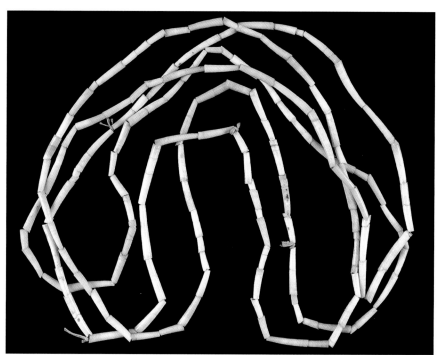

THREE

# THE MIDDLE EAST AND THE ARABIAN GULF

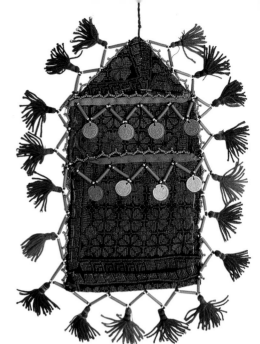

**B**EADS OF SILVER, amber, semi-precious stones and glass are used extensively in the traditional jewelry of the Arabian Gulf, but beadwork, of small glass beads, is mainly found on the traditional clothing of the tribal groups living on the western coast and in parts of Yemen, and is considered to be the result of an African influence. The dress styles of this region vary from village to village and though the regional styles are disappearing in favour of a more universal style using imported materials, they are still made and worn by some of the remoter nomadic tribes.

## SOUTH-WESTERN ARABIA

SOUTH-WESTERN Arabia extends from Ta'if in the north to Najran in the south. Both towns are important centres for trade, where traditional garments can be purchased in the markets. In the south-western region around Asir, the woman's dress is a variation of the standard 'kaftan' shape, in dark, plain fabric, embroidered in predominantly reds and yellows. White and silver beads are used to outline the bodice area and to decorate the sleeves. The white beads are considered to be 'African' and the silver beads 'Arabian'.

Cowrie shells and pearl buttons are also used extensively as embellishment. Women's burqa (face masks) may be heavily beaded, as well as decorated with the more usual coins and tassels. Seed beads are stitched to the cloth, and made into woven strands to form a fringe of beadwork and coins which hangs from the bottom edge of the burqa. These highly decorated burqa are the traditional attire of Bedouin and village women, townswomen prefer a plainer style. In the past, the decoration of the burqa, as much as the style of the rest of the dress, would have identified the wearer's home village or region. Small silver beads ornament the asayib (head ring) worn by women to hold the headcloth in place, and are also used to support decorative pendants.

## BEDOUIN

AMONG the Bedouin, both men and women make and use leather articles. These are often embellished with appliqué, fringes, tassels and beadwork. Small metal beads threaded onto leather thongs are stitched to the edges of garments. Camel trappings and saddle-bags, always important items for a nomadic people, are similarly decorated.

Glittering bead and sequin work of a type once made in the fashion houses of Europe – though now more likely to be made in the Far East – is popular on the more modern styles of dress worn by the wealthier classes on special occasions.

OPPOSITE, ABOVE, LEFT; AND RIGHT: *Contemporary bead embroidery for the European market; made in Dubai.*

OPPOSITE, ABOVE, RIGHT: *Piece of traditional cross-stitch embroidery from Palestine.*

OPPOSITE, BELOW: *Woman's headdress, from Sanaa, Yemen, with small red beads, possibly coral.*

OPPOSITE, INSET: *Bands said to be used for decorating the edge of a shelf, from Jordan.*

LEFT: *Water carrier made by the Rashaida.*

ABOVE: *Woman's* burqa *(face veil), from Israel.*

THREE

FAR LEFT: *Beads worked on canvas.*
LEFT: *Norwegian beaded stomacher.*
RIGHT: *Turkish amuletic necklaces.*
BELOW: *Small Turkish coin purses.*
BOTTOM LEFT: *Beads on evenweave
linen, Eastern Europe.*
BOTTOM RIGHT: *Devotional bag.*

# EUROPE

FOUR

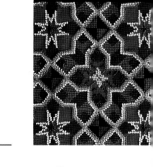

# THE HISTORY OF BEADWORK IN EUROPE

**B**EADS HAVE been made of semi-precious stone, pearl and other materials since ancient times, though perhaps not as prolifically in Europe as in Asia. Beads, or more usually the raw materials with which they were made, were traded along established routes between Asia and the eastern Mediterranean region during the Bronze Age. The Phoenicians were trading glass beads by 1200 BC.

LEFT: *Bride from northern Russia.*

ABOVE, RIGHT: *Norwegian girl in bridal costume of heavily beaded and embroidered waistcoat, stomacher and bridal crown.*

BELOW: *Young woman from the Bulgarian–Macedonian border region, wearing a headdress similar to the example on page 165.*

LEFT: *Suede coin purse, with a simple stitched pattern of steel beads, probably late 18th century.*

RIGHT: *Contemporary woman's cap, in traditional style, from the area around Archangel, northern Russia, with embroidery and 'veil' of imitation pearls.*

## THE RAW MATERIALS

Scotland, as well as Russia, produced quantities of freshwater pearls, the smallest of which were used for embroidery and beadwork. Coral is found in the Mediterranean off the coast of North Africa, and around the islands of Sicily, Corsica and Sardinia. Jet has been worked in Whitby, England, since 2000 BC, though it was not until the beginning of the 19th century that beads were produced in large numbers. Large quantities of 'jet' beads were used during the 19th century – they were considered appropriate mourning attire and the whole country went into mourning following the death of Prince Albert – but most of the very small beads were in fact black glass. Crystal, gold and silver, and the humbler materials of wood or bone, as well as glass, were all used to make beads, many of which were small enough to be used for embroidery or beadwork, though it was not until the advent of very small drawn-glass beads from Venice that beadwork became widespread.

BELOW, LEFT: *Detail of beaded cape, late 19th or early 20th century. The embroidery and beadwork have been produced on a Cornely machine.*

BELOW, RIGHT: *Bulgarian girls, in beaded festival costume, taking part in a May Day dance.*

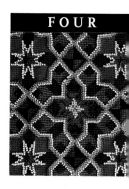

**FOUR**

SOCIETÀ VENEZIANA CONTERIE
VENICE
(ITALY)

CAPE CARD VII          Ed. 1928

White 99   Black 100   Turquoise 101   Turquoise 102   Turquoise 103   Med Lapis 120   Dark Lapis 123   Ungazi 115

SOCIETÀ VENEZIANA CONTERIE
VENICE
(ITALY)

Orange 105   Green 121   Yellow 112   Pink 106   Lavender 124   Green 120   New Yellow 113   Cornelian 810

SOCIETÀ VENEZIANA CONTERIE
VENICE
(ITALY)

Ruby 803   Brown Glass 120   Amber 116   Pink 107   Royal Bleu 119   Coral 812   Striped 94   Different Colors

ABOVE, LEFT: *Flowers of French-made beads; used for wreaths and other grave furniture.*

LEFT: *Necklace of Venetian rocailles and larger handmade beads, c. 1920.*

ABOVE: *Sample cards of Venetian beads.*

BELOW: *Woman from the Carinthian border.*

## GLASS BEADS

VENICE HAD been an important centre for glass production for centuries, but the mass production of seed beads did not begin until the end of the 15th century, on the island of Murano. These beads were traded throughout Western Europe and, by the beginning of the 17th century, tiny glass beads were used to make or decorate a range of articles. This period also coincided with the age of European exploration – Europeans landed in the 'New World' of the Americas in 1492, and the sea route to India and the Spice Islands was discovered in 1498. Traders soon followed the explorers, taking beads as gifts, and to barter and trade. If the glass beads were enthusiastically received by the peoples of southern Africa and North America, the profits for the traders were immense – a return of 1,000 percent was reported in the 17th century. Especially in the East, European traders followed routes that had been in use for centuries.

146

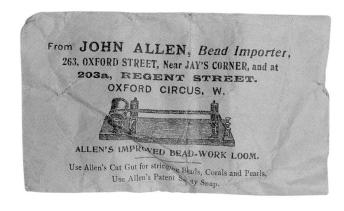

## DRAWN-GLASS BEADS

WHILE GLASS had been made in Bohemia since the 11th century, it was not until the late 18th century that drawn-glass beads were made. Bohemian beads were sold in vast quantities to North America, by then a major market for beads. Bohemian beads also satisfied the markets nearer home – as production increased, they were sold throughout Europe, particularly Austria, Russia and the Ukraine. The use of beadwork in traditional dress in Europe very closely follows the route from Bohemia through Transylvania, Romania and Turkey, along the beginning of the old Silk Route to Iran and the Central Asian oasis towns. Though Murano and Bohemia were the main centres of production in Europe, beads were also produced in Germany (by beadworkers from Bohemia), France and Holland, and very briefly in England during the 17th century and Russia in the mid-18th century. The Amsterdam beadworks supplied the trade in the Dutch East Indies, though the volume of trade between Europe and South-East Asia was so great that virtually all centres of production supplied beads to the region. Cut steel beads, made in Birmingham, England and France, were sold not only in Europe, but were also particularly popular among the Chinese community of the Malaccan Straits, as were glass beads from France, favoured because of their muted, opalescent colours.

ABOVE, LEFT: *How to make a rosette of beads; a diagram from a women's monthly magazine, 1867.*

ABOVE, RIGHT: *Advertising on a needle packet, showing a bead loom – loom beading as a hobby became popular in the second half of the 19th century, and was often referred to as 'Apache' or 'Indian' beading.*

BELOW: *Two beaded and crocheted bags from Turkey; the many triangular amulets are typical of Turkish beadwork, so much so that a crocheted amulet will almost certainly identify a piece as Turkish.*

The 20th century saw the decline of seed bead production in Murano, with the gap in the market largely filled by Bohemia. Today, Bohemian beads are exported to Europe, North America, Turkey and Egypt as well as, to a lesser extent, Africa and India.

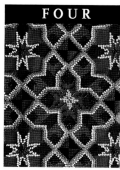

FOUR

# WESTERN EUROPE

F RESHWATER SEED-PEARL beadwork has been used throughout Europe for centuries, both on domestic dress and artefacts, as well as religious vestments. Much of the beadwork made for secular use would have been produced by professional workers, and the vestments would most probably have been made in convents by highly skilled embroiderers. Glass beads also have a long history of use in embroidery, some of the oldest surviving examples can be found on religious vestments from Germany; in this instance perhaps they were used to extend, or even replace, the more costly gold, silver and pearls that would have been more usual on this type of work. An example survives from Spain, dated 1275, with seed pearls and small beads of coral, mixed with small glass beads, worked onto fabric and formed into a cap – this would have been a precious and rare garment, available only to a wealthy minority.

ABOVE: *Basket of beads on wire, made by Elizabeth Clarke in c. 1675 when she was about twenty years old. These baskets are thought to have been made to celebrate betrothals, and were used to hold sprigs of rosemary given to wedding guests.*

RIGHT: *Top and front of a box of raised beadwork on satin, made by Anne Melinge in c. 1660. As well as a leopard, lion and camel, the figures depict the Roman goddess of plenty with a cornucopia.*

## Techniques

A S VERY small glass beads became more readily available from the beginning of the 17th century, beadwork became fashionable as a pastime. There was already a tradition of making small 'sweete' bags as gifts, and of making boxes or caskets decorated with embroidery and the three-dimensional figurative work known as stumpwork. This tradition was adapted to use the new, readily available seed beads – small bags were constructed entirely of threaded beads, and beads were used to decorate the sides and lid of a casket or mirror frame, either partly or wholly. Some examples from this period are entirely decorated with beads stitched onto fabric, others combine beads with embroidery and/or a small amount of painted detail – this mixing of media was particularly popular in Italy for a short period. Threading or stitching the beads

onto fabric would not have been difficult – fine steel needles had been made in Germany and Spain since the beginning of the 16th century and by the end of the century were being produced in London. Beads were also threaded onto fine iron wire and shaped into three-dimensional flowers and fruit, which were then constructed into a basket or tray.

Much less beadwork survives from the early 18th century than the 17th, which perhaps indicates a change in fashion, or maybe new difficulties in construction – as the manufacture of the beads developed, and ever smaller beads were produced, threading the beads could prove something of a problem. The end of a thread could be stiffened with wax or shellac, which could then be made to pass through the beads, but this stiffened thread would not pass through fabric. The strung beads could be couched onto cloth using another thread; otherwise, to embroider the beads directly onto fabric, the needle would have to be laboriously threaded and unthreaded with each stitch. Some surviving examples of beadwork from this period were made by threading the beads into the spaces on fine hand-made net, or over the crossed threads of the net, techniques that would not necessarily require a needle.

TOP LEFT: *Beadwork bag in right-angle weave lined with green silk, in the style of the 'sweete' bags of the 17th century. The inscription, which runs around both sides of the bag, reads 'remember the pore'.*

ABOVE: *Late 18th-century velvet bag embroidered with steel beads; steel beads were made in Sheffield, England. In the early 19th century, the steel bead industry fell into difficulties and King George IV commissioned a hat with 5,000 steel beads on it in an attempt to revive the trade.*

TOP: *Panel of point de sable, c. 1760, possibly intended to be mounted as a face screen. The design is reminiscent of the dress brocades of this period.*

ABOVE: *Georgian needlecase of fine blue silk, with white beads; an early example of beaded knitting.*

**FOUR**

LEFT; AND DETAIL: *Bag of very fine bead knitting, depicting a parrot and pet dog. The thousands of beads required for a bag like this had to be strung on the thread in the correct order before knitting commenced.*

ABOVE: *Small crocheted coin purse of steel beads. Purse making was a popular pastime and the frames or handles could be bought from a haberdasher.*

OPPOSITE, ABOVE: *Very fine knitted purse – this design may have been published in a women's magazine or book of patterns as several variations of this design can be found. It would have been finished with a lining, fringe and fastening.*

By the late 18th century, needle making had developed to such an extent that needles of extreme fineness were readily available, and the exceedingly small beads then popular were again sewn onto small articles such as purses and needle cases. During this period knitting in fine, coloured silks was an increasingly popular pastime, especially in Germany and Austria. Very small beads in brilliant colours were readily available and were used with knitting to make small bags and purses. Initially added to the knitting in a single-coloured pattern, the technique soon developed to produce a complete fabric of knitted beads in complex multicoloured designs. For this method, the beads had to be strung on the thread

before knitting, in precise order, following a printed chart. Most of these pieces were worked in the round, on four needles. Beaded purses were also made on a wooden 'purse mould' that allowed the worker to build up the design one bead at a time, threading through the beads of previous rows. By the beginning of the 19th century, beads were also used in crocheting in a similar manner – again the beads had to be strung on the thread before commencing.

As the 19th century progressed, the divergence between beadwork done as a domestic pastime and professional work, and high fashion and traditional costume, became more apparent. In 1770 work-rooms making beadwork for the French court were established in Paris by Charles de Saint-Aubin. During his lifetime, the tambour hook, already used for chain-stitch embroidery, was first employed to attach beads to fabric, though it was not until almost a hundred years later that this development was fully exploited by Louis Ferry of Luneville, near Strasbourg. In the hands of a skilled worker, this method was considerably faster than attaching each bead singly, thus making the heavily beaded trimmings and dresses of the period more readily available and affordable. As in crocheted beadwork (the French word for hook is *le crochet*), the beads must first be strung on the working thread. Though the method of embroidery and the English word *tambour* (an oriental drum) have clearly been adopted from the East, the method of attaching the beads with the hook is different from that used in the Indian Sub-continent.

LEFT: *German notebook of beadwork and leather, 19th century.*

RIGHT: *These beaded tassels would have been bought ready made and incorporated into a dress by a dressmaker. The sleeves, made for the original dress, have been detached, possibly to be re-used.*

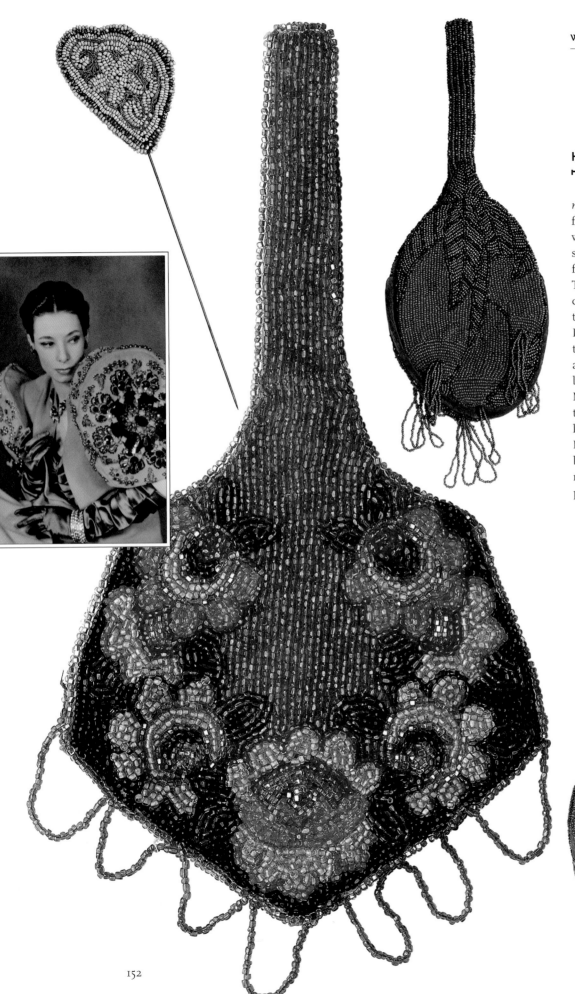

## High fashion

THROUGHOUT the 19th and early 20th centuries vast quantities of *passementerie* (corded and beaded trimmings for dress and furnishings) and beading were produced in the workrooms and sweatshops of Europe to supply the fashion houses of the major capitals. Though Paris was, and is, an important centre for both fashion and embroidery, this work was also produced elsewhere. Introduced in London towards the end of the 19th century, it was known for a time as *Luneville work*, and later as 'French beading'. In 1868 the workrooms of Michonet had been established in Paris; they worked for the house of Worth, and later for the designers Paul Poiret and Madame Paquin. The business was bought in 1924 by Albert Lesage, whose name it now bears, and they continue to produce beadwork and embroidery for

today's major designers. During the 19th century both the Cornely machine, patented in 1865, and the schifflé machine, built the same year, were used, with varying degrees of success, to produce embroidered beadwork for the fashion industry.

Beadwork on dress, having fallen from favour at the turn of the century, underwent a brief but intense revival during the 1920s. Hardly a 'flapper' dress was made without a lavish amount of beadwork on it and beadwork, combined with sequins, continued to be popular for evening wear. The workrooms of Norman Hartnell, dressmaker to the British royal family, were famous for the quantity and quality of their beadwork.

OPPOSITE, ABOVE, LEFT: *This hatpin from the 1920s has beads dyed a pale turquoise.*

OPPOSITE, INSET: *A Norman Hartnell model – his workrooms were famous for beaded gowns.*

OPPOSITE, CENTRE: *French tambour beaded bag; the workrooms of Paul Poiret, the couturier, were renowned for high-quality beading.*

OPPOSITE, ABOVE, RIGHT: *Tambour beaded 'plum' bag – small novelty bags were fashionable for the first two decades of the 20th century.*

OPPOSITE, BELOW, RIGHT: *Commercially made bag of tambour beading, c. 1920; typical of the items produced for the fashion market.*

RIGHT: *Late 1920s dress – the cut has changed from the early 1920s to this more flattering bias-cut skirt.*

BELOW, LEFT: *Cap, early 1920s, with a long, elegant beaded fringe.*

BELOW, RIGHT: *White satin and beadwork bridal shoes from the beginning of the 20th century. Every fashionable bride had shoes handmade to match her gown.*

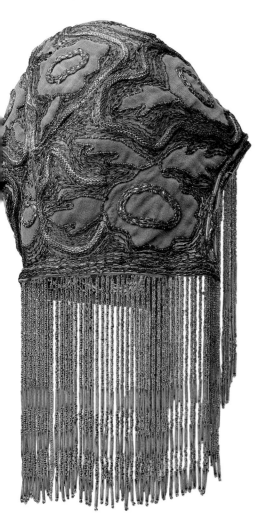

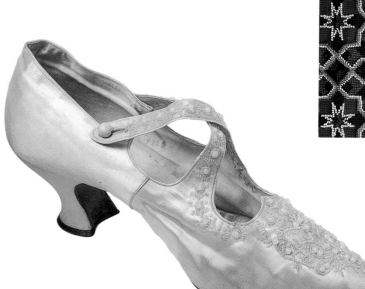

FOUR

**FOUR**

FAR LEFT: *Choker of loom-woven steel beads, stitched to a velvet ribbon. Loom weaving, quick and simple to produce, became a popular pastime in the late 19th century.*

LEFT, MIDDLE: *Tambour beaded dress, in the straight shape of the early 1920s.*

NEAR LEFT: *Long, loom-woven strip, probably intended as a belt, with fashionable 'Oriental' motifs.*

ABOVE: *Commercially made beaded dress from c. 1960. The label reads 'made in Hong Kong', though it was intended for the Western market.*

OPPOSITE, RIGHT: *Two tea cosies of Berlin woolwork and beads. The patterns for Berlin woolwork printed in magazines could very conveniently be used for beadwork; items could combine beads with cross stitch or be worked entirely in beads.*

OPPOSITE, BELOW, LEFT: *Part of a long altar frontal of net, embroidered with images of a chalice and grapevine in beads and sequins; probably Spanish.*

## Beadwork as a pastime

DOMESTIC beadwork, by contrast, increasingly became a somewhat frivolous pastime of ever reducing skill to occupy the leisured classes (who would have worn the work of the highly skilled but poorly paid beadworkers of the sweatshops). The purses and bags finely worked in minute beads, of the early part of the 19th century, gradually gave way to a wealth of trinkets – spectacle cases, wall tidies, all manner of domestic ephemera – decorated with larger, coarser beadwork. It was possible to buy the beads for a knitted purse ready strung in the correct order, so that the purchaser could have the pleasure of making the purse without the tedious and exacting task of threading the beads; this work was done by outworkers in the Netherlands, and the ready strung beads were then sold throughout Europe. From about 1850 onwards, Berlin work, a craze for embroidering wools on canvas following a printed pattern, dominated all domestic needlework – those looking for yet another novelty were soon using beads in place of some, or all, of the wool stitches. Fire screens, tea cosies, slippers, chairbacks could all be decorated with beads, or beads and wool. At about the same period, 'Apache' beadwork, as it was called, was introduced from North America. This was beadwork produced on a small wooden loom, which could very conveniently use the same squared printed patterns used for Berlin work.

*ABOVE: Two Bavarian brides wearing the traditional wired and beaded headdress.*

*RIGHT: Bonnet, from Moravia, with lace, brocade ribbons, blown-glass beads, bugles and sequins.*

*INSET: Newly married couple from Schapbach in the Black Forest, Germany. The bride is wearing a padded headdress, decorated with strands of beads.*

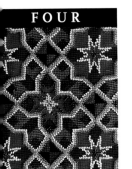

**FOUR**

## CENTRAL EUROPE

WHILE the fashionable women of the wealthier classes followed the current trends in dress and pastimes, beadwork in Central Europe was in the traditional colours and patterns of each region, supplementing embroidery and lacework in elaborate displays of the workers' skill. Beads were added to the existing decorations, particularly in those areas where beads were manufactured, or on the main trading routes. In Bavaria and the Tyrol they were stitched in formal repeating patterns, around Prague they were used to decorate the festival lace aprons, in Moravia (see also p. 165) they were embroidered onto bodices and caps, and in southern Bohemia they were worked alongside openwork embroidery. In Austria beads, imitation pearls and gold 'purl' were used for Klosterarbeiten (church work) and for girls' traditional hair decorations and costumes.

*OPPOSITE, ABOVE: Bead and bugle embroidery on, from left to right, a woman's cap; woman's bodice and stomacher; young girl's cap; all from Hardanger, Norway.*

*OPPOSITE, BELOW: Woman's bodice, from Moravia, part of the same costume as the bonnet opposite. Sections of the glass cane used in making the beads have been stitched on and encircled using smaller beads.*

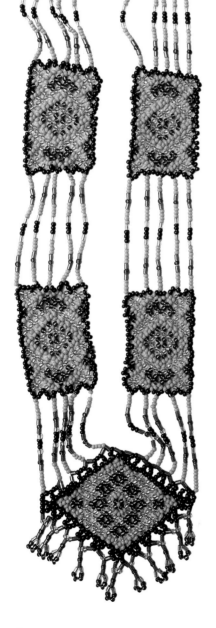

A CORAL OR terracotta bead necklace is part of the Ukrainian national costume, but beadwork using drawn-glass beads is not universal throughout the Ukraine – it is mostly concentrated in western and south-western Ukraine, particularly in the Podillia region.

## Gerdany

NECKLACES, known generically as *gerdany* (which roughly translates as 'garland') were constructed during the Middle Ages from glass beads made within the Ukraine. Following the Tartar invasions of the 12th century, the knowledge of beadmaking was lost and, consequently, the making of *gerdany* died out.

Beadwork was revived during the 17th century following the mass production, and export, of well-made glass beads from Venice, and, later, from Bohemia. By the 19th century, beadwork was a recognized part of regional dress, each district having a distinct style that reflected the colours and patterns of the embroidery of the area. Originally threaded on horsehair, gradually cotton or linen threads were used to construct the *gerdany* – a number of techniques were used of which loom weaving, one-bead netting and right-angle weave were the most common.

While most beadwork is commonly known as *gerdany* (though in the village of Vovkivtsi it was known as *dziumbaly*), this name properly refers to the long, slim necklaces with a central medallion shape. Other necklaces are referred to as *sylinnka*, a beaded strip used as a choker for women, or a hat band for men; and *zubchyky*, a type of beaded collar, usually with serrated edges. Necklaces with strands of larger, blown-glass beads, part of almost every festival costume, were known as *luskavky*. In the south-west region, beads were stitched on top of, or instead of, the counted-thread embroidery on the women's traditional shift – the placement, patterns and colours echoing the regional embroidery styles. *Leibyky*, sleeveless

LEFT: *The colours are contemporary, but the shape is the traditional* gerdany, *made of sections of netting linked with strands of beads.*

ABOVE: *Small trinket box, from Kolomyia, decorated with beads pressed into the wood while it is still soft.*

BELOW: *Eggs are an important part of the traditional Easter celebrations. The egg on the right is older, dating from before 1940. Made of wax, two have been decorated by pressing beads into the wax when soft, while on the above left-hand example the beads have been threaded and the thread wound around the egg. The bottom left egg is from Chernivets, the other smaller one from Lviv.*

OPPOSITE: *The subversive bead – this traditional shift from Bukovina, decorated with beads sewn onto linen, was hidden beneath the floorboards for 50 years during the period of Soviet domination, when all traditional aspects of Ukrainian culture were discouraged. The placement of the beads, slanting in alternate directions, is typical of bead embroidery from Eastern Europe.*

**FOUR**

UKRAINE

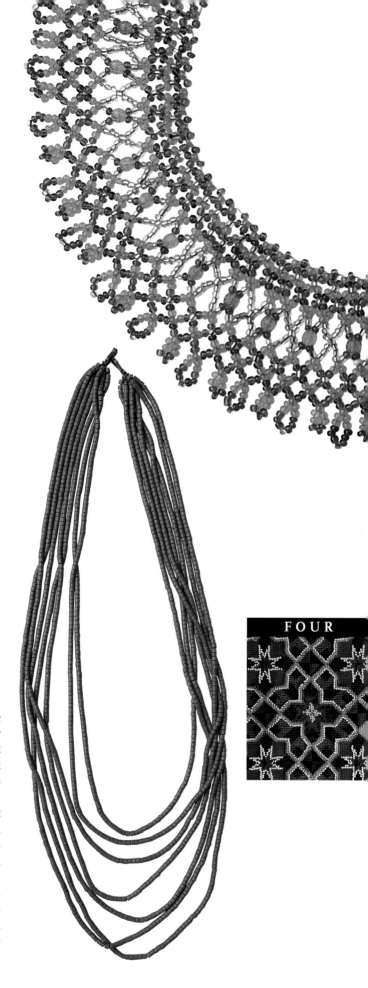

OPPOSITE: *The traditional collar,* zubchyky, *in colours reminiscent of the cross-stitch embroidery of this region, made before 1940.*

OPPOSITE, INSET: *Collar in the favourite red and black.*

LEFT: *Necklaces like these, of coral beads and silver coins, form part of the national costume. The wealthier the family, the more strands of coral and the more coins a girl would wear.*

ABOVE, RIGHT: *Netted* zubchyky *(collar) with an edging of small loops.*

RIGHT: *Strands of small terracotta beads – necklaces of these beads were worn by the poorer girls, whose families could not afford coral beads and silver coins.*

**FOUR**

sheepskin waistcoats, were worn by both men and women, throughout the year; those made for festival wear would be decorated with seed beads as well as the more usual wool embroidery, or appliqué.

Young men, approaching marriage, would wear hats decorated with *gerdany*, beaded strips or a beaded and sequinned ornament, called a *triasenytsia*. Young, unmarried women would make straw braids decorated with beads to wrap around their hair, and many *gerdany* would be worn. The wedding costume for a girl would also include many *gerdany*, and beaded ribbons for her headdress.

## THE SOVIET REPUBLIC

THE Soviet dominance of the Ukraine following the Second World War meant that the materials for beadwork became scarce; as traditional beadwork therefore declined, a *gerdany* factory was established to mass produce beadwork. Sadly, the beadwork thus produced lost much of the original regional variation and had the uniformity of government-approved designs. Following the secession of Ukraine from the Soviet Republic, beadworkers can once again design and market their own work, and beadwork is undergoing something of a revival, with new designs and colours used alongside the more traditional patterns.

# EASTERN EUROPE

O VER THE centuries the countries of Eastern Europe have experienced a number of boundary changes and changes of rule and are home to several ethnic groups. Dominated, at different times in history, by the Ottoman Empire, the Austro-Hungarian Empire and, latterly, Russia, the culture of the region has also been influenced by trade with Western Europe, and, more importantly, by trade with Central Asia. Goods travelled the Silk Route from as far away as China, arriving in Turkey and crossing the Bosphorus into Eastern Europe.

In Eastern Europe the difference between the traditional dress of the rural villages and the fashionable dress of the wealthier elite is more marked than in Western Europe. For instance, in Hungary, at the end of the 18th century, 90% of the population were defined as 'peasant', while only 7% were urban bourgeois or nobility. The traditional 'peasant' dress was retained for longer and was more widely worn – perhaps as an expression of identity in a region subject to so much change.

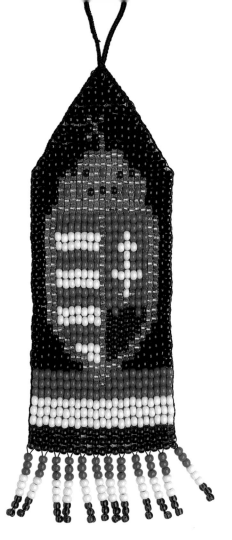

BELOW: *Man's hat, from Transylvania, with elaborately beaded hat band with a netted edging; it would have been worn for festivals and weddings.*

RIGHT: *Man's loom-woven watch fob, depicting the Hungarian flag. Hungarian men wore very little beadwork other than a small watch fob.*

## TRANSYLVANIA AND POLAND

S EED beads were used extensively, especially on women's festival dress, in Transylvania (at times part of the Hungarian Empire, but now within Romania), and to a lesser extent in Poland. The beads were mostly embroidered onto fabric in richly coloured floral patterns, by one of two methods – the beads were stitched to an evenweave fabric, following the weave in a counted design in the same way as counted-thread embroidery, which was also widely used in this region, or stitched to velvet. For this, the design was executed in long stitches holding several beads, often of more than one colour, and a small amount of padding could be incorporated beneath the beads to give a slightly raised appearance to part of the beadwork. The design to be worked would be drawn onto the velvet using a thin flour and water paste; this was available in every household and had the advantage that when dry, any unworked parts of the design could be easily brushed away. In Romania, men's belts were made,

originally of leather with small pockets, and covered in bead embroidery. During the communist era, all traditional crafts were discouraged, but since 1988 these are being revived, and the belts are made once more, though now of velvet rather than leather. While the women of Transylvania wore so much beadwork, the men would simply wear a beaded watch fob, and a wide beaded hat band. The headdress (*parta*) of pearly beads worn by young women was a symbol of virginity.

ABOVE; AND RIGHT (DETAIL): *Woman's traditional blouse, from Romania, decorated with fine counted-thread embroidery, beads and sequins.*

BELOW: *Heavily beaded belt, from Romania, which, though made after 1989, is in the traditional style. The fabric is velvet rather than the leather that would have been used previously.*

BOTTOM: *Velvet belt, from Poland, with individual floral motifs worked in a combination of lazy and appliqué stitch.*

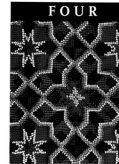

FOUR

163

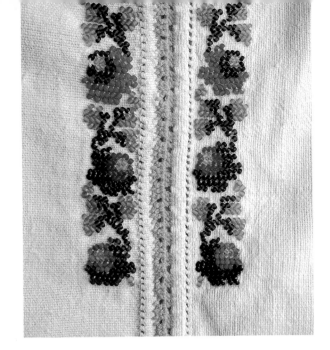

FOUR

TOP, LEFT (DETAIL): *Romanian woman's shift – beads have replaced counted-thread embroidery.*

ABOVE, LEFT: *Polish netted bag, lined with silk.*

RIGHT (FROM TOP TO BOTTOM): *Transylvanian woman's apron; waist band of bead embroidery similar to that on the apron above; beadwork on an apron (detail) which again resembles that on the apron above.*

164

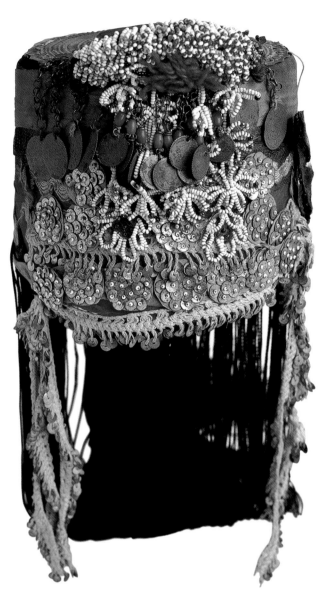

ABOVE: *Man's belt from Moldavia. The beads have been stitched to an evenweave or canvas backing, the rows of beads slanting in alternate directions. The beadwork has then been mounted on leather.*

NEAR RIGHT: *Loom-woven strip from Moravia. These strips were worn by men as hat bands, and by young women around their hair, or wound around their necks or wrists.*

FAR RIGHT, ABOVE: *Woman's headdress from the Bulgarian–Macedonian border, decorated with metal discs to imitate coins, and beaded 'flowers' and sequins.*

FAR RIGHT, BELOW: *Child's wristlets of knitted wool and steel beads, from the Former Yugoslavia.*

## THE BALKANS AND BULGARIA

BEADS were used sparingly in the Balkans, with small red, black and white beads – the typical colours of this region – almost hidden among the dense embroidery decorating traditional costume. In Bulgaria, too, while the festival dress – so similar in style to the dress of Romania and the Ukraine – was lavishly embroidered, beads were used little, the women preferring silver jewelry as their ornament. Almost the only use of beads seems to have been the leather pouches of the Rhodope shepherds, decorated with tassels and a few small blue beads.

In Poland beads were used in greatest quantity for the elaborate wreath-like headdresses of beads, flowers and ribbons worn by young women for festival dress. Hollow, fragile, blown-glass beads were strung on wire and fixed between artificial flowers and other decorations.

Throughout this region, traditional dress is now worn only for special occasions, or as costume for 'folklore' events.

# TURKEY AND THE EASTERN MEDITERRANEAN

WHAT IS now modern Turkey, with its long history of periods of regional power, sits at the convergence of trade routes between Europe, Arabia and Asia. The Assyrian, Hittite, Byzantine and Ottoman empires each helped to influence the culture and trade of the region.

Fine textiles and jewelry have been made and used in this region since the earliest times; embroidery embellished with small blue beads has been discovered at Aksaray-Acemhöyük, dating to 2,000 BC. Embroidery has been a widespread and important means of decorating household textiles and costume for centuries; though frequently metallic threads have been used rather than beads. In the 19th century, as ornamentation of all objects including textiles became more elaborate, glass beads were incorporated into folk embroideries and small pearls and coral beads were used to embellish embroideries for the wealthier classes.

LEFT: *Crocheted Turkish amuletic coin purse.*

CENTRE: *'Miser's' purse, so called because of the supposed difficulty in extracting coins.*

TOP RIGHT: *Beads woven into handwoven cloth.*

RIGHT: *Netted bag, typical of prisoner-of-war work made during and after the 1914–18 war.*

ABOVE, LEFT: *Lizard of crocheted beads. Both lizards and snakes were made by prisoners, often with an elongated tail. These could be worn as a necklace, with the 'tail' in the reptile's mouth.*

ABOVE RIGHT; AND RIGHT: *Waistcoat and cap decorated with large, coarse white beads, belonging to a shepherd from Macedonia.*

LEFT: *Loom-woven amulet for the rear-view mirror of a vehicle. The two birds swing freely. These amulets are currently made by prisoners.*

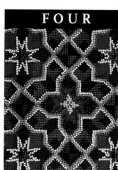

**FOUR**

## 'Prisoner work'

TODAY, Turkey is a major importer of beads from the Czech Republic. From the early 20th century beadwork was taught to prisoners, as it was in Greece, and this practice continues today. This 'prisoner work', particularly the earlier examples made by prisoners of war from the 1914–18 war, is sought after by collectors. Prisoner work said to be from this period often bears the date, or the legend 'WWI', worked into the beadwork, although the date of items with the latter inscription is questionable since the 1914–18 war was surely not referred to as the *first* world war until at least the start of the *second*. The two most commonly used techniques are netting and crochet; netting is used mainly in the prisoner-work bags and purses, and crochet used for the beaded lizards and snakes produced in great numbers in Turkey. Fine beaded crochet was also used in a domestic setting to make small bags and amuletic purses, and more recently to decorate the edges of women's scarves. These scarves, worn as a symbol of modesty, were once edged with fine and intricate knotted needle-lace flowers and fruit, but today are more likely to be edged with beaded crochet – the decorative edgings are collectively known as *oya*.

Loom-woven beadwork is also used today, by prisoners making amulets to hang from a car's rear-view mirror; these often bear the word *mashallah*, which roughly translates as 'may Allah protect', or alternatively they may use the colours and name of a favourite football team. The interest in Europe and North America in Arabic or Turkish dance has meant that a great deal of crocheted beadwork, in the form hip scarves and other accessories, is made for export.

## GREECE

WHILE beadwork was, at least until the mid-20th century, also taught in Greek prisons, beadwork has not assumed the same importance in Greece, though beads have been used to decorate shepherds' clothing in Macedonia.

# RUSSIA

**F**RESHWATER PEARLS rather than glass seed beads were used in the earliest beadwork made in Russia – this is considered to have been because of contacts with Asia Minor and the Byzantine Empire. Russia's many rivers provided an abundant supply of pearls, and by the 10th century the industry was well established – the largest and best-quality pearls were used for jewelry and the smaller, inferior pearls for embroidery. Pearls were sewn on garments for the wealthy, and all but the poorest women aspired to have elaborate pearl encrusted headdresses. The industry paid an annual tithe to the church in pearls, which were used abundantly on religious vestments and other ecclesiastical embroideries, in particular, religious icons. The facial details of the image to be venerated were often painted, and the surround embroidered. The embroidery pearls, once drilled, were worked either into a threaded netting, or stitched directly to the fabric. The pearls were usually strung on a thread, which was wound onto a bobbin, and the pearl-laden thread was couched to the fabric.

## Glass beads

**W**ITH the growth in the manufacture and export of glass beads from Venice, and, later, Bohemia, the use of beads and beadwork increased; by the 18th century beadwork was used for large ornamental panels depicting landscapes, or arrangements of flowers and birds, many copied from paintings or engravings. The beads and bugle beads were often combined, as in Italy, with painted details. Glass beads were used alongside pearls in the decoration of religious articles and vestments. As in much of Western Europe, by the 18th century the women of the wealthier classes had the leisure time to indulge in making beaded trinkets for the home; small purses, paperweights, fire screens, bell pulls and so on. Serf girls could learn beadwork by being apprenticed to another worker, so beadwork was also produced commercially.

Beads were used to decorate the many different regional costumes of the rural population. Imitation pearls as well as glass beads could be used in place of the costly real pearls which meant they were within the means of a larger section of the population. Beads were incorporated on costume both west and east of the Urals, though the most elaborate, crown-like women's headdresses of pearls or

LEFT: *Traditionally constructed modern necklace.*

ABOVE, RIGHT: *Right-angle weave and netting necklace.*

ABOVE; AND BELOW: *Contemporary necklaces.*

OPPOSITE: *Icon of the Madonna and Child, heavily decorated with beads and seed pearls.*

imitation pearls came from the western and north-western regions around Novgorod, Archangelsk and Kursk. Coloured glass beads were used on festive garments, particularly those of a bride or groom; and in the districts surrounding Moscow, women's pill-box shaped hats were decorated with beads, and had a fall of netted beadwork covering the back of the neck. Women wore a great variety of breast, neck and throat ornaments, mostly netted beadwork, as well as beaded hair decorations for their plaits.

The peoples of Siberia decorated their hide and fur outer clothing with beads, stitched to the hide, or strung on sinew. Small bags for carrying pipe and tobacco were covered with beads. The Yakut people made bridal dowry boxes of birch bark decorated with hide and beads, and horse trappings were similarly ornamented. In the Turukhansk region men wore a breastplate of hide, fur and beads. The style of decoration is reminiscent of the sub-Arctic tribes of North America.

Beadwork continues to be made and worn in Russia, both in contemporary high fashion and traditional styles; many of the latter echo the regional embroidery styles in colour and pattern, with red, black and white being the dominant colours.

**FOUR**

# GREENLAND

BEADWORK USING glass seed beads has a comparatively short history in Greenland, though very small beads of fish vertebrae were used long before the arrival of the whaling ships and missionaries, who were responsible for bringing beads to trade and as gifts in the early 18th century.

## EAST GREENLAND

THE fish vertebrae were used in their natural off-white colour, as well as dyed red (with blood) and blue (with the juice of berries), to construct the hargrime (hair-halter), chest amulet and arm amulets worn by young men, and the hair decorations worn by women in East Greenland. With the arrival of glass beads, the favoured colours were initially white, red and blue, worked into items of similar design to the older fish vertebrae articles.

## WEST GREENLAND

IN WEST Greenland, loops of larger beads were initially used to decorate the hem, cuffs and hood edge of the women's parkas. Over a century or more the shape of the women's parka gradually changed; the large hood became smaller until a vestigial hood in the form of a wide standing collar was all that remained. Skin or hide clothing was replaced by cloth, and the use of beads increased. The beaded cuff edging became wide beaded bands,

OPPOSITE, TOP LEFT: *Detail of the bottom left-hand collar from West Greenland.*

OPPOSITE, ABOVE, RIGHT: *Two beaded mats in typical colours – the lower mat depicts the Danish flag, a frequent motif.*

OPPOSITE, CENTRE: *Cigarette holders; many small household items were made or decorated with beads.*

OPPOSITE, BELOW: *Two wide collars of netted beadwork – these are typical of West Greenland work.*

RIGHT: *The complete West Greenland woman's costume – velvet, cloth, lace, fur, leather, beadwork and leatherwork patterns are all used for this festival outfit. The very fine leatherwork decorating the* kamiks *(boots) is a craft older than beadwork.*

while the beads that once decorated the edge of the hood appeared around the neck edge. In the early 20th century this was a narrow band of netted beadwork, but by the middle of the 20th century this beadwork 'collar' had increased in size, reaching to the elbows. The geometric patterns used in the beadwork echo the fine leatherwork patterns used to decorate the women's *kamiks* (boots).

From the early 20th century beadwork – almost invariably netted, and using a range of bright colours – was being used to decorate many household items such as candleholders, table mats, cigarette holders and serviette rings. Beadwork is still made, and women continue to wear the wide beaded collar for special occasions, even if the other items of traditional clothing are now seldom worn.

FAR LEFT: *English panel, 17th century.*
SECOND FROM LEFT: *Hanging from Pakistan, North-West Province.*
THIRD FROM LEFT: *Russian necklace.*
NEAR LEFT: *Three-bead netting, Borneo.*
ABOVE: *European loom-woven beadwork.*
BELOW, LEFT: *Russian necklace.*
BELOW, RIGHT: *Straits Chinese panel of beads embroidered onto velvet.*

# CONSTRUCTION
## AND
# TECHNIQUES

FIVE

# CONSTRUCTION AND TECHNIQUES

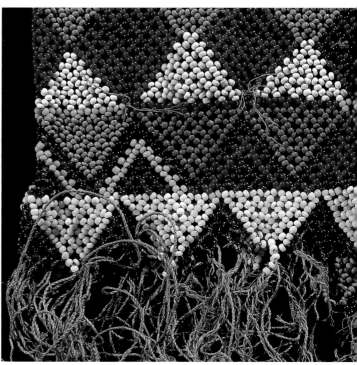

A CAREFUL EXAMINATION of the construction of a piece, as well as the more obvious characteristics of colour and intended use, can be of help in identifying a piece. There are very many methods of constructing beadwork, although a few are quite distinctive, many are variations of a well-known and widely used method. Old or seldom used methods are still being discovered and researched, but the more usual methods of construction which a collector is likely to encounter are discussed here.

ABOVE, LEFT; AND ABOVE, RIGHT: *Netted beadwork, possibly Tsonga; Ndau raphia beadwork, from southern Africa, made using the netting technique.*

BELOW, LEFT; BOTTOM LEFT; AND BELOW, RIGHT: *'Castillane' girdle, 1867; Zipper edgings, possibly Zulu; and Ndebele strips of beadwork being constructed.*

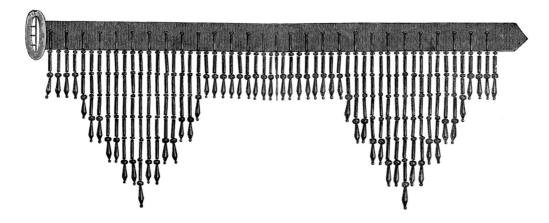

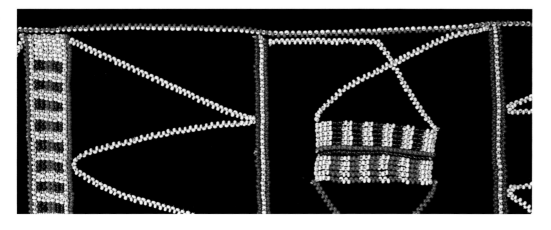

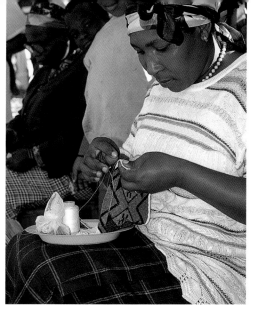

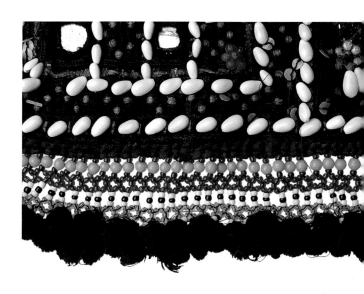

LEFT: *Zulu women making beadwork to sell to followers of the Shembe religion, near Durban, KwaZulu Natal, 2001.*

RIGHT: *Detail of the netted edging of a woman's blouse from Sind, Pakistan.*

Some methods will be found to be common to cultures as far apart as Borneo, Central Asia and Greenland – this should not be taken as evidence of ancient contact between the cultures, but rather demonstrates that each culture approached the problem of constructing beadwork in a similar way. A few methods are unique to a particular location, and the method of construction alone will probably be sufficient to identify the origin of the piece.

BELOW, LEFT: *Instructions for working loomed beading from a women's magazine of 1867, with the basket (shown below) to be covered in the beadwork.*

BELOW, RIGHT: *Ceremonial shoulder cloth with beads woven into the fabric by adding them with the weft, from Sumatra.*

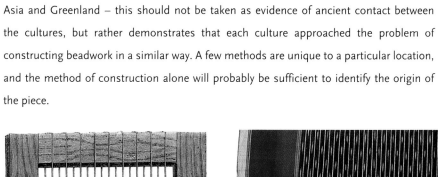

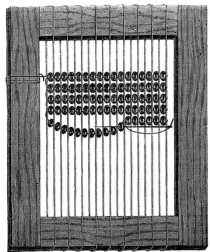

FIVE

In some regions the preferred colour and patterning of the beadwork closely follows that of an existing technology – weaving, embroidery or quill work, for example, while in other areas this relationship is not so apparent. Because the nature of the construction method very often places constraints upon the design, beadwork from widely differing cultures can appear, superficially, similar. It is then that colour, intended use and viewing of similar articles can help to identify the origin of the piece.

# BEADS ON EVENWEAVE FABRIC AND CANVAS

FAR LEFT: *Detail of the embroidery on a Romanian blouse (see page 163).*

LEFT: *The beads on the left are set in parallel rows, the method used in Western Europe; while on the right, the beads are set in opposing rows, typically Eastern European.*

Beads embroidered onto evenweave fabric are attached singly, and the design almost always, in colour and pattern, follows that of the region's counted-thread embroidery. The beads may be combined with embroidery stitches and sometimes sequins. Beads embroidered onto canvas are attached in the same manner; the canvas can be entirely covered with beads, or the principal design worked in beads and the background in wool cross stitch. The designs are very often found in patterns published in women's magazines of the period, for working in Berlin woolwork.

## Distribution

Bead embroidery on evenweave fabric was used in Eastern Europe, particularly Transylvania, Hungary and the Ukraine, all regions where counted-thread embroidery was also used extensively. Berlin woolwork reached a peak of popularity in Western Europe during the late 19th century, and the designs could be easily adapted for working partly or wholly in beads.

## Construction

The method is the same for evenweave on fabric or canvas; the bead is picked up, and the stitch made diagonally across the threads of the weave. The beads lie next to each other; on Eastern European embroideries, the beads are often set in opposing pairs, giving a herringbone-like

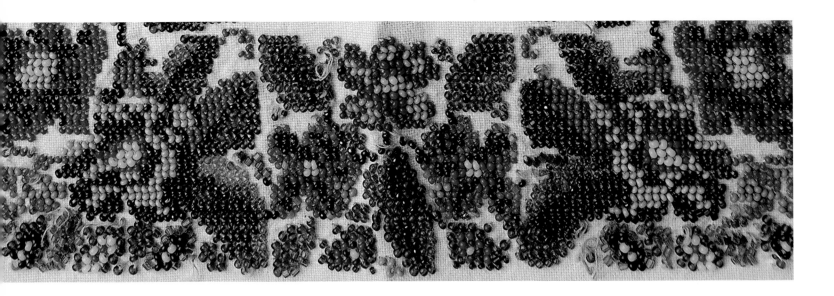

OPPOSITE, ABOVE, RIGHT: *Detail of a tea cosy (see page 155); a typical late 19th-century piece.*

OPPOSITE, BELOW: *Detail of a Ukrainian shirt (see page 159), which shows clearly how the beads have been stitched in opposing rows.*

ABOVE: *Typical 19th-century Berlin woolwork and beads.*

LEFT: *An entirely beaded piece, not yet made up, showing the canvas backing. This is a double-thread or 'Penelope' canvas.*

appearance, but on canvas, with or without woolwork, the beads all need to lie in the same direction to give a uniform surface. Ideally the beads should completely cover the area of each stitch, so that the canvas is not visible. In a recent innovation, canvas is placed onto a fabric with no discernible weave – satin, for instance – and the bead embroidery worked over the canvas into the fabric, taking care not to pierce the threads of the canvas. When the embroidery is completed, the canvas threads are removed, leaving the 'counted' bead embroidery on the fabric.

**FIVE**

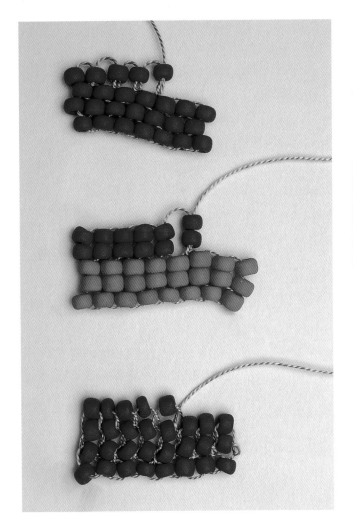

# BRICK STITCH

TOP (FROM TOP TO BOTTOM): *Single brick stitch (top); 'two-drop', that is, using two (or more) beads as one (middle); a variation of brick stitch sometimes found on English 17th-century beadwork, a method very probably related to needlelace or the detached buttonhole stitch used for stumpwork (bottom).*

FIVE

ABOVE: *Zulu bandolier band worked in multiple-drop brick stitch. Four of the smaller white beads are needed to make a block the same size as one created with three of all the other colours. This method of construction is known in KwaZulu Natal as the Shembe method.*

THE most obvious characteristic of brick stitch is the placement of the beads, which, as the name suggests, lie in staggered rows, although this also applies to one-bead netting (see page 190). It is impossible to determine whether a piece is constructed in one-bead netting or brick stitch by looking at a photograph – careful examination of the passage of the thread through the beads, or an examination of the working edge, is required to make an accurate identification. Brick stitch will generally produce a firm – sometimes stiff – fabric of beads, making it an ideal method for the construction of vessels. The ease with which it can be shaped, by increasing or decreasing within the working row, has led to its use by many contemporary bead workers for three-dimensional pieces.

In common with a number of other methods of construction, patterns of lozenge shapes, triangles and diagonal lines are easily formed, as are horizontal lines following the line of construction. Straight vertical lines can only be produced by working a multiple-drop variation (see below).

## Distribution

WIDELY used in South Africa, particularly by the Zulu and Xhosa, it was also found in some areas of North America, referred to there as Comanche stitch. Though it is now one of the most widely known and used methods of construction, its historic use would appear to have been restricted to South Africa and North America, though a method so similar that it could be called a variation of brick stitch was used during the 17th century in Europe. It was almost certainly a development of needlelace and stumpwork.

## Construction

THE main body of the work is formed thus: as each new bead is threaded, the thread is passed under a loop of thread on the previous row, and then back through the bead. It is this method of adding beads by looping *around the thread*, rather than passing through a previously threaded bead, that gives the firmness so appreciated by the Zulu and Xhosa beadworkers. This characteristic of threading around a thread is typical of many Zulu techniques.

The first row can be worked into an edge of hide or fabric, or over a cord or safety pin, in which instance the construction is as before. If the beadwork is not to be attached to an edge or cord, the first row must consist of a 'ladder' of beads which then forms the foundation for the rest of the piece.

A variation of the basic method is a multiple drop, where two or more beads are threaded together as one (long) bead – this can be used to speed up the work, to add a little more flexibility, or to vary the design.

The 17th-century variant has the thread following exactly the same path as for brick stitch, but does not pass back through the bead, but loops around itself, in a manner identical to blanket stitch or needlelace. The beads thus sit at right angles to the working edge. This means a bead fabric can be made without a needle, using just a thread with a stiffened end.

OPPOSITE, ABOVE, RIGHT: *Small triangular pennants worked in brick stitch hanging lose from a Tsonga skirt. The triangular shape is echoed in the beadwork embroidered onto the skirt beneath.*

ABOVE: *The colours and the design, executed in brick stitch, are typical of beadwork made by Zulu women in the Nongoma area of KwaZulu Natal. The seeds, Job's tears, added to the bottom of the fringe are commonly found in Zulu beadwork.*

RIGHT: *In brick stitch, where each bead is attached to the stitch between two beads in the previous row, the beads are staggered making diagonal and horizontal colour changes a natural choice for pattern making, so triangle and diamond motifs were frequently used. These Zulu examples show how they were further subdivided into smaller areas – diagonally into smaller diamonds on the left, and on the right and above, diamonds in decreasing sizes within each other. The diamonds above are further subdivided into triangles.*

# DIAGONAL WEAVE AND HERRINGBONE STITCH

## DIAGONAL WEAVE

THIS is an unusual method, producing beading that can look, superficially, like a cross between loom weaving and one-bead netting. The beads are in straight rows in relation to each other, but the rows are set diagonally, or 'on the bias'. It produces a flexible fabric, the threads of which are frequently held at the beginning and possibly also the end of the work by a strip of hide. Patterning tends to be confined to very simple geometric designs.

## Distribution

OLD examples of this technique are relatively uncommon; it was apparently used solely by some tribes of the north-eastern Woodlands region in North America, and is considered to have developed from finger weaving, a technique also practised in this area. Finger-woven sashes, using just a few beads woven in as embellishment, survive and may represent a transitional stage.

## Construction

THE technique differs from loom weaving in that pairs of weft threads, having passed across the width of the weave, become warp threads; the furthest pair of warp threads then become the next weft pair. This pair is threaded with beads, and passes across the weave. The technique is related to braiding. It is said that Native American beaders would thread all the beads needed before

*ABOVE: Working sample of diagonal weave, showing how the pair of threads that were the farthest right warp threads have become the working weft. This will then form the far left warp threads, and the next pair of threads on the right will become the weft.*

*RIGHT: Wide strips of beadwork are constructed, usually using herringbone stitch, and then sewn onto woollen blankets. Strong geometric designs, often architectural in shape, are used in Ndebele designs.*

beginning, but this requires considerable familiarity with the technique as well as the ability to visualize the finished piece.

## HERRINGBONE STITCH

ERRINGBONE stitch, so called because of its appearance, is quite unlike any other method of beadwork, and is therefore easily identified. The beads are set at a slight angle, in pairs. The setting of the beads gives a very distinctive appearance and determines the design – horizontal lines appear to 'zig zag' very slightly. The only other method of beadwork where the beads are set at an angle in this way is bead embroidery on evenweave fabric from Eastern Europe and the Ukraine, but this cannot be confused with herringbone stitch since with one technique the beads are stitched to fabric and not with the other.

### Distribution

RADITIONAL usage of herringbone stitch is confined to southern Africa among the Ndebele and some Zulu tribes. It is often referred to Ndebele herringbone or Ndebele stitch, but it is also used to a lesser extent by some Zulu women. The Ndebele use the stitch extensively, in their characteristic bold geometric patterns in strong primary colours with black and white.

### Construction

FTER the initial row, the beads are added in pairs, each new pair being placed between a pair in the previous row.

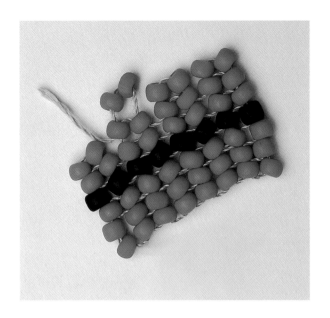

ABOVE: *This shows how in herringbone stitch the beads are attached in pairs. This method of construction results in a very geometric patterning – curves cannot be created.*

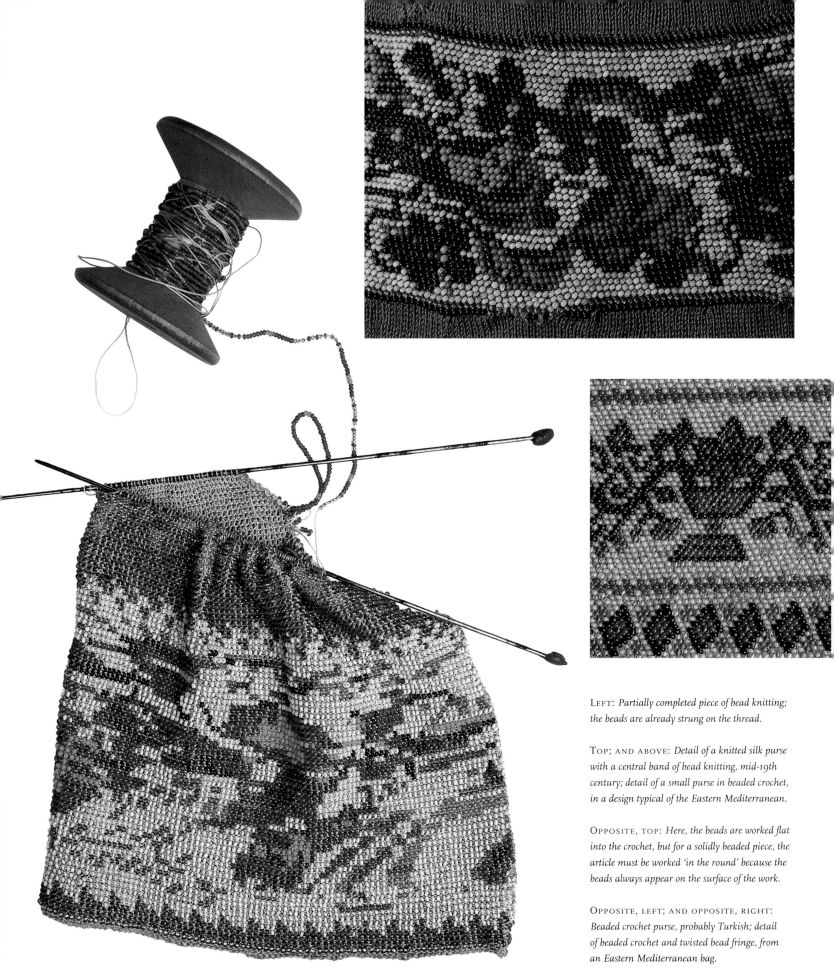

LEFT: *Partially completed piece of bead knitting; the beads are already strung on the thread.*

TOP; AND ABOVE: *Detail of a knitted silk purse with a central band of bead knitting, mid-19th century; detail of a small purse in beaded crochet, in a design typical of the Eastern Mediterranean.*

OPPOSITE, TOP: *Here, the beads are worked flat into the crochet, but for a solidly beaded piece, the article must be worked 'in the round' because the beads always appear on the surface of the work.*

OPPOSITE, LEFT; AND OPPOSITE, RIGHT: *Beaded crochet purse, probably Turkish; detail of beaded crochet and twisted bead fringe, from an Eastern Mediterranean bag.*

# Knitting and Crochet

Both knitting and crochet produce a flexible fabric – knitting more so than crochet – with the beads on the face of the work, and the knitted or crocheted fabric visible behind the beads. If just a few beads are worked into the fabric as an embellishment, it is easy to ascertain whether the piece is knitted or crocheted if one is familiar with either or both of the techniques. If the beads more or less cover the face of the work, then examination of the piece should determine which technique has been used, again if one has knowledge of either method. Crochet is generally more visible than knitting on the face of the fabric. Both techniques are usually worked in the round rather than flat.

## Distribution

Both knitting and crochet with beads became popular as a pastime throughout Europe and North America from the early 19th century onwards. It was possible to buy the beads ready strung, for making up into the article required, an early example of kits for the domestic hobby market. Women's magazines of the period contain patterns and instructions for many varied articles decorated with beads. So popular were beaded purses and bags that these were also produced, by poorly paid outworkers, to be sold to those women unable or unwilling to make their own.

Prisoners in Turkey and Greece also learnt crocheted beadwork, and it is used in Turkey for *oya*, the decorative edgings of women's scarves. Today, crochet with beads is found in Egypt and Turkey on beaded hip scarves and costumes for Egyptian or Arabic dance. Much of this is exported to Europe and North America.

## Construction

For both techniques, the beads must be threaded on the yarn before commencing. If a pattern is to be worked in beads of different colours, care must be taken to thread the beads in exactly the correct order – no small undertaking for a purse with several thousand beads in a complex floral pattern using a dozen or more colours and very small beads.

When knitting or crocheting, the beads appear on the face of the work; if worked as a flat piece, the return row is either unbeaded, or the beads appear on the 'wrong' side. While this is not a problem for a lightly beaded piece, for a complex picture this is unwelcome, so most items are worked in the round, if knitted, on four needles, so that the work constantly progresses in the same direction. In crochet the piece is generally also worked in the round.

For both techniques the bead to be used is pushed along the yarn to sit on the fabric before the next stitch is formed; the stitch is then made, and then next bead pushed into place.

# Lane, or Lazy, Stitch and Appliqué

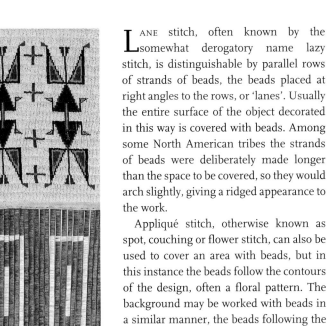

Lane stitch, often known by the somewhat derogatory name lazy stitch, is distinguishable by parallel rows of strands of beads, the beads placed at right angles to the rows, or 'lanes'. Usually the entire surface of the object decorated in this way is covered with beads. Among some North American tribes the strands of beads were deliberately made longer than the space to be covered, so they would arch slightly, giving a ridged appearance to the work.

Appliqué stitch, otherwise known as spot, couching or flower stitch, can also be used to cover an area with beads, but in this instance the beads follow the contours of the design, often a floral pattern. The background may be worked with beads in a similar manner, the beads following the contours of the design, or filled with beads in parallel lines, or the background may be left unbeaded, allowing the ground fabric – hide, velvet or cloth – to be seen.

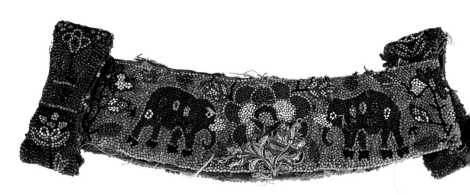

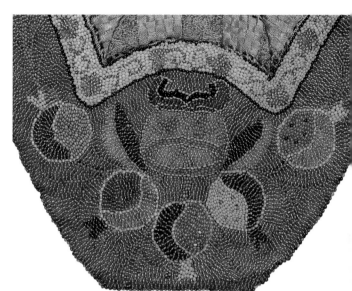

OPPOSITE: *Lane-stitch beadwork, Plains style, North America (far left); Iroquois beadwork in lane stitch. The method of working can be seen, as can the parchment used as a template (right); lane and appliqué stitch on a leather apron, Ntwane, North Sotho (below).*

THIS PAGE: *Lane or lazy stitch (above, left); spot or appliqué stitch (above, middle); Straits Chinese bridegroom's appliqué-stitch crown (above, right); panel with white beads worked in appliqué stitch from Gujarat, India (near right); appliqué-stitch beading on a slipper, probably Straits Chinese, but the design shows a strong Korean influence (far right); appliqué-stitch beading on a small North American pouch, Woodlands region (below right).*

## Distribution

BOTH the methods described above were used extensively throughout North America; lane stitch is also used in southern Africa, mostly by the Ndebele on the women's and girls' 'aprons', and appliqué stitch, worked without a background of beads, was used in Romania and Poland. During the late 19th century, appliqué stitch beadwork from North American was copied in Western Europe, in the floral style typical of the eastern Woodlands tribes. Couching a thread containing beads is a very widespread method for embroidering with beads.

## Construction

FOR lane stitch, the 'lanes' must first be marked upon the piece to be worked; the thread emerges at the lowest marking, the required number of beads are threaded, and then a small stitch is taken along the next lane marking. (When beading buckskin, Native American beaders would make this stitch through part of the thickness of the hide without it being visible on the back of the work. If working on cloth or leather the short stitch would be visible on the wrong side.) The next line of beads are then threaded, and the stitch made through the lowest marking, next to the row already made.

Appliqué stitch requires two threads; one holds the beads and follows the contours of the pattern, and the other is used to couch, or stitch over, the thread holding the beads, at intervals.

A hybrid of the two methods – straight lines of beads that follow a shape – is sometimes seen worked over a shape cut out of paper, card, or thin leather, or over a lightly padded shape to give a raised appearance.

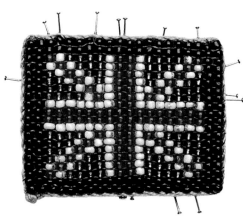

LEFT: *Basketry rather than loom weaving is an indigenous craft in southern Africa, so this woven beadwork from Mozambique is very unusual. (Afri-Karner Collection)*

ABOVE: *Patriotic British pin cushion, early 20th century. The top and bottom of the pin cushion are small panels of loomed beadwork.*

BELOW: *This sample shows the method of attaching a complete row of beads at a time. The warp threads are visible between the beads.*

OPPOSITE, ABOVE, RIGHT: *Loomed beadwork made into a belt,* c. 1920s, *from the Czech Republic.*

OPPOSITE, BELOW: *Loomed beadwork strip, probably intended as a belt, possibly from North Africa, although the designs are typical of those found in Mali.*

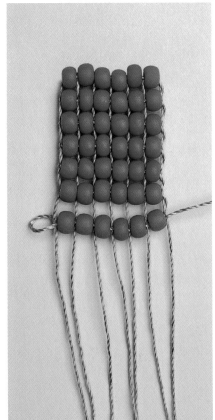

# LOOM WEAVING

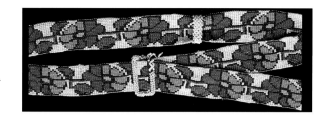

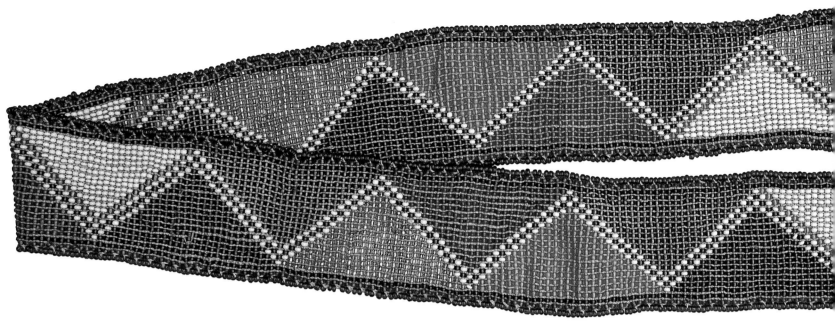

LOOM weaving, like square stitch, is easily recognized as the beads are set in straight rows, both vertically and horizontally. The long warp threads are visible between the rows of beads. Loom weaving is relatively quick to construct and complex designs can be produced with reasonable ease. Depending on the thread used for the warp, it usually produces a supple and flexible fabric. One of the disadvantages of loom work is the number of warp threads that must be finished off securely after weaving, though this can be overcome by working in the round, or using the continuous warp technique, both of which appear to be fairly recent innovations. In older works, loom weaving is sometimes, a little confusingly, referred to as 'square weave'. (At one time even-weave cloth was called 'square cloth'.)

Another form of weaving incorporating beads was developed during the late 19th century where strings of beads were woven into cloth on a commercial cloth loom. The beads could be added as embellishment in what was predominantly cloth or could be used to produce a completely beaded fabric. A pattern could be created by stringing the beads in pattern order before weaving.

In South-East Asia beads were also incorporated into hand-woven cloth.

## Distribution

HISTORICALLY, loom weaving was mainly used in the Americas, both North and South. Various Amazonian tribes used loom weaving – though a variation where the warp rather than the weft threads were manipulated – to make 'aprons' for women's festival wear. In the north the Plains and Woodlands tribes used loom weaving, which is thought to have developed from the older technique of quill work. A form of loom weaving was chosen for some of the surviving wampum belts. As interest in beadwork as a hobby spread during the 19th century, the bead loom and loom work was introduced to white American society, and to Europe – it became known as 'Apache' beadwork. A number of women's magazines of this period give instructions about making beadwork using an 'Indian' loom.

The commercially produced beaded cloth was made in Bohemia, and possibly elsewhere, until the early 20th century. Following the Second World War and the

eviction of German workers from Czechoslovakia, the technology was lost.

Handwoven cloth incorporating beads was used as a status-conferring cloth exchanged at weddings in Sumatra, and a few examples of a similar technique, thought to be from Greece or the Balkans, survive.

## Construction

THE basic method is thus: after the loom is prepared with the warp thread, the beads are added one complete weft row at a time, the thread of beads being passed under the warp threads and then the same or another weft thread passed back through the beads *over* the warp threads. Two warp threads may be used as one at each edge for added strength. This is the standard method, but there are a number of slight variations. It is possible to work the weaving using a heddle, as when weaving cloth. As previously mentioned, the Amazonian tribes use a technique whereby the warp threads are each in turn passed through the weft, and another, probably older technique from North America, is a combination of weaving and twining, and may have developed from basketry.

# NETTING

ONE of the simplest of techniques, netting can be easily identified by the mesh-like structure of beads and spaces produced by this method of construction. The spaces between the beads give a flexibility to the fabric, and also render the piece lighter in weight than a piece constructed of solid beading. It is relatively straightforward to work, but it is extremely difficult to execute any but the simplest of designs in this technique – lozenge shapes and diagonal lines are the most common. Close examination is needed to determine if a piece has been constructed horizontally or vertically. It can be worked in the round, over an object to cover it, or used as an edging, or as a complete fabric.

## Distribution

NETTING in its various forms must be one of the most widely used techniques for constructing beadwork – almost every culture that produces beadwork has knowledge of a variation of netting. Particularly fine pieces of very elaborate designs were made in Borneo,

Gujarat in India, and by the Chinese community in the Straits of Malacca. In Gujarat two variations (see below), rarely seen or unknown elsewhere, are worked, one of which attaches the beadwork to a cloth backing as the work progresses.

## Construction

NETTING is very often characterized by the number of beads used for a single mesh, so it would therefore be referred to as 'three-bead netting' or 'five-bead netting' and so on. It can be worked so that the beads are added horizontally or vertically along the working edge. After the foundation row, which may be a strand of beads or a fabric edge, enough beads for a single mesh are picked up, and the needle passed through the central bead of the mesh of the previous row.

There are two variations made in Gujarat in India – in one, after picking up

OPPOSITE, ABOVE: *Tightly worked three-bead netting, southern Africa.*

OPPOSITE, BELOW: *Large apron or skirt, from Mozambique, made using three-bead netting. The zig-zag design forms along the construction lines.*

LEFT: *Netting, in a loop of seven beads, covering a purse from the Czech Republic, first half of the 20th century.*

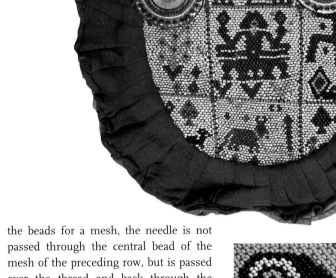

ABOVE: *Three-bead netting worked horizontally (top); five-bead netting worked vertically (centre); variation of the technique frequently found in western India – the thread passes into a space between the beads of the previous row and returns through the bead (bottom). The contrast colour shows the direction of working.*

LEFT: *Fan, from Gujarat, India, worked in the version of three-bead netting typical of much beadwork from this region. Pictorial motifs such as these are difficult to execute in this method.*

the beads for a mesh, the needle is not passed through the central bead of the mesh of the preceding row, but is passed over the thread and back through the last bead of the new mesh; and in the other, the needle, at this point, takes a small stitch into the backing fabric, and then passes through the last bead of the new mesh.

RIGHT: *Detail of three-bead netting, from Borneo, in typical colours and pattern. The beaders of Borneo surpassed even those of Gujarat in India in their ability to produce complex curvilinear motifs.*

# 'PEYOTE' OR ONE-BEAD NETTING

'P EYOTE' IS the most common name for this stitch, but it should only be used for the slightly different stitch (also called gourd stitch) employed to decorate objects in the Native American peyote ceremony. This variation of the stitch can only be worked in the round, but the stitch that is widely used and usually referred to as 'peyote' can be worked flat as well. Its old English name is 'twill' weave, but this could be confused with herringbone stitch – which has a twill-like appearance – so it is referred to throughout as 'one-bead netting'.

## Characteristics

W HILE the method of working is very different, one-bead netting super-ficially looks the same as brick stitch – the beads are held in staggered rows. Only close examination of the piece, and if possible the working edge, will determine if a piece is constructed in brick stitch or one-bead netting. The difference in con-struction generally results in a somewhat more flexible fabric than that produced by brick stitch, and one-bead netting is more likely than brick stitch to be used to cover a solid object.

## Distribution

O NE-BEAD netting is one of the most widespread of all techniques – surpassed only by netting – and is used

*ABOVE: The most usual version of one-bead netting (top) shows why 'one-bead netting' may be an appropriate name – the beads are attached by passing the thread through a bead in the previous row; in the 'two-drop' version (bottom) two or more beads are added at a time. This variation is widely used in South Africa.*

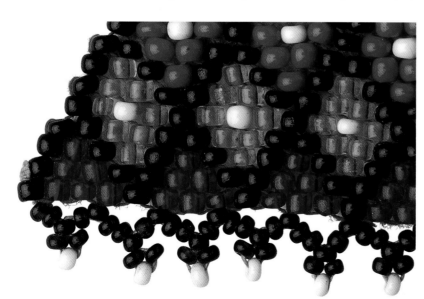

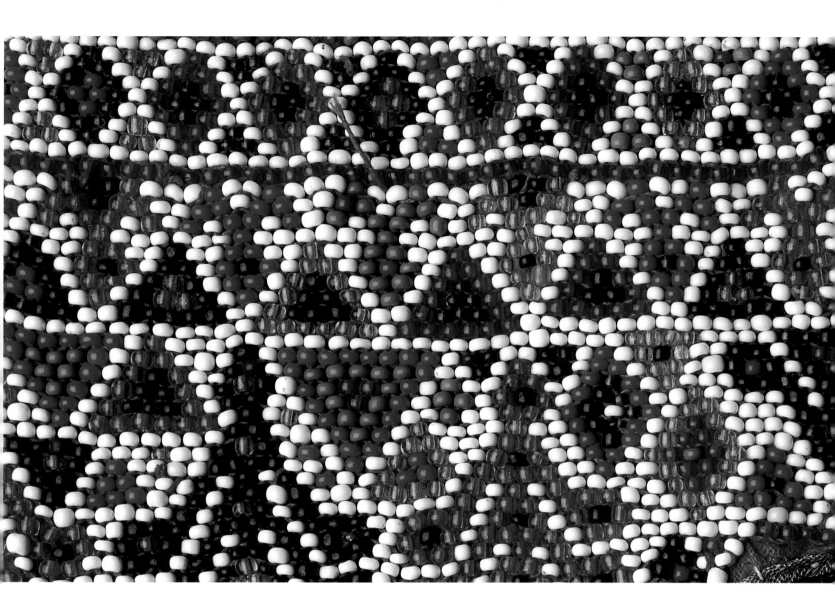

extensively in Central Asia, Indonesia, Europe, Russia, the Ukraine and North America. Today, it is a widely known and used method of construction.

## Construction

THE standard method used now is 'one drop'; after the foundation row, the beads are in a castellated line – each new bead is attached by being threaded into the space between two beads of the previous row. The stitch can be worked using two (or more) beads in the place of one bead, which is known as 'two drop' (or 'three drop').

The traditional Native American method, used solely for covering objects, is usually known as 'unit of three', and can only be worked in the round, and will spiral diagonally up the object to be covered.

ABOVE: *Section of one-bead netting covering a pistol holster from Afghanistan.*

LEFT: *Section of one-bead netting from Central Asia – the colours and small, stylized floral motifs are typical of items from this region.*

OPPOSITE, BELOW, LEFT: *Corner of a triangular amulet from Central Asia. This detail also shows the three-bead or clover-leaf end so typical of this region.*

OPPOSITE, RIGHT: *Ornamental tassel of large metal beads and small glass beads from Afghanistan. The strands at the base of the tassel have been made of narrow strips of one-bead netting.*

FIVE

# RIGHT-ANGLE WEAVE

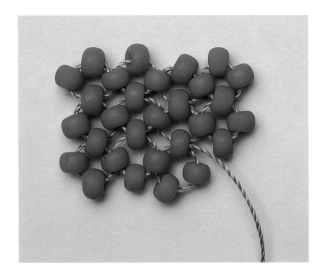

ABOVE, RIGHT: *Small elephant, originally attached to a key ring, from Bombay, India. Because of the way right-angle weave is constructed it can be added onto any edge; it makes a flexible fabric which is ideal for three-dimensional objects.*

BELOW: *Part of a Ukrainian gerdany (traditional necklace); the strands connecting the motifs are made in right-angle weave.*

## Construction

A FOUNDATION ring of four beads is threaded, then three beads added at a time, working in a 'figure-of-eight' movement. For subsequent rows, first three beads, then two at a time, are added, in the same manner. In a variation, producing a very much more open fabric, extra beads are added in between the beads that hold the fabric together.

R IGHT-ANGLE weave is very easily identified since this is the only construction method in which the beads are set at right angles – hence the name – to each other. It produces a flexible, somewhat open fabric that can be added to, or joined, at any edge. Because of the placement of the beads, any design tends to have a rather angular, stylized appearance.

## Distribution

O NE of several techniques used in Russia and the Ukraine, it is also used, worked as a single strip, in Afghanistan. This single strip, almost invariably in white beads, is used as a trimming, fastened to clothing as a braid, or used as embellishment on small bags where it forms part of a fringe. It is also one of the oldest methods of construction used in Western Europe – many of the 17th-century beaded 'sweete' bags are constructed in right-angle weave.

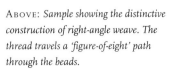

ABOVE: *Sample showing the distinctive construction of right-angle weave. The thread travels a 'figure-of-eight' path through the beads.*

# SQUARE STITCH

S QUARE stitch has a very similar appearance to loom-woven beadwork, in that the beads are in straight lines both vertically and horizontally. Close examination of the work will determine which of the methods has been used – square stitch lacks the long warp threads running through the work and can produce a somewhat firmer fabric than loom-woven beadwork. The advantage of square stitch over loom-woven work is that it can be worked in the hand, without a loom; a disadvantage is that it requires the thread to pass through the beads several times.

## Distribution

W HILE the use of square stitch is reasonably widespread now, historically it seems to have been confined to pieces from Russia and the Ukraine, and these communities in North America and Canada. Surviving pieces date from the late 19th or early 20th centuries.

## Construction

A FTER the initial string of beads is threaded, the beads are added one at a time, the passing of the thread through the beads forms a series of adjoining circles.

ABOVE: *Square stitch is superficially similar to loom weaving, but the warps are not visible.*

BELOW: *Central medallion of a Ukrainian necklace. The centre is worked in square stitch.*

FAR LEFT: *Reed mask with fringes, used by Sotho girls during initiation.*

ABOVE: *Detail of zipper edging on an Iroquois bag, North America.*

BELOW, FAR LEFT: *Central Asian hair tassel of wrapped beadwork and twisted beadwork fringe.*

BELOW, MIDDLE: *Hanging from Pakistan, North-West Province. The fringes have divided ends.*

NEAR LEFT; AND BELOW: *A wrapped cord incorporating beads (near left); below: zipper edging (above); three-bead or clover-leaf end (below, left); divided strands (below, right).*

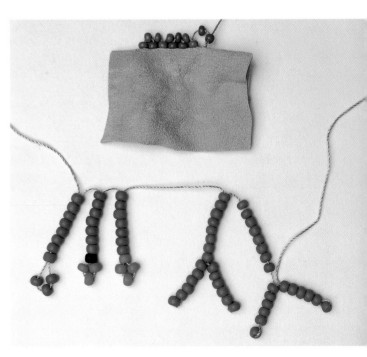

# STRANDS, FRINGES, TASSELS AND EDGING

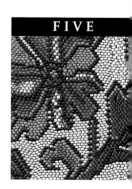

THE variety of decorations used to embellish a piece of beadwork, or, on occasion, to form the body of the beadwork, is almost limitless. Only a very few of the most widespread methods are discussed here.

## Distribution

STRANDS of bead fringe are used almost universally, but most particularly in South Africa and North America, and on dresses and other fashion items dating from the 19th and early 20th centuries. The three-bead or clover-leaf strand ending is as widely used as fringe.

A fringe of twisted thread incorporating small blue or white beads is found widely throughout north Pakistan, Afghanistan and Central Asia, as is a wrapped cord incorporating beads. The so-called zipper edging is used in this same region, as well as in North America and southern Africa.

## Construction

A PLAIN strand of beads is made by threading the required number of beads, and then passing the thread back through the last but one bead, and the subsequent beads, back to the start of

*ABOVE, LEFT: Central Asian amuletic decoration; the strands are finished with a clover-leaf end.*

*ABOVE, RIGHT: Tassels of netting embellishing on an Uzbek tent hanging, Central Asia. The left-hand tassel shows the construction.*

*BELOW: Zulu edgings, from South Africa, used to cover an entire piece; the overlapping layers suggest fur or feathers.*

the strand. A clover-leaf end is made in the same way, but the thread is passed through the fourth bead from the end, then through the remaining beads.

Divided ends are made by threading a strand of beads, missing the last bead and passing the thread back through the bottom part of the strand, then adding more beads, and completing the strand in the usual way.

A wrapped cord is made by winding one thread around one or more other strands forming a central core. The cord is secured by changing the wrapping strand for one of the strands in the core, and wrapping with the new strand. To incorporate beads, the beads are threaded onto the wrapping strand, and tightly wound around the core, before changing to another wrapping thread to secure them.

Zipper edging is done by picking up three beads on the thread, taking a small stitch into the fabric, and passing the thread back through the last bead. From there on, two beads are picked up each time, and the thread passed through the last bead as before.

Tassels can be made by gathering together a number of strands, or by making a narrow tube of netting.

# TAMBOUR AND ARI

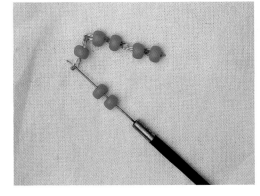

BOTH tambour beading and beading worked with an ari hook are easily identified by the appearance of a fine chain stitch on one side of the work. If the piece is European tambour work then the chain stitch is on the wrong side of the work, and the beads are held in place by a single, straight stitch rather than the chain. If the piece has been worked with an ari hook, the beads are held by the chain part of the stitch, which therefore appears on the surface of the work. Ari work very often includes chain-stitch embroidery, sequins, bugles, beads of different colours and metallic threads, known as *purl* or *zardozi*.

## Distribution

TAMBOUR beading was used extensively by the fashion houses and *passementerie* workshops of Europe until the mid-20th century. It is still used by couture houses and in workshops in the Czech Republic producing beaded accessories for the fashion market.

The ari hook is employed throughout the Indian sub-continent to embroider and bead accessories for the Western fashion market, and saris and other textiles for home consumption and export.

## Construction

THE method is very much the same for both tambour and ari work – the fabric to be beaded must be tightly stretched on a frame, and the beading worked with a continuous thread. When using the tambour hook the beads must first be threaded onto the continuous thread. A loop of thread is drawn up through the fabric, the hook advanced slightly, then another loop drawn up – making a chain stitch – with the bead placed on the straight part of the stitch underneath the fabric. Therefore the worker is working on the 'wrong' side of the work, and designs such as lettering must be worked in reverse. If changes of colour or size of bead are required, these are best worked as separate areas.

For ari work, the chain-stitch technique is the same, but as the ari hook is much finer the seed beads can be threaded onto the hook, and then released onto the chain part of the stitch. This means the beads are applied on the 'right' side of the work, and it is a simple matter to change colour or size of bead at will, as work proceeds.

**FIVE**

TOP: *Neck edging on a garment commercially produced in Pakistan. Embroidery incorporating beads and lengths of coiled gold or silver wire (purl) are produced with an ari hook in commercial workrooms.*

ABOVE: *Detail of commercially produced tambour embroidery, mid-20th century.*

RIGHT: *Tambour beadwork made in Western Europe, early 20th century (detail).*

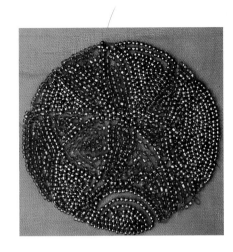

OPPOSITE, ABOVE, RIGHT: *Attaching beads with tambour hook (top) – this is the 'wrong' (non-working) side. The hook pulls the thread through the fabric, in between the beads. Using an ari hook (bottom) – the beads are placed on the hook and then slipped onto the loop of thread drawn through the fabric.*

THIS PAGE: *Small motif of tambour beading produced as a sample, European, 1960s (above); part of a dress bodice in tambour beading and embroidery, early 20th century (right); detail of tambour beading from a French purse, early 20th century (below).*

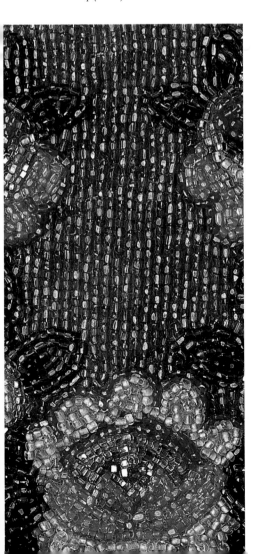

# THREE-DIMENSIONAL STRUCTURES

THERE are a number of ways to create a three-dimensional structure using beads, but the two most common methods are threading the beads on wire rather than thread, or covering a rigid, usually padded, structure with strands or a network of beads.

## Distribution

BEAD and wire structures were widely made throughout the latter half of the 19th and early 20th centuries. These structures were generally constructed to resemble flowers, sometimes fruit, and were used as ornaments under a glass dome – wax, leather and other artificial flowers were displayed in the same way – or, particularly in France, as beaded floral wreaths or grave furniture. The beaded flowers were superseded by porcelain flowers during the second half of the 20th century. Bead and wire structures were also employed to make miniature 'doll's house' furniture, a popular hobby during this period. While the miniature furniture was a domestic hobby, the making of the wire and bead was done as a hobby or professionally.

The most notable examples of beads over a padded structure are the 'crowns' made by the Yoruba of West Africa for their kings. In Cameroon carved thrones and items of regalia were also made, and in some instances were covered with cloth which would then be entirely covered with beads, stitched at intervals to the cloth.

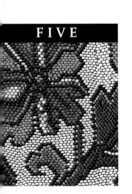

FIVE

ABOVE, LEFT: *Small turned horn egg cup, covered in one-bead netting using exceptionally small beads, early 19th century. This is still a common method of covering a three-dimensional piece.*

RIGHT: *Maasai disc neck ornaments are either made from wire-threaded beads, or as in this one by applying strings of beads to a stiff leather or plastic backing. Many layers are worn to create a profusion of colour.*

Small animals of wood or grass, covered with netted beadwork, or whimsical items – cups and saucers of bead and wire, for example – have been produced for the tourist market in many places, particularly in southern Africa.

## Construction

For bead and wire construction, once the beads of the appropriate colour are threaded onto the wire, the skill lies in shaping the wire to the desired form, and finishing each wire length both neatly and securely.

First of all rigid constructions need a base, which is usually padded and covered with cloth – unless it is to be covered with bead netting when the cloth is not required – and the beads are stitched to the cloth, generally in long strands, anchored at the beginning and end of each strand.

ABOVE: *Ethiopian food cover made from beads threaded on wire.*

RIGHT: *Beads made of beads – small beads have been used to cover larger, probably wooden, beads, 1920s.*

BELOW: *This unique horned hat was made by the Kuba in the Democratic Republic of the Congo. (Afri-Karner Collection)*

# COLLECTING BEADWORK

THE VARIETY of beadwork that can be collected is almost limitless, but collections definitely benefit from a focus or theme – beadwork from a particular area or period; or certain objects such as pipe bags or moccasins from North America; or construction techniques, such as netting; or a particular material – Venetian glass or beads of natural materials. The beauty and integrity of a personal beadwork collection ultimately depends on the choices made and the budget allowed.

A primary goal for any collector is to become as knowledgeable and familiar with the material they are collecting as possible. A large variety of publications are available in numerous formats, aimed at beginner and advanced collectors; local libraries are useful. Subscriptions to journals or magazines are often helpful in keeping attuned to new developments in a collecting area. Valuable information is also available through viewing museum and private collections, exhibitions, shows and auctions. Cultural centres such as those in North America can assist in the gaining of knowledge. Additionally, contact with tribal arts dealers, organizations, or other collectors can be especially rewarding. Listening to a dealer or advanced collector review the qualities of a particularly important piece can both inspire and educate. This network of information from others who share your interest can save you both time and money, it can expose you to material that will help develop your aesthetics, and, most importantly, educate you regarding authenticity.

Make a note of when and where each item was bought, how much was paid for it, and, if bought in the field, the local name and as much information as possible about the item and what it was used for. Keep an open mind! When buying from a dealer, particularly one who does not specialize in beadwork, bear in mind that the piece may be wrongly attributed. It is not unusual for almost any beadwork to be described as 'African' or 'American'; many dealers are unfamiliar with beadwork from the Indian Sub-continent, South-East Asia, or Eastern Europe.

If you are collecting relatively inexpensive pieces of recent beadwork you may not consider the authenticity of a piece to be important. If, however, you are collecting beadwork with a known market value – Native American beadwork is a prime example – then the authenticity is of importance. As in any collecting area, as soon as a type of item establishes a market value, facsimiles will be created to deceive. Learning this can be an expensive lesson, but one that few collectors have been totally able to avoid. Also, if not a complete fabrication, some pieces have been heavily restored; again the more valuable or rare the piece, the more likely it is that extensive restoration will be worth someone's time. Some collectors – of American pieces particularly – prefer to buy damaged pieces as they are more likely to be authentic and unrestored.

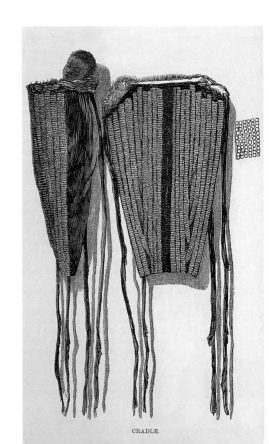

CRADLE.

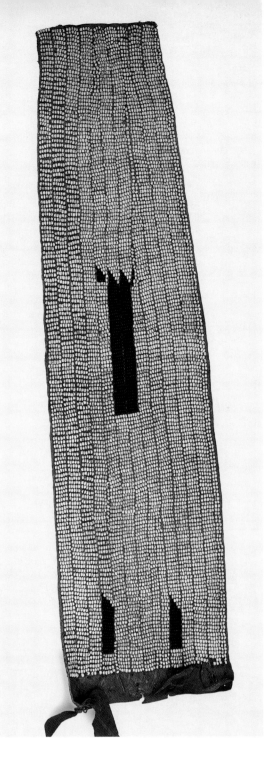

## Conserving beadwork

**B**EADWORK IS MADE to be used and worn and is fairly resilient, but a few simple and common sense rules can be applied here.

• Direct sunlight will fade the colour of beads and damage the thread that holds a piece together.

• Very heavily beaded items, such as Ndebele blankets, are best stored flat, as the weight of the beads puts too great a strain on the fabric or thread used in its construction.

• Wire, nails or pins should not be used to hold or suspend a piece for display as this will cause damage and probable discolouration through rust.

• Older pieces of work may be held together with animal sinew, which, if it dries out, may shrink and curl, causing the beads to break. Try gently moistening with distilled water.

## Cleaning

**S**OME OLD PIECES can look quite dull with ingrained dirt, but be very careful about washing a piece. First, try gently brushing away loose dirt with a soft brush – work slowly, over a clean cloth, and carefully examine any debris. Ask a qualified conservator if you want to do more than simple cleaning, or if the piece is valuable.

• Threads holding a piece can be damaged by water, or may expand when wet, causing the beads to break. Loose beads may be lost.

• Any piece on hide or leather will be irreparably damaged by washing – the skin will become rigid and shrink.

• Some discolouration occurs to silverlined beads and bugles with age – the silver lining becomes tarnished where it is exposed to the air – cleaning cannot reverse this.

• Not all that appears to be ingrained dirt should be removed; organic materials were sometimes rubbed into pieces by the wearer. For instance, the Xhosa of the Eastern Cape used red ochre extensively, and traces of it can be found rubbed into their beadwork, and this has become an integral part of it. The Sioux of North America used kaolin powder on animal hides, some of which coats the beads.

*OPPOSITE: Portrait of a Fingo Woman (1851), attributed to W. H. F. L. Langschmidt, shows a beaded headdress similar to the one shown opposite, below, right. The headdress, illustrated as a baby carrier, appeared in* The Natural History of Man, Africa *by J. G. Wood, published in 1868.*

*RIGHT: Mid-19th century headdress beaded in lane stitch. It is always interesting to research a piece – pictured opposite are two references the present owner of this headdress has found. (Afri-Karner Collection)*

## Storage

• When it is necessary to reduce the size of a piece for storage, roll if possible, rather than folding, but whether rolled or folded do so with the beads outwards. Items can be rolled around a cylinder for support.

• If a piece must be folded, it needs to be re-folded from time to time to prevent the creasing always being in the same place.

• Store pieces between layers of acid-free tissue to prevent their chafing against each other. Plastic packaging is best avoided, as it can encourage condensation.

• Moth repellents all have potentially damaging effects – even cedar chips (an otherwise safe repellent) can damage some beadwork.

# ACKNOWLEDGMENTS

The authors should like to thank the following: Celia Ankers; Anne Bahnson and Poul Mork at the National Museum of Denmark, Copenhagen; Irene Barnes at Manor House Museum, Bury St Edmunds; Rayda Becker, who wrote the Tsonga section; Frank Bergevin; Caroline Bevan; The Burrell Collection, Glasgow; Brigit Carlstein at the McGregor Museum, Kimberley; Kate Chisholm and Tracy Rushmere at African Image; DeAnn Dankowski at the Minneapolis Institute of Art; Joyce Doel; Terry Dokis; Brian and Jean Douglas; Eiluned Edwards; Embroiderers' Guild, Yorkshire Branch Collection; Ann Evans; John Gillow; Vera Grey; Tessa Halfpenny; Jan Harvey; Sithembile Haya at the Queenstown and Frontier Museum; Steve Henrikson at the Alaska State Museum; Margaret Herbert; Gillian Hill; Professor Lewis Hill at the Centre for South-East Asian Studies, Hull University; Miloslav Hlousek of Jablonex; Colleen Hobman; Lindsay Hooper and June Hosford at the South African Museum; Ann Mary Johnstone; Ken Karner; Lynn Kirk; Maria Kirk; Gerald Klinghardt, who wrote the San and Ovambo section; Bob Knoops for photographs of the Standard Bank Collection;

Yan Krupka, ex-director of Ornela; Katerina Krupkova of Yani, Zasada; Mark Lewis; Steven Long; Jean Lord; Midori Matsushima; Lalou Meltzer at the William Fehr Collection at the Castle, South Africa; Michael Methven from the Pan African Market in Cape Town; Irvine Meyer; Alysyn Midelow-Marsden; Ann Mockford; Professor Anne Morrell; Carole Morris; Karel Nel; Moira Noonan at the Kelvingrove Art Gallery and Museum, Glasgow; Pusetso Nyabela at the Morija Museum in Lesotho; Robert Papini and Phindi Mabuza; Diana Pardue and LaRee Bates at the Heard Museum, Arizona; Stephanie Poissons at the McCord Museum of Canadian History, Montreal; the Rabari of Kachchh; Fiona Rankin-Smith, who wrote the Ndebele section; Peter Rich; Colin Sayer from The Collector; Mark Sedgman; Bryan Sentance; Josie Shepherd at York Castle Museum; Mary Anne Slemmons at the Alaska State Library; Torben Sode; Rod Stallebrass; Betty Starrey; Mark Sykes Collection; Shiro Tamakoshi; Colin Taylor; Mr Hideho Tezuki of Miyuki Shoji Co., Angela Thompson; Stefany Tomalin; Barbara Tyrrell; Sue van Langelaar; Lesley Verrinder; Olivia Wells; Ian West; Sandra Winter at the Killie Campbell Collection; Marilee Wood

# SOURCES OF ILLUSTRATIONS

The following abbreviations have been used: *a*, above; *b*, below; *c*, centre; *i*, inset; *l*, left; *m*, main picture; *r*, right; *t*, top; PS Pam Stallebrass.

African Image (photos PS) 18r, 69ar, 69bl, 69br, 70ar, 70br, 72b, 73al; Afri-Karner Collection (photos PS) 21b, 37m, 48ar, 48ari, 49l, 62 all, 63al, 64br, 65ar, 66al, 66cl, 66bl, 188b, 199b, 200br, 201; Courtesy Alaska State Library 80cl, 84al, 103bl, 103ar; Alaska State Museum 77bl, 102b, 103br; Frank Bergevin 13ar, 77ar, 90br, 194ar; Tessa Bunney 2, 3, 6bl, 6br, 7 all, 8l, 8r, 9t, 9cl, 9b, 10a, 10bl, 11bl, 11br, 12tr, 12cr, 13c, 13b, 20ar, 23ar, 25ar, 27t, 31t, 63br, 72a, 73ar, 74 all, 75 all, 76, 77br, 78a, 79, 80cr, 81al, 81ar, 86ar, 86cr, 86bl, 86br, 87 all, 88al, 88ar, 88bl, 88br, 89ar, 89cl, 89bl, 89br, 90al, 90ar, 91ar, 91bl, 91br, 92ar, 93l, 93br, 94ac, 94bl, 94r, 95bl, 96l, 96r, 97 all, 98bl, 101l, 101r, 102r, 104r, 105tr, 105b, 106ar, 108, 109 all, 111bl, 112al, 113al, 114bl, 114br, 115 all, 116bl, 116br, 117a, 117br, 118ar, 118b, 119 all, 120 all, 121al, 121bl, 122 all, 123am, 123ar, 123b, 124 all, 125, 126 all, 127 all, 128al, 128am, 128ar, 128b, 129 all, 130 all, 131 all, 132 all, 133 all, 134 all, 135 all, 136 all, 137l, 139t, 140 all, 141 all, 143 all, 145al, 145ar, 145bl, 146al, 146c, 147ar, 147bl, 147br, 149bl, 149br, 150 all, 151a, 151bl, 151br, 152al, 152c, 152ar, 154cr, 156ar, 157 all, 158 all, 159 all, 160 all, 161 all, 162 all, 163 all, 164al, 164cl, 165c, 165ar, 165br, 166 all, 167t, 167bl, 168 all, 172, 173a second from left, 173ar, 173bl, 174al, 174cl, 174bl, 175ar, 175bl, 175br, 176al, 176ac, 176b, 177b, 178al, 180al, 181ar, 182 all, 183 all, 184al, 184ar, 185tl, 185tm, 186ar, 186br, 187b, 188a, 189al, 189ar, 189c, 189al, 190ar, 191a, 192 all, 193 all, 194c, 194bl, 194br, 195ar, 195b, 196 all, 197bl, 197r, 198l, 199al, 199ar; Burrell Collection, Glasgow 148al; Calico Museum, Ahmedabad, India (photos Professor Anne Morrell) 111tr, 121ar; Killie Campbell Collection, Durban (photos PS) 35ar, 53tl, 58al, 58bl, 180r; The Collector (photos PS) 28, 68a, 68b, 69al; Gina Corrigan 110b, 114ar; Caroline Crabtree 27cr, 27bl; Brian Douglas 112br; Alfred Duggan Cronin (photos McGregor Museum, Kimberley) 30a, 31b , 33ac, 34bl, 37i, 38a, 39bl, 50b, 56tl, 61i; Local History Museum, Durban (photos PS) 32bl, 43i, 46ar, 46cl, 46bc, 47b, 48tl, 48cl, 48bl, 49ar, 179 all; Dr Eiluned M. Edwards 111al, 123al; Embroiderer's Guild, Yorkshire branch collection 197al (photo Tessa Bunney); Courtesy William Fehr Collection 200al; John Gillow 11al, 64bl, 65al (photo PS), 67bl (photo PS), 70bl, 78b, 80t, 80b, 89tl, 95ar, 96bi, 107bl, 144al, 144ar, 145br, 146br, 156l, 156br; Mike Harding, South American Pictures 13tl; Heard Museum, Phoenix 99a, 104l, 105cr; Courtesy of Jablonex 22bl, 22br, 23bl, 23br; Kelvingrove Art Gallery and Museum, Glasgow (photos Glasgow Art Galleries and Museums photographic service) 1, 65br, 107t, 107c, 138bl, 139c, 139bl, 139br; Mark Lewis 51ar, 52ar, 74br; Library of Congress, Washington, DC 92bl, 92br, 94al, 98ar, 101br; Steven Long (photos PS) 21a, 25br, 29bm, 33bl, 38b, 39lc, 39tri, 40b, 41a, 41cl, 41bl, 42bl, 44l, 45r, 45bl, 58ar; Manor House Museum, Bury St Edmunds (photos Tessa Bunney) 5, 20l, 148c, 148b, 149ar, 151br, 152l, 152i, 152br, 153 all, 154al, 154cl, 154r; Ian Martin 8br, 63ar; McCord Museum of Canadian History, Montreal 83l (ME937.3), 84ar (M7059), 84br (ME927.1.8.1), 103al (M12529); McGregor Museum, Kimberley 12 bm; Minneapolis Institute of Art 67br; courtesy of Miyuki Shoji Co. 19b, 27br; Ann Mockford 18al, 18bl, 173bl, 173a third from left, 173br, 185tr, 189b, 190b, 191b, 194bm, 195al; Morija Museum, Lesotho (photos PS) 58br, 59al, 60bl, 61br; Carole Morris Collection 33al, 73br, 112ar, 137br; Tony Morrison, South American Pictures 106bl, 107br; Courtesy National Museum of Denmark, Copenhagen 82a, 82b, 83ar; reproduced by kind permission of Oxford University Press, India 116ar, 117bl, 118al; Pan African Market, Cape Town 64al (photo PS), 64ar (photo PS), 66ar (photo PS), 71 all, 198r; Maggie Pederson Campbell 169; Queenstown and Frontier Museum (photos PS) 39r, 50br, 60ar; Ruth Rathke 125i; Peter Rich 10br, 33ar; Bryan Sentance 6ar, 24b, 25al, 25bl, 100ar; Torben Sode 14, 15a, 15b, 17ar, 19t, 19c, 26 all, 164ar, 164cr, 164br, 165al, 170 all, 171 all, 185cl, 185cr, 185b; South African Museum, Cape Town 13lm, 29bl, 29br, 32ac, 33cr, 34a, 34c, 34br, 36cl, 36cr, 36bl, 36br, 39tl, 40a, 41br, 42al, 42ar, 42br, 43m, 44r, 45a, 47al, 47ar, 47rc, 59ar, 60c; Pam Stallebrass 9cr, 12bl, 13cr, 16a, 16b, 17al, 17b, 20br, 22al, 22lm, 22ar, 23al, 23ac, 24al, 24ar, 32al, 32ar, 46bl, 46br, 67al, 67ar, 106br, 175al, 178bl, 186l; Standard Bank Collection (photos Bob Knoops unless stated otherwise) 36t, 37bl, 49b, 50al, 50ar, 51al, 51b, 51bi, 52al (photo PS), 52bl, 53bl, 53ar, 53cr, 53br, 54 all (photos PS), 55 all, 56ar (photo PS), 56bl, 56br, 57a, 57b, 59br, 60al, 61al, 61bl, 70al, 73bl, 174ar, 178ar, 184b; Taylor N. A. Indian Archives, Hastings 77bc, 81b, 83r, 84bl, 85a, 85b, 90bl, 92al, 93ar, 95br, 98br, 99br, 100al, 100b, 105al, 105ac; Angela Thompson 128i, 144b; Barbara Tyrell (photos PS) 61tr, 194al; York Castle Museum (photos Tessa Bunney) 142, 149al, 155a, 155br, 176ar, 177a; Paul Weinberg, University of Cape Town 30b; Sue van Langelaar (photos PS) 35tl, 35al; Yani Studio 187t (photo PS).

# COLLECTIONS

## BRAZIL
**Rio de Janeiro**
Museo do Indio
Rua Mata Machado 127, 20000 Rio de Janeiro
*Brazilian Indian costume*

**São Paulo**
Folklore Museum
Pavilhao Garcez
Parque Ibirapuera, 01000 São Paulo
*Brazilian folk costume*

## BRITISH ISLES
**Bury St Edmunds**
Manor House Museum
Honey Hill, Angel Corner
Bury St Edmunds IP33 1UZ
*19th- and 20th-century items and dresses designed by Norman Hartnell*

**Exeter**
Royal Albert Memorial Museum
Queen Street, Exeter EX4 3RX
*Yoruba crowns*

**Glasgow**
Burrell Collection
Pollok Country Park, Glasgow GA3 1AT
*20th-century dresses and bags*

**London**
British Museum
Great Russell Street, London WC1B 3DG
*Worldwide collection, including Yoruba crowns*

Victoria and Albert Museum
Cromwell Road, London SW7 2RL
*Sweete bags and beaded boxes*

**Oxford**
Pitt Rivers Museum
South Parks Road, Oxford OX1 3PP

## CANADA
**Hull**
Canadian Museum of Civilisation
100 Laurier Street, Hull, Quebec J8X 4H2

**Montreal**
McCord Museum of Canadian History
690 rue Sherbrooke West
Montreal, Quebec H3A 1E9
*Arctic and Sub-Arctic beadwork*

**Toronto**
Royal Ontario Museum
100 Queen's Park
Toronto, Ontario M5S 2C6

**Vancouver**
Museum of Anthropology at the University of British Columbia
6393 N. W. Marine Drive
Vancouver, BC V6T 1Z2

## CZECH REPUBLIC
**Jablonec nad Nisou**
Muzeum skla a bizuterie (Museum of Glass and Jewellery)
Jiráskova ul 4, 46600 Jablonec nad Nisou

## DEMOCRATIC REPUBLIC OF THE CONGO
**Kinshasa**
Museum of Ethnology and Archaeology
Université National du Congo, BP 127, Kinshasa
*Central African collection*

## DENMARK
**Copenhagen**
National Museum of Denmark
Department of Ethnology
Ny Verstergade 10, Copenhagen
*Beadwork from Greenland, North America and Africa*

## EGYPT
**Cairo**
Arabic Museum
Midal Babel-Hkalk
Cairo
*Islamic costume*

## FINLAND
**Helsinki**
The National Museum of Finland
Mannerheimintie 34, FIN-00100 Helsinki

## FRANCE
**Paris**
Musée de l'Homme
17 place du Trocadéro
75016 Paris
*Worldwide collections*

Musée National des Arts d'Afrique et d'Océanie
293 avenue Daumesnil
75012 Paris
*African and Oceanic collections*

## GERMANY
**Berlin**
Museum für Völkerkunde
Staatliche Museen zu Berlin – Preussischer Kulturbesitz
Lansstrasse 8
14195 Berlin

## GUATEMALA
**Ciudad de Guatemala**
Museo Nacional de Artes e Industria Populares
Avenida 10 No. 10–70
Zona 1 Ciudad de Guatemala
*Guatemalan folk costume*

## INDIA
**Ahmedabad**
The Calico Museum of Textiles
Shanti Bagh Area
Ahmedabad, Gujarat

## MEXICO
**Mexico City**
Museo Nacional de Historia
Castillo de Chapultepec
11580 Mexico City
*Mexican and European collections*

## PERU
**Lima**
Museo Nacional de Antropologia y Arqueologia
Plaza Bolivia s/n, Pueblo Libre, Lima

## RUSSIA
**St Petersburg**
Peter the Great Museum of Anthropology and Ethnology
nab Universitetskaja 3
St Petersburg

Staatliche Eremitage (Hermitage Museum)
Dworzowaja Nabereshnaja
34–36 St Petersburg
*Beaded panels*

## SINGAPORE
Singapore Art Museum
71 Bras Basah Road
Singapore 189555
*Straits Chinese collection*

## SOUTH AFRICA
**Cape Town**
South African Museum
49 Adderley Street
Cape Town

**Durban**
African Art Centre
8 Guildhall Arcade
35 Gardiner St, Durban

Durban Art Gallery
Second Floor
City Hall
Smith Street
Durban

Killie Campbell Collection
220 Marriott Road
Durban 4001

Local History Museum
Aliwal Street
Durban 4001

**Grahamstown**
Albany Museum
Somerset Street
Grahamstown 6139

**Johannesburg**
Gertrude Posel Gallery
University of the Witwatersrand
Johannesburg 2050

Johannesburg Art Gallery
Klein Street, Joubert Park
Johannesburg

Museum Africa
121 Bree Street
Johannesburg 2001

**Kimberley**
McGregor Museum
2 Egerton Rd
Belgravia, Kimberley 8300

**Pietermaritzburg**
Natal Museum
237 Loop Street
Pietermaritzburg

**Port Elizabeth**
King George VI Art Gallery
1 Park Drive, Port Elizabeth 6001

## COLLECTIONS

**Queenstown**
Queenstown and Frontier Museum
PO Box 296, Queenstown 5320

**UNITED STATES OF AMERICA**
**Austin**
Texas Memorial Museum of Science & History
2400 Trinity Street
Austin, TX 78705

**Berkeley**
Phoebe A. History Museum of Anthropology
(formerly the Lowie Museum of Anthropology)
Kroebber Hall, Bancroft Way
University of California
Berkeley, CA 94720
*Worldwide collections, including beadwork from
the West Sub-Arctic*

**Bloomington**
Mathers Museum
416 North Indiana Ave
Bloomington, IN 47405

**Cambridge, Mass.**
Peabody Museum of Archaeology & Ethnology
Harvard University
11 Divinity Ave
Cambridge, MA 02138

**Chamberlain**
Atka Lakota Museum
St Joseph's Indian School
Chamberlain, SD 57325

**Chicago**
Field Museum of Natural History
Roosevelt Rd at Lake Shore Drive
Chicago, IL 60605

**Cody**
Buffalo Bill Historical Centre
720 Sheridan Ave
Cody, WY 82414

**Denver**
Colorado Historical Society
1300 Broadway
Denver, CO 80203
*Plains collection*

The Denver Art Museum
100 West 14th Ave, Parkway
Denver, CO 80204

Denver Museum of Natural History
2001 Colorado Boulevard
Denver, CO 80205–5798

**Idaho**
Shoshone-Bannock Tribal Museum
Fort Hall N. of Pocatello at Fort Hall
Off Interstate 15, Idaho

**Juneau**
Alaska State Museum
395 Whittier Street, Juneau, AK 99801

**Los Angeles**
Fowler Museum of Cultural History
University of California
405 Hilgard Ave, Los Angeles, CA 90024
*Beadwork from around the world, and a strong
African collection*

Lost and Found Traditions Collection
Natural History Museum of Los Angeles
County
900 Exposition Boulevard
Los Angeles, CA 90007

The Southwest Museum
234 Museum Drive
Los Angeles, CA 90065

**New York**
American Museum of Natural History
79th Street and Central Park West
New York, NY 10024
*Beadwork from North and South America*

George Gustav Heye Centre
Alexander Hamilton
US Custom House
One Bowling Green
New York, NY 10004

Rochester Museum and Science Center
657 East Avenue
Rochester, NY 14607–2177
*Old trade beads*

**Pendleton**
Tamastslikt Cultural Institute
72789 Highway 331
Pendleton, OR 97801

**Philadelphia**
Choctaw Museum of the Southern Indian
Choctaw Indian Reservation
Highway 16 West
Philadelphia, MS 39350

University of Pennsylvania Museum of
Archaeology and Anthropology
33rd and Spruce Streets
Philadelphia, PA 19104

**Phoenix**
Heard Museum
2301 N. Central Ave
Phoenix, AZ 85004

**Pierre**
The Museum of the South Dakota State
Historical Society
Cultural Heritage Center
900 Governors Drive
Pierre, SD 57501–2217
*Plains collection*

**Santa Fe**
Museum of Indian Arts and Culture
Laboratory of Anthropology
Camino Lejo off Old Santa Fe Trail
Santa Fe, NM 87504

Museum of International Folk Art
706 Camino Lejo
Santa Fe, NM 87505
*Central and South American beads and
beadwork*

**Seattle**
Seattle Art Museum
Eugene Fuller Memorial Collection
Downtown
100 University Street
Seattle, WA 98101–2902

**South Dakota**
Sioux Indian Museum
515 West Blvd Rapid City
South Dakota, SD 57709

**Spokane**
Cheney Cowles Museum
2316 West First Avenue
Spokane, WA 99204

**Suitland**
National Museum of the American Indian
Cultural Resources Centre
4220 Silver Hill Road
Suitland, MD 20746

**Taos**
Millicent Rogers Museum of Northern New
Mexico
1504 Millicent Rogers Road
Taos, NM 87571

**Tucson**
Arizona State Museum
1013 E. University Boulevard
University of Arizona
Tucson, AZ 85721

**Tulsa**
The Gilcrease Museum
1400 North Gilcrease Museum Road
Tulsa, OK 74127–2100
*Plains collection*

**Warm Springs**
Museum at Warm Springs
2189 Highway 26
Warm Springs, OR 97761
*Plateau collection*

**Washington**
Indian Arts and Crafts Board
US Department of the Interior
1849 C Street, N.W.
Washington, DC 20240

Library of Congress
101 Independence Avenue, S.E.
Washington, DC 20540
*Archival photographs, including Edward Curtis
photographs*

National Museum of Natural History
Smithsonian Institution
10th St and Constitution Ave, N.W.
Washington, DC 20560
*Worldwide collections*

OTHER USEFUL ADDRESSES
**Bead Society of Great Britain**
1 Casburn Lane
Burwell
Cambridge CB5 0ED

**The Beadworkers' Guild**
PO Box 24922
London SE23 3WS

# Bibliography

## General

Beaded Splendor (exh. cat.), National Museum of African Art, Washington, DC, 1994
Bead Society of Great Britain, newsletter 48, 1999 and newsletter 52, 2000
Coles, Janet, and Robert Budwig, *World Beads*, London, 1997
Dubin, Lois Sherr, *The History of Beads: From 30,000 BC to the Present*, London and New York, 1995
Edwards, Joan, *Bead Embroidery*, London, 1966
Mack, John (ed.), *Ethnic Jewellery*, London, 1995
Rivers, Victoria Z., *The Shining Cloth: Dress and Ornament that Glitters*, London and New York, 1999
Van der Sleen, W. G. N., *A Handbook on Beads*, Liège, 1967
Wolters, Natacha, *Les Perles*, Paris, 1996
Wright, Margot M. (ed.), *Ethnographic Beadwork: Aspects of Manufacture, Use and Conversion*, London, 2001

## Africa

*African Arts* magazine, UCLA, Los Angeles
*Art and Ambiguity: Perspectives on the Brenthurst Collection of Southern African Art*, Johannesburg, 1991
Bedford, E. (ed.), *Ezakwantu: Beadwork from the Eastern Cape*, Cape Town, 1993
Bigham, Elizabeth, *Fun with African Beads*, London and New York, 1999
Bothma, J. du P., Anthony Hall-Martin and Clive Walker, *Kaokoveld, The Last Wilderness*, Johannesburg, 1988
Broster, Joan, *Red Blanket Valley*, Johannesburg, 1967
Broster, Joan, *The Thembu: their Beadwork, Songs and Dances*, Cape Town and London, 1976
Broster, Joan, and Alice Mertens, *African Elegance*, Cape Town, 1973
Carey, Margaret, *Beads and Beadwork of East and South Africa*, Princes Risborough, UK, 1986
Clarke, Duncan, *African Hats and Jewelry*, Rochester, UK, 1998
Costello, Dawn, *Not Only for its Beauty: Beadwork and its Cultural Significance among the Xhosa-Speaking Peoples*, Pretoria, 1990
Courtney-Clark, M., *Ndebele: the Art of an African Tribe*, Cape Town, 1986; New York, 2002
Davison, Patricia, 'Lobedu Material Culture: A Comparative Study of the 1930s and 1970s', *Annals of the South African Museum*, 94, 3, Cape Town, 1984
Davison, Patricia, and June Hosford, *Conserving Ndebele Beadwork*, Cape Town, 1988
Fisher, Angela, *Africa Adorned*, London, 1984
Hammond-Tooke, D., and A. Nettleton (eds), *Ten Years of Collecting (1979–1989): the Standard Bank Foundation Collection of African Art*, Johannesburg, 1989
Kasule, Samuel, *The History Atlas of Africa: From the First Humans to the Emergence of a New South Africa*, New York, 1998
Klopper, Sandra, *The Art of Zulu-speakers in Northern Natal-Zululand: an Investigation of the History of Beadwork, Carving and Dress from Shaka to Inkatha* (PhD), Johannesburg, 1992

Kuckertz, Heinz J., 'Tlokwa Material Culture as it Relates to the Usage of Beadwork', *Journal of Humanities*, vol. 12, Pietermaritzburg, 2000
Mack, John (ed.), *Africa: Arts and Cultures*, London, 2000
Magubane, Peter, *Vanishing Cultures of South Africa: Changing Customs in a Changing World*, Cape Town and London, 1998
Mertens, Alice, and H. Schoeman, *The Zulu*, Cape Town and London, 1975
Meyer, Laure, *Black Africa: Masks, Sculpture, Jewelry*, Paris, 1992
Morcom, G. M., *The Sacred and the Profane: the Religious and Commercial Significance of Church Adornment in the Nazareth Baptist Church of Amos Shembe*, Durban, 1994
Morris, Jean, and Eleanor Preston-Whyte, *Speaking with Beads: Zulu Arts from Southern Africa*, London, 1994
Nell, K., *Evocations of the Child: Fertility Figures of the Southern African Region*, Cape Town, 1998
Nuytten, Phil, 'Money from the Sea', *National Geographic*, 1993
Peires, J. B., *The House of Phalo: A History of the Xhosa People in the Days of their Independence*, Johannesburg, Berkeley and London, 1982
Phillips, T. (ed.), *Africa: the Art of a Continent*, New York and Munich, 1995
Saitowitz, Sharma Jeanette, 'Classification of Glass Trade Beads', *SAMAB*, vol. 18, 1988
Schwager, Dirk, and Colleen Schwager, *Lesotho*, Maseru, Lesotho, 1986
Shaw, E. M., and N. J. van Warmelo, 'The Material Culture of the Cape Nguni', *Annals of the South African Museum*, 58 (4)
Stevenson, M., and M. Graham-Stewart, *South East African Beadwork, 1850–1910: From Adornment to Artefact to Art*, Cape Town, 2000
Stokes, D., 'Rediscovered Treasures: African Beadwork in the Field Museum, Chicago', *African Arts* 32 (3)
Tyrrell, Barbara, *Tribal Peoples of Southern Africa*, Cape Town, 1968
Tyrrell, B., *Her African Quest*, Cape Town, 1996
Wannenburgh, Alf, *The Bushmen*, Cape Town and London, 1979 and 1999
Wood, M., *Making Connections: Relationships between International Trade and Glass Beads from the Shashe-Limpopo Area*, South African Archaeological Society, Johannesburg
*Zulu Treasures of Kings and Commoners: A Celebration of the Material Culture of the Zulu People*, Durban, 1996

## Americas

Adam, Hans Christian, *Native Americans: Edward S. Curtis*, London, New York, Cologne, Madrid, Paris and Tokyo, 2001
Barth, Georg J., *Native American Beadwork: Traditional Beading Techniques for the Modern-Day Beadworker*, Stevens Point, WI, 1993
*Beads: their Use by Upper Great Lakes Indians* (exh. cat.), Grand Rapids, MI, 1977 and 1981
DeVore, Steven Leroy, *Beads of the Bison Robe Trade: The Fort Union Trading Post Collection*, Williston, ND, 1992
Dubin, Lois Sherr, *North American Indian Jewelry and Adornment: from Prehistory to the Present*, New York, 1999
Johnson, Michael G., *The Native Tribes of North America: A Concise Encyclopedia*, London, New York and Toronto, 1993
Orchard, William C., *Beads and Beadwork of the American Indians: A Study Based on Specimens in the Museum of the American Indian, Heye Foundation*, New York, 2nd edn, 1975
Penney, David W., *Art of the American Indian Frontier: The Chandler-Pohrt Collection*, London, Detroit and Seattle, 1992
Phillips, Ruth B., *Trading Identities: the Souvenir in Native North American Art from the Northeast, 1700–1900*, Washington, DC, 1998
Taylor, Colin F., *Native American Arts and Crafts*, London and New York, 1995
Taylor, Colin F., *The Native Americans: The Indigenous People of North America*, London 1996 and San Diego, 1999
Vincent, Gilbert T., *Masterpieces of American Indian Art: From the Eugene and Clare Thaw Collection*, New York, 1995
Waldman, Carl, *Encyclopedia of Native American Tribes*, New York, 1999

## Asia

Allen, Jamey, *Magical Ancient Beads: From the Collection of Ulrich J. Beck*, Singapore, 1998
Askari, N., and R. Crill, *Colours of the Indus: Costume and Textiles of Pakistan*, London, 1997
Elwin, Harry Verrier Holman, *The Tribal Art of Middle India*, Bombay, London and New York, 1951
Garrett, Valery M., *Traditional Chinese Clothing in Hong Kong and South China, 1840–1980*, Oxford, Hong Kong and New York, 1987
Hamilton, Roy W. (ed.), *From the Rainbow's Varied Hue: Textiles of the Southern Philippines*, Los Angeles, 1998
Harvey, Janet, *Traditional Textiles of Central Asia*, London and New York, 1996
Hitchcock, M., *Indonesian Textiles*, London, 1991
Ho Wing Meng, *Straits Chinese Beadwork and Embroidery: A Collector's Guide*, Singapore, 1987
Kock, J., and Torben Sode, *Glass, Glassbeads and Glassmakers in Northern India*, Denmark (n.d.)
Lewis, Paul and Elaine, *Peoples of the Golden Triangle: Six Tribes in Thailand*, London and New York, 1984
Newman, Thelma R., *Contemporary Southeast Asian Arts and Crafts: Ethnic Craftsmen at Work with How-to Instructions for Adapting their Crafts*, New York, 1977
Ross, Heather Colyer, *The Art of Arabian Costume: A Saudi Arabian Profile*, Switzerland and Studio City, Calif., 1981
Sode, Torben, 'Papanaduipet' (article), 2002
Sode Torben, 'Mangal Sutra – The Smallest Handmade Glass beads in the World', *Bead Society Newsletter* (53), UK

## Europe

*Borshchiv: Folk Art, Customs and Traditions*, New York, 1994
Groves, Sylvia, *The History of Needlework Tools and Accessories*, London, 1966
Hughes, Therle, *English Domestic Needlework, 1660–1860*, London and New York, 1961
Jones, Mary Eirwen, *A History of Western Embroidery*, London and New York, 1969
Kendrick, A. F., *English Needlework*, London, 1933; 2nd edn, 1967
Poli, Doretta Davanzo, *Arts and Crafts in Venice*, Cologne and Venice, 1999
Sander, Helga, and Wolfgang Peschl, *Klosterarbeiten*, Munich, 1997
Stadnychenko, Tamara, *Baubles, Bangles and Beads: An Overview of Ukrainian Gerdany*, 2001
Wingfield Digby, George, *Elizabethan Embroidery*, London, 1963

# Index